M000273595

Building Geography Skills for Life

Student Text-Workbook

Richard G. Boehm, Ph.D.
Professor of Geography and
Jesse H. Jones Distinguished Chair
in Geographic Education

Department of Geography

Southwest Texas State University
San Marcos, Texas

Glencoe
McGraw-Hill

New York, New York   Columbus, Ohio   Chicago, Illinois   Woodland Hills, California   Peoria, Illinois

Acknowledgments

The Global Pencil lesson on pages 151–153 is an adaptation of "The International Pencil: Elementary Level Unit on Global Interdependence," by Lawrence C. Wolken, *Journal of Geography,* November/December, 1984, pp. 290–293. Used by permission.

Photo Credits

6 PhotoDisc; **60** PhotoDisc; **77** PhotoDisc; **81** PhotoDisc; **84** PhotoDisc; **98** PhotoDisc; **109** PhotoDisc; **113** PhotoDisc; **118** PhotoSpin, Inc.; **143** PhotoDisc; **147** PhotoDisc; **152** PhotoDisc; **158** PhotoDisc; **178** PhotoDisc; **181** Shepard Sherbell/CORBIS; **183** PhotoDisc; **187** PhotoDisc; **194** PhotoDisc; **208** PhotoDisc.

Cover

David Teal/CORBIS

Send all inquiries to:
Glencoe/McGraw-Hill
8787 Orion Place
Columbus, Ohio 43240-4027

Printed in the United States of America.

ISBN 0-07-825799-9 (Student Text-Workbook)
ISBN 0-07-825800-6 (Teacher Annotated Edition)
1 2 3 4 5 6 7 8 9 10 047 08 07 06 05 04 03 02 01

Table of Contents

# To the Student

Do you live in a city, or in a small town? Or do you live on a farm or a ranch? Has your family lived there a long time or a short time? How does living where you do affect the way you live? For example, do you need special clothes in the winter? Is your favorite food grown nearby, or is it brought in from far away?

All these questions have to do with **geography.** Geography is the study of our home—the earth—and how our lives are affected by it. Almost every detail of our lives is affected by geography. The clothes we wear, the food we eat, the things we do for fun, and the kinds of homes in which we live are all connected to geography.

Ask yourself these six questions about a food in the store where you shop. Where was it grown? What is the place and how it is like other places on Earth? Why does the place look the way it does? How do the people who grow the food live? How do the people use the resources in their environment? What problems do the people living in the place have to solve?

These six questions deal with the very heart of geography. As you look for answers to these questions, you are studying geography.

When we study a place on the earth, we ask six questions that are very similar to the six above. We ask (1) where a place is, (2) what the place is like and how that place is like other places on the earth, (3) how were the physical features in the place formed, (4) how the people there live, (5) how do people interact with their environment, (6) what does geography tell us about the past and how does it help us plan for the future. These questions deal with the six essential elements of geography. These elements are **the world in spatial terms, places and regions, physical systems, human systems, environment and society,** and **the uses of geography.**

This book is divided into six units. Each unit is organized around one of the six essential elements of geography. Each unit introduction identifies and explains more fully the element being covered in that unit.

Each unit introduction is followed by a series of short lessons that deal with the topic of that unit.

Numerous maps, graphs, and tables will be used to present information. You will receive a great deal of instruction and practice in reading these special ways of presenting information. A **Unit Review** checks your understanding of the important concepts and information presented in each unit. A **Final Review** at the end of the book is an overall check on your learning.

Vocabulary study is an important part of this book. Geographers use many special words in order to understand the world in which you live. The terms you should know after completing the lesson are listed at the start of each lesson. All the words are also listed in the **Glossary** at the end of the book, so that you may easily look them up at any time. The Glossary tells how to pronounce each word and gives the meaning of the word.

As you progress through the book, you will learn some of the skills you need to learn about places on the earth. You will learn some of the language of geography. You will learn how to read the maps, charts, and tables that geographers often use to present information about the earth and its peoples. You will study examples of how people interact with each other and with their environment. And you will learn how to organize your study of the earth by regions that are alike in some way.

Almost every day in the newspaper or on television, we learn of some place of which we might have never heard before. Often we find that in some way our lives are affected by that place. Events in places such as Afghanistan, the Gaza Strip, Macedonia, and Rwanda influence our lives as part of a global community. We may know someone from those parts of the world. We at least have read about and heard about their misfortunes. Perhaps we have donated money to help buy food for war-torn areas, or to help establish homes for orphans.

All of us, everywhere, are affected in some way by what happens everywhere else. We study geography to help us deal with the things that affect our lives. The skills you will learn in this book can help you make better decisions about where and how you will live. In that sense, this book is designed to help you gain more control over your own life.

Unit 1

The World in Spatial Terms

The earth is covered with land and water divided into seven continents and four oceans.

Objectives

After completing this unit, you will be able to:

- describe locations in absolute and relative terms;
- locate places on a map using latitude and longitude;
- locate major landmasses and bodies of water;
- read map symbols, legends, and scales;
- compare different types of maps and map projections.

A radio announcer breaks into regular programming to announce the devastating consequences of a flash flood, hurricane, forest fire, or other disaster. People immediately wonder where the disaster occurred. Often the disaster has only local consequences, affecting the people living in the area where the disaster happened. In some cases, however, the disaster has a far-reaching impact, and affects the lives of people in other areas.

One of the most notable disasters took place in 1986, when a series of human errors caused the reactor at the nuclear power plant in Chernobyl, Ukraine, to explode and catch fire. Deadly radioactive material spewed into the air. Winds began carrying the particles to the northwest into other European countries and eventually around the world. Dozens of people were killed. Hundreds more became very ill.

When news of the disaster became known, most people's first question was, "Where is Chernobyl?" That is, they wanted to know exactly where on the face of the earth it was located. The nuclear reactor at Chernobyl is at a precise position on the earth. This is called its **absolute location.**

Within days after the disaster, news outlets reported on the spread of the radioactive cloud from the explosion. Poland, Sweden, and England reported increases in radiation. Farmers across Europe were forced to destroy crops covered with radioactive dust. People were afraid to drink the water. Now people were asking a different question about the location of Chernobyl: "Where is it *from here*?" People needed to know in what direction, and how far, Chernobyl was from their own location. This is called **relative location.** By knowing their location in relation to Chernobyl, people could tell whether the wind was carrying the radioactive material closer or farther away.

Geographers use latitude and longitude to describe absolute location. Lessons in this unit will teach you how to use latitude and longitude. Geographers also use absolute location to make maps. This unit will teach you how to read several kinds of maps. You will also learn about relative location and its importance to you.

The world in spatial terms is one of the six essential elements of geography. Spatial relations refers to the connections that people, places, and environments have to one another because of their location on the earth's surface. While location does not determine how we live, it does influence our lives.

Direction and Distance

WHAT YOU WILL LEARN

To identify direction and distance information from maps

READING STRATEGY

Create a diagram like the one below to list the cardinal and intermediate directions.

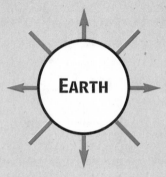

TERMS TO KNOW

compass rose, cardinal directions, intermediate directions, scale, scale bar

Have you ever drawn a map in the dirt to show someone where you live? Such drawings were some of the earliest maps. Other early maps were made of sticks tied together, or pieces of wood sewn to a piece of sealskin. People have used maps for thousands of years to show *where* places are, *how far* it is from one place to another, and the *direction* to travel to get from here to there.

Maps are important tools. Maps tell us where to catch a bus and where that bus will take us. Maps help us find a friend's house in a part of town that is new to us. Maps help us plan vacation trips. They help us learn about the town or state to which we are moving.

Direction

Direction is one of the most important things we can learn from a map. You use direction every day—left, right, forward, back, up, down. But these directions depend on where you are and which way you are facing. Maps use the directions north, south, east, and west. These directions do not change. North is always toward the North Pole of the earth. If you stand facing the North Pole, east will be to your right. West will be to your left. South will be behind you.

Usually, north will be at the top of a map. However, this is not always true. You must check to be sure. Mapmakers use a **compass rose** or a north arrow to show directions. If there is no compass rose, north arrow, or other symbol to indicate direction, you can assume that north is at the top of the map.

Look at the examples below. Find north, south, east, and west on Figure 1-1. These are the **cardinal directions.** Turn your book so that north on the compass rose points north (toward the North Pole). Face north yourself. Now east is to your right, west is to your left, and south is behind you.

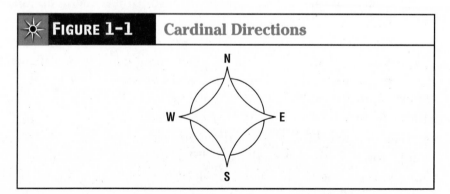

☀ **FIGURE 1-1** | **Cardinal Directions**

Look straight north. Hold your right hand straight out to the side. In what direction are you pointing? You are correct if you said *east*. Now turn your head just halfway toward your right arm. You are no longer looking north. But you are not looking east, either. You are looking *northeast*. Look at Figure 1-2. Find northeast, southeast, northwest, and southwest. These are known as **intermediate directions.**

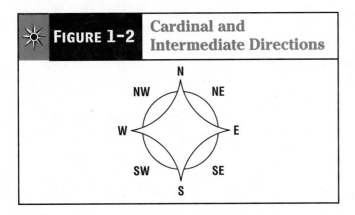

☀ FIGURE 1-2   Cardinal and Intermediate Directions

Notice that Figure 1-3 is just an arrow with its point labeled *N*. The *N* stands for north. The arrow points north. When you see a north arrow, remember that east is to the right, west is to the left, and south is in the opposite direction from north.

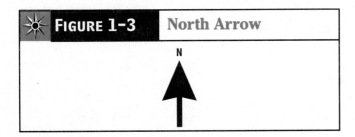

☀ FIGURE 1-3   North Arrow

Distance

If you make a drawing of a person, you will probably not make the picture as large as the person. That would take a piece of paper the same size as the person. A map is a drawing of a part of the earth. A map as big as the earth would be too large to put in your pocket and carry with you across Africa! Maps are drawn so that a certain distance on the map represents a much larger distance on the earth. This is called **scale.** Scale makes it possible to show the whole earth on a piece of paper the size of this page.

Not all maps are the size of this page, of course. Your classroom may have maps hanging on the wall. These maps are much larger than the ones in your book. But they both show the same earth. Maps have a **scale bar** to tell you what distance on the earth is represented by a certain distance on the map.

Using Map Scale Bars

Here are some examples of map scale bars. Notice that all lines are the same length, but that each line represents a different distance on the earth. Also notice that the same scale bar can represent distance in miles and kilometers on the map.

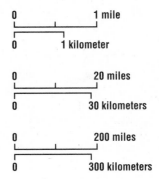

Using the scale bar to measure distances between places on a map is easy. Use a piece of paper. Put the edge of the paper between the two points you wish to measure. Make a mark on the paper at each point. Then put the piece of paper on the scale bar with one mark at zero. Note where the other point falls on the scale. This gives you the distance.

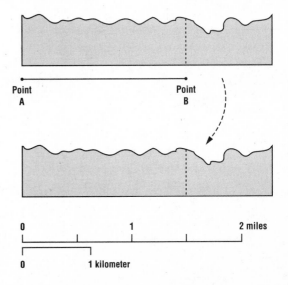

If the scale bar is not long enough, mark where it ends on the paper. Then slide the paper to the left to line up the new mark with zero. Do this as many times as necessary. Then multiply the number of spaces between marks by the distance each length of the scale bar represents. For example, if the scale bar represents 100 miles, and you marked off three spaces, then multiply 3 by 100. The distance between the two points on the map is 300 miles.

Using Your Skills

Ⓐ REVIEWING KEY TERMS

Place each phrase in the box under the correct heading.

helps you find directions on a map can be marked in miles	helps you find distances on a map may be marked N, S, E, W

     Compass Rose   **Scale**

1. _____   3. _____

2. _____   4. _____

Ⓑ RECALLING FACTS

Fill in the missing directions on these compass roses. Notice that north is not always in the same place.

1.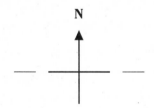

2.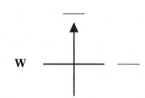

3.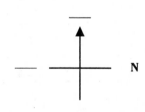

4.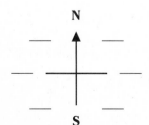

5.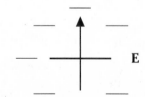

6.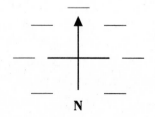

ⓒ PRACTICING MAP SKILLS

Use what you have learned about direction and distance to answer the questions about Map 1-1: The United States on page 12.

1. What part of this map shows direction? _____

2. What part of this map shows distance? _____

3. If you were in Kansas, in which direction would you have to travel to reach each of the states listed below? Use intermediate directions when necessary.

    a. South Dakota _____

    b. Virginia _____

    c. Utah _____

    d. Texas _____

    e. Washington _____

    f. Florida _____

    g. New Mexico _____

    h. Michigan _____

4. How many miles does the full length of the scale bar on the map

    represent? _____

5. About how many miles is it from east to west across Colorado?

    _____

6. About how many miles is it from north to south across Texas at its

    widest point? _____

7. How would you measure a distance on the map that is longer than the scale bar?

    _____

    _____

    _____

    _____

    _____

    _____

    _____

8. About how many miles is it from Ohio to Oklahoma when traveling

    southwest? _____

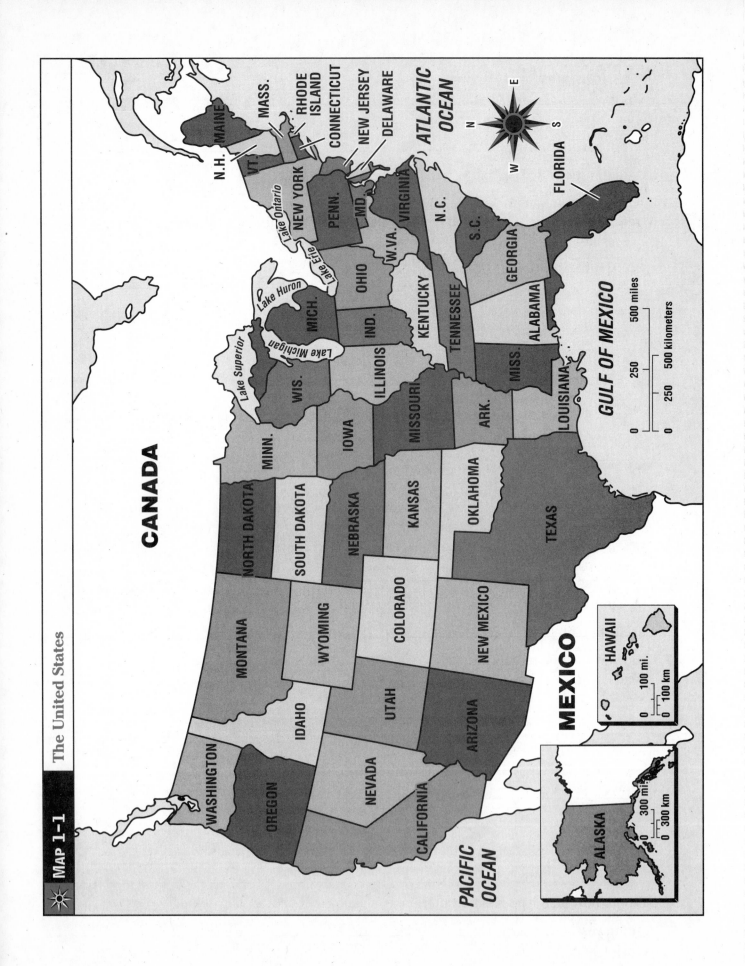

The United States

MAP 1-1

Importance of Distance and Relative Location

WHAT YOU WILL LEARN

How to describe locations in terms of relationships with other locations

READING STRATEGY

Create a chart like the one below. List three examples of the importance of relative location in your life.

RELATIVE LOCATION →

TERMS TO KNOW

relative location, interdependence

Have you ever been lost? Or have you just not been sure about how to get somewhere you wanted to go?

From the specific spot where you stand on the earth, you are different directions and distances from many other spots on the earth. You may be 22 miles south of your home. At the same time you may be 150 miles northeast of the capital of your state. You may also be three feet from the front door of your favorite pizza place. Your location can, in fact, be compared to the location of any other spot on Earth. This is called **relative location.**

Distance and location affect your life in many ways. If you live eight miles from school, you must wake up earlier each morning than someone who lives eight blocks away. If you live 2,500 miles from the nearest volcano, you will be much less concerned about its latest eruption than someone who lives in the valley below it.

The story of Houston, Texas, is an example of the importance of distance and relative location. One of the greatest oil strikes in history took place near Houston in 1901. The Spindletop Field was the first great oil discovery in Texas. Within a few years Houston, Texas, was an important center for the oil industry. Why? Because Houston's relative location was near the early oil fields. It was also located near the Gulf of Mexico. This made it possible to ship oil and equipment by water. Many oil companies built plants near Houston to make products from oil. These products were then shipped to other parts of the country, and around the world by water. As a result, Houston became one of the largest ports in the United States.

Global Interdependence

Distance and relative location are important because we depend on people in other places for things we need. Depending on other people is called **interdependence.** We depend on them for certain goods and services, and they depend on us for others.

Interdependence links us together in the larger global community in many ways. For example, the United States imports and buys from other countries much of the oil that runs its cars and factories. A great deal of this oil comes from countries in Southwest Asia. This is why the United States is so interested in wars and other events in the region. Because of the location of oil fields in Southwest Asia, a war there could cut off the supply of oil to the United States. This could result in oil shortages and economic changes in the United States.

Ⓐ PRACTICING MAP SKILLS

Use Map 1-2: Panama below to decide whether each statement about relative location is true or false. Write *T* if the statement is true. Write *F* if the statement is false.

_____ 1.   Panama has water to the north and south.

_____ 2.   The country of Colombia is located to the west of Panama.

_____ 3.   The Caribbean Sea is located to the north of Panama.

_____ 4.   The Canal Zone is located in the central part of Panama.

_____ 5.   When a ship enters the Panama Canal at Colón, it is northwest of the other end of the canal at Panama City.

_____ 6.   Costa Rica is located northwest of Panama.

_____ 7.   According to this map, all parts of the Caribbean Sea are east of the Pacific Ocean.

_____ 8.   The city of Rio Hato is about 300 kilometers west of La Palma.

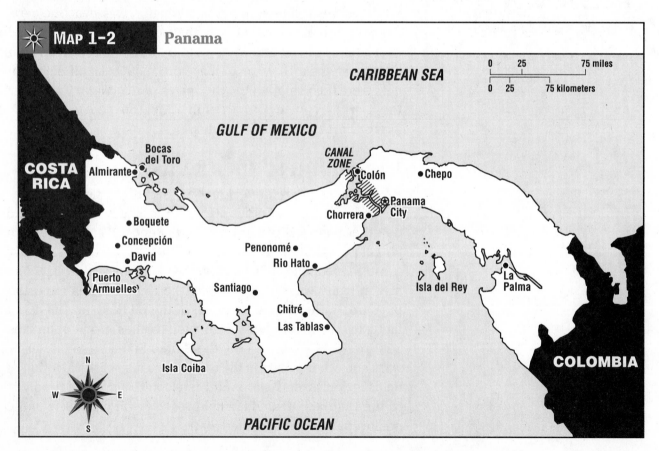

MAP 1-2   Panama

ⓑ PRACTICING MAP SKILLS

**Use Map 1-3: The World below to answer the questions about relative
location. Use intermediate directions where necessary.**

1. Where is the United States located on this map?

   _____

2. What country is to the north of the United States? _____

3. What country is to the south of the United States? _____

4. What direction is South Africa from the United States? _____

5. What direction is Australia from the United States? _____

6. In what direction would you travel to go from Japan to the United

   States? _____

7. In what direction would you travel to go from India to the United

   Kingdom? _____

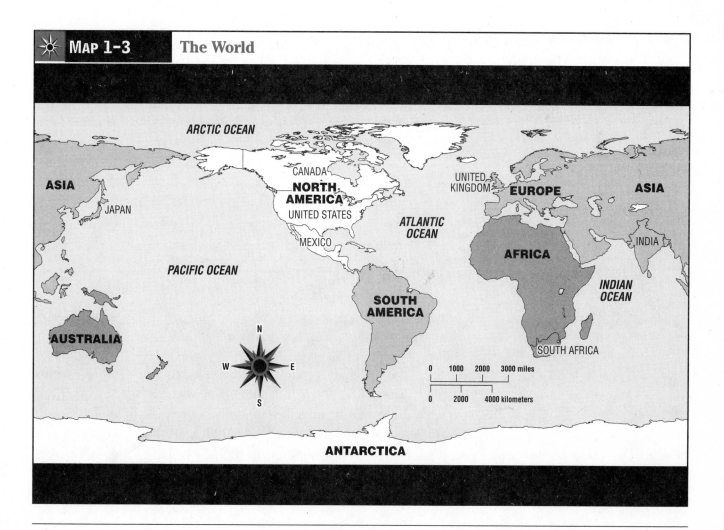

Locating Places Using a Grid

WHAT YOU WILL LEARN

To locate places using grids

READING STRATEGY

Use a table like the one below to list the major elements of a map grid.

ELEMENTS OF MAP GRIDS
•
•
•

TERMS TO KNOW

grid, cell, index

I magine that you have just landed on this planet. You have been told to find the center of government for the place where you landed. Someone hands you a map, points out your current location, and identifies the city where the center of government is located. You have heard of maps, but you have never seen one. On your planet, you simply enter your destination into a tracking device in your vehicle and the course is automatically programmed.

As you examine the map, you notice that there are lines running vertically and horizontally on the map. You also notice many symbols, colors, and words on the map. You are fairly certain that the words tell the names of places, but you are not certain what all the labels and symbols mean. You need something that will tell you about where the center of government is located.

Using Map Grids

The something you need to help you find the center of government in this new place is called a **grid.** A grid is a set of vertical and horizontal lines used to identify locations on a map. An alpha-numeric grid uses letters and numbers around the edges of the map to label the areas marked off by the lines. Look at Figure 1-4 at the top of the next page for an example of an alpha-numeric grid.

Place your left index finger on the letter *B* on the left side of the grid. Place your right index finger on the number *3* at the bottom of the grid. Move your left finger straight across and your right finger straight up until they meet. There should be a star in the box at your fingertips.

The four spaces to the right of the letter *B* form a *row.* We call this row B. The four spaces above the number *3* form a *column.* We call this column 3.

The area where a row and a column meet is called a **cell.** Notice that only one cell can be at the area where row B and column 3 meet. We call this cell B-3.

Practice using the grid in Figure 1-4. Which cell is closer to the top of the grid, cell A-1 or cell E-4? Now draw a star in cell C-2. Then draw a circle in cell A-4. Finally, write your name in cell D-1. You should be able to draw a straight line through all four cells on the grid that have something in them.

Many cities and towns are described as being built on a grid. This means that horizontal and vertical streets and roads cross

FIGURE 1-4   An Alpha-Numeric Grid

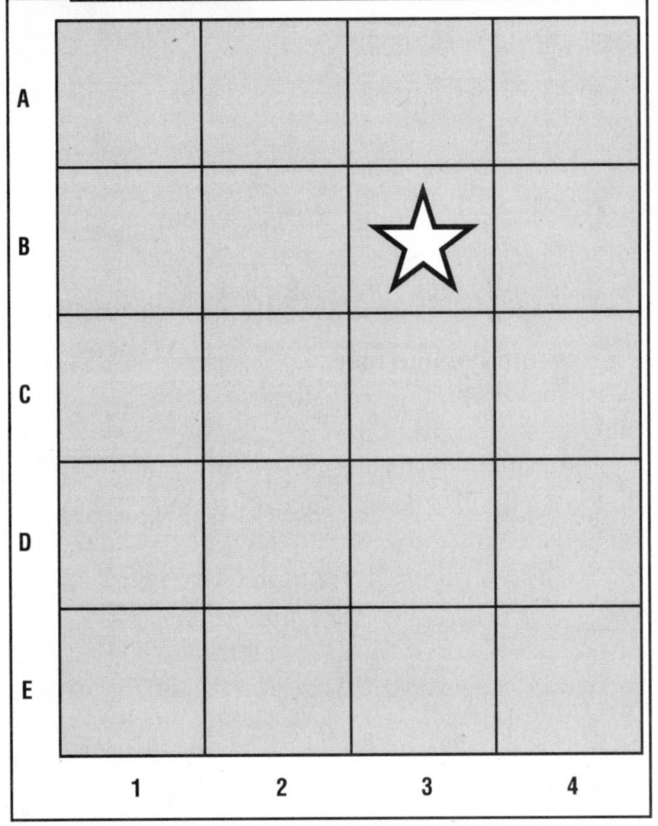

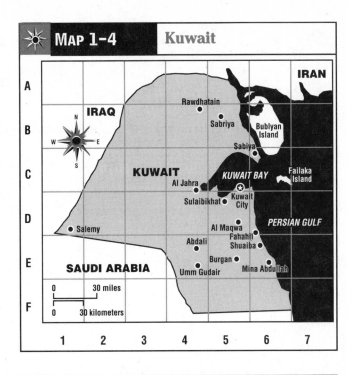

MAP 1-4   Kuwait

Index for Map 1-4

Abdali E-4

Al Jahra. D-4

Al Maqwa D-5

Burgan. E-5

Fahahil E-6

Kuwait City. C-5, D-5

Mina Abdullah E-6

_____ B-4

_____ C-6

_____ B-5

_____ D-1

_____ E-6

_____ D-5

_____ E-4

each other to form a grid. The names of the streets and roads are used to locate places in the city or town. For example, the high school may be located at the intersection of Main Street and Third Avenue. Or the post office is located on Sunset Boulevard between Fifth Avenue and Sixth Avenue. Is your town or city built on a grid?

Using a Grid Index

Mapmakers often use a grid to help us find places on maps. We use letters and numbers to identify cells on the map in which specific places are located. The grid is used with an **index.** The names of places on the map are listed in alphabetical order in the index. Following each name is the letter and number of the cell in which that place can be found.

Look at Map 1-4 and its index. Notice that the index is not complete. Use the map to help you fill in the name of the missing city for each cell number. Be sure you spell the name of each city correctly.

Using Your Skills

Ⓐ REVIEWING KEY TERMS

Match each term at left with its meaning.

_____ 1. cell   a.   an alphabetical list of places on a map, with cell numbers

_____ 2. row   b.   a set of lines used to identify locations on a map

_____ 3. column   c.   the space where a row and column meet

_____ 4. grid   d.   a set of spaces that goes across a map

_____ 5. index   e.   a set of spaces that goes up and down a map

Ⓑ PRACTICING MAP SKILLS

Use **Map 1-5: London, England** to answer these questions.

1. What is located in cell B-3?

   _____

2. What is located in cell C-2?

   _____

3. What is located in cells F-2, F-3, F-4, F-5, E-5, D-5, and C-5?

   _____

4. What is located in cells B-3 and B-4?

   _____

5. About how many miles is it from the London Zoo to the Planetarium?

   _____

6. About how many miles is it from Buckingham Palace to Kensington Palace?

   _____

7. Complete the following index for the map of London. Remember that all names in an index are in alphabetical order. If there is more than one possible answer for a cell, see which answer will fit in alphabetical order.

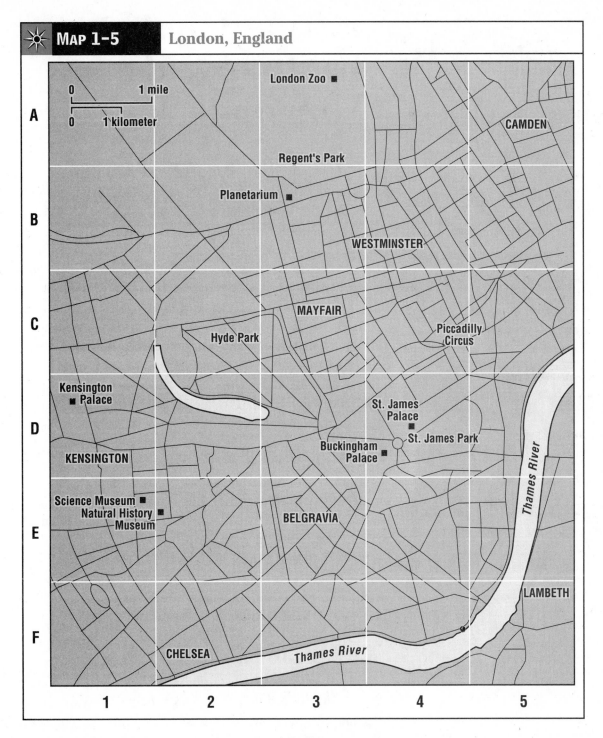

MAP 1-5 London, England

0 — 1 mile
0 — 1 kilometer

A
London Zoo ■
CAMDEN

Regent's Park

B
Planetarium ■
WESTMINSTER

C
MAYFAIR

Hyde Park
Piccadilly Circus

D
Kensington Palace ■
St. James Palace ■
St. James Park
Buckingham Palace ■
Thames River

KENSINGTON

E
Science Museum ■
Natural History Museum ■
BELGRAVIA
LAMBETH

F
CHELSEA
Thames River

1   2   3   4   5

Index

Introduction to Latitude and Longitude

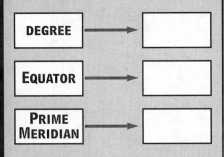
Do you know how ships measured their speed long ago? Do you know why a ship's speed is given today in knots rather than miles per hour or kilometers per hour?

Long ago, each ship carried a piece of wood fastened to a rope. The rope had knots tied in it. Each knot was a certain distance from the next. To measure the ship's speed, the piece of wood was thrown overboard. It pulled the rope out behind it. The faster the ship was going, the faster the rope went out. Someone counted how many knots passed over the side of the ship in a certain length of time. If seven knots were pulled out, the ship was said to be traveling at a speed of seven knots. Today, one knot is about 1.15 miles per hour.

Ships of long ago had to keep track of their speed on long voyages because they had no other way to tell how far they had traveled. Ships often became lost. For example, a storm might blow them far away from where they wanted to go.

What people needed was a way to tell exactly where they were on the earth's surface—their **absolute location.** They also needed to be able to find their way to any other absolute location.

What they needed was a grid system that covered the entire earth. You know that a grid is made up of two sets of lines that cross each other. A grid system that covered the whole earth would let anyone find any location on Earth. We have such a grid today. We call it **latitude** and **longitude.**

Using Latitude and Longitude

Latitude lines, called *parallels,* run east and west around the earth. Longitude lines, called *meridians,* run north and south. Latitude and longitude are measured in **degrees.** The shape of the earth is a sphere. It is 360 degrees around a sphere. Each degree of latitude or longitude is 1/360th of the distance around the earth. The symbol for degree is °.

The starting point for measuring degrees of latitude is the **Equator.** The Equator is a line of latitude. It divides the earth into two equal parts. The Equator runs east and west all the way around the world, halfway between the North and South Poles. Figure 1-5 shows that the Equator is at zero degrees (0°) latitude. When we give the latitude of a place, we must state whether the place is north or south of the Equator. For example, the North

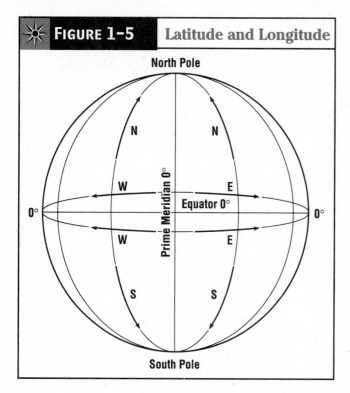

☀ FIGURE 1-5   Latitude and Longitude

North Pole

N   N

W   E

Prime Meridian 0°

Equator 0°

0°   0°

W   E

S   S

South Pole

Latitude and longitude are determined by measuring the angle between the Equator or Prime Meridian and any point on Earth. Look at Figure 1-6 and find the Equator. Now find the line 10° north of the Equator. The angle between the Equator, the center of the earth, and this line is 10°.

Now look at Figure 1-7 and find the Prime Meridian. Now find the line 10° west of the Prime Meridian. The angle between the Prime Meridian, the center of the earth, and this line is 10°.

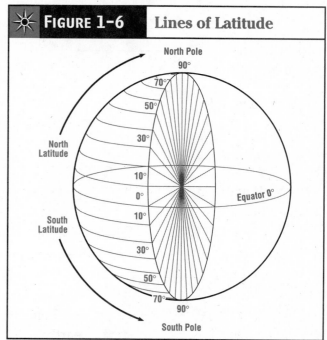

☀ FIGURE 1-6   Lines of Latitude

North Pole
90°
70°
50°
North Latitude
30°
10°
0°   Equator 0°
10°
South Latitude
30°
50°
70°
90°
South Pole

Pole is at 90° north latitude. If we said only that a place was at 90° latitude, we would not know if the place was the North Pole or the South Pole.

The starting point for measuring longitude is called the **Prime Meridian.** Meridian is another name for a longitude line. The earth does not have an east pole and a west pole. Therefore, some point had to be chosen as the starting point for measuring longitude. Through international agreement, Greenwich, England, was chosen as this place. All longitude is measured from the Prime Meridian that runs from the North and South Poles through Greenwich, England.

Figure 1-5 shows the Prime Meridian is at 0° longitude. When we give the longitude of a place, we must state whether the place is east or west of the Prime Meridian.

Lines of latitude run all the way around the earth, but lines of longitude do not. On the other side of the earth from the Prime Meridian is the line of longitude marked 180°. This line is the ending point for measuring longitude. The area west of the Prime Meridian and 180° is west longitude. The United States is located west of the Prime Meridian.

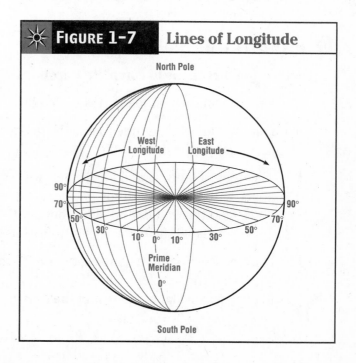

☀ FIGURE 1-7   Lines of Longitude

North Pole

West Longitude   East Longitude

90°   90°
70°   70°
50°   50°
30°   30°
10° 0° 10°

Prime Meridian
0°

South Pole

Using Your Skills

Ⓐ REVIEWING KEY TERMS

Explain the meaning of each of the following terms.

1. degree

   _____

   _____

2. latitude

   _____

   _____

3. longitude

   _____

   _____

4. Equator

   _____

   _____

5. Prime Meridian

   _____

   _____

Ⓑ PRACTICING MAP SKILLS

Follow the directions to complete Map 1-6: The World.

1. Find the line of latitude that is the Equator. Write Equator on the line.

2. Find the line of longitude that is the Prime Meridian. Write Prime Meridian on the line.

3. The lines of latitude and longitude shown on the map are spaced 30° apart. Find the first latitude line north of the Equator. Label the line 30°N. Find the first latitude line south of the Equator. Label the line 30°S. Now label the rest of the latitude lines correctly.

4. Find the first longitude line east of the Prime Meridian. Label the line 30°E. Find the first longitude line west of the Prime Meridian. Label the line 30°W. Now label the rest of the longitude lines correctly.

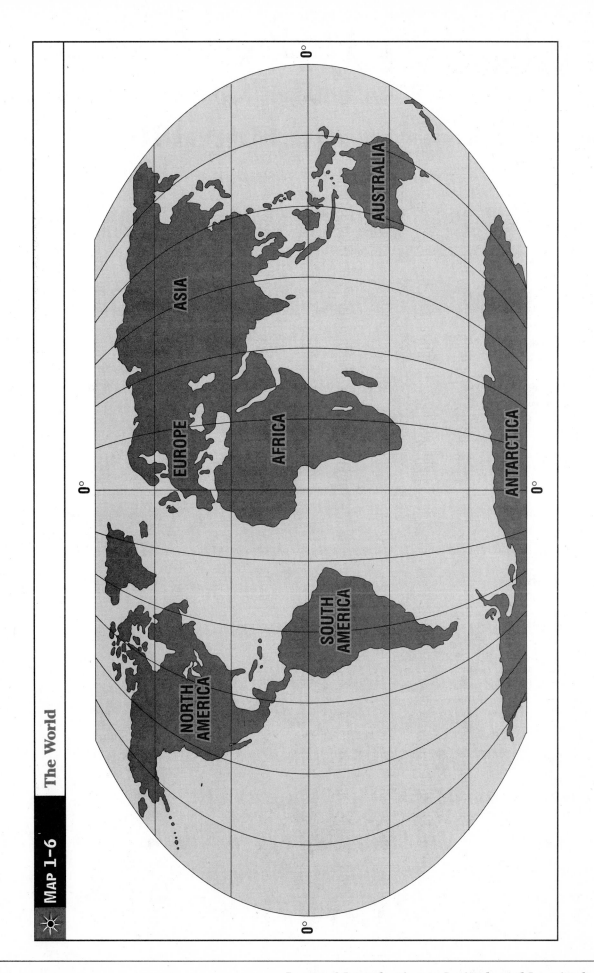

MAP 1-6

The World

0°

0°

0°

0°

NORTH AMERICA

SOUTH AMERICA

EUROPE

AFRICA

ASIA

AUSTRALIA

ANTARCTICA

Lesson 5 — Finding Places Using Latitude and Longitude

Lesson 5

Finding Places Using Latitude and Longitude

WHAT YOU WILL LEARN

To locate places using latitude and longitude

READING STRATEGY

Create a flowchart like the one below to explain how to find a place using latitude and longitude.

Finding places using latitude and longitude is just like using a grid, as you learned about in Lesson 3. Look at Map 1-7. Notice that each degree of latitude and longitude is shown. Find the line for 40°N latitude. What city is located at this latitude? What line of longitude is closest to this city? We say that Boulder is located at about 40°N latitude, 105°W longitude. Remember that when we write the location of a place using latitude and longitude, latitude is always written first.

Now look at the city of Delta. What line of latitude is closest to Delta? What line of longitude runs through Delta? We say that Delta is located at about 39°N latitude, 108°W longitude. This is Delta's absolute location. What is the absolute location of Durango?

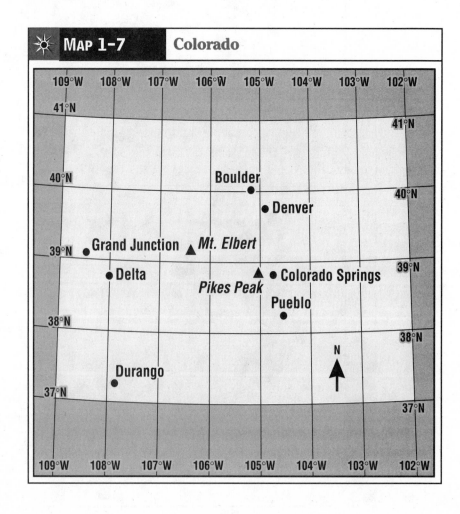

MAP 1-7   Colorado

Ⓐ PRACTICING MAP SKILLS

Answer these questions about Map 1-7: Colorado.

1. Which line of latitude runs near Pikes Peak? _____

2. Which line of longitude runs near Pikes Peak? _____

3. Write the location of Pikes Peak using latitude and longitude.

   _____

4. Which line of latitude runs nearest Pueblo? _____

5. Which line of longitude is closest to Pueblo? _____

6. Write the location of Pueblo using latitude and longitude.

   _____

7. What city is near 39°N latitude, 105°W longitude? _____

8. What city is located at about 39°N latitude, midway between 108° and 109°W longitude?

   _____

9. Which line of longitude is at Colorado's eastern border? _____

10. Which line of latitude runs nearest Mt. Elbert? _____

Ⓑ PRACTICING MAP SKILLS

Use a map of your state that includes lines of latitude and longitude to complete the following activities.

1. Write the approximate location of your city using latitude and longitude.

   _____

2. Write the approximate location of your state capital using latitude and longitude.

   _____

3. Select a popular recreation area in your state, such as a national park, national forest, or large lake. Write the name of this recreation area and its approximate location latitude and longitude.

   _____

   _____

⑥ PRACTICING MAP SKILLS

Use Map 1-8: Africa to answer the following questions. Be sure always to begin counting degrees of latitude from the Equator and degrees of longitude from the Prime Meridian.

1. What body of water is located at 0° latitude, 0° longitude?

    _____

2. What body of water is located between 30°N and 40°N latitude?

    _____

3. What city is located near 30°S latitude, 30°E longitude?

    _____

4. In what country do the lines of 10°N latitude, 0° longitude cross?

    _____

5. In what country do the lines of 10°S latitude and 20°E longitude cross?

    _____

6. Write the approximate location of Cairo, Egypt, using latitude and longitude. (Remember that the lines of latitude and longitude on this map are spaced 10° apart. Give locations to the nearest degree.)

    _____

7. Write the approximate location of Kigali, Rwanda, using latitude and longitude.

    _____

8. Write the approximate location of Cape Town, South Africa, using latitude and longitude.

    _____

9. Write the approximate location of Abidjan, Côte d'Ivoire, using latitude and longitude.

    _____

10. Write the approximate location of Freetown, Sierra Leone, using latitude and longitude.

    _____

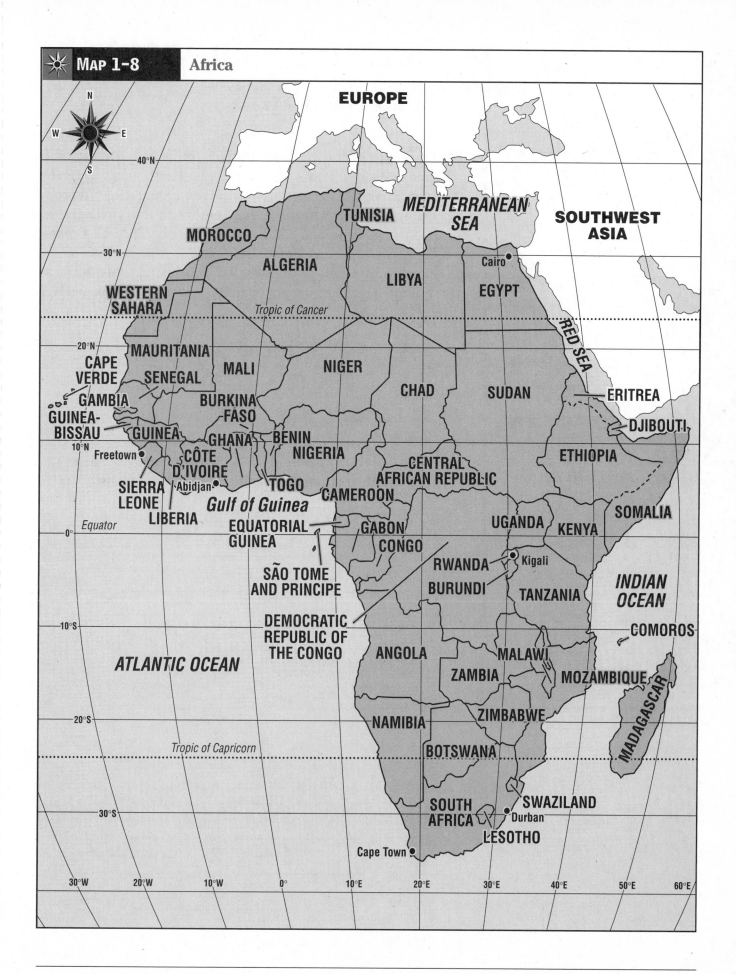

MAP 1-8   Africa

EUROPE

N
W   E
S

40°N

TUNISIA

MEDITERRANEAN
SEA

SOUTHWEST
ASIA

MOROCCO

30°N

ALGERIA

LIBYA

Cairo •

EGYPT

WESTERN
SAHARA

Tropic of Cancer

RED SEA

20°N

MAURITANIA

CAPE
VERDE

SENEGAL

MALI

NIGER

CHAD

SUDAN

ERITREA

GAMBIA

BURKINA
FASO

DJIBOUTI

GUINEA-
BISSAU

GUINEA

GHANA

BENIN

NIGERIA

ETHIOPIA

10°N

Freetown •

CÔTE
D'IVOIRE

TOGO

CENTRAL
AFRICAN REPUBLIC

SIERRA
LEONE

Abidjan •

CAMEROON

SOMALIA

LIBERIA

Gulf of Guinea

UGANDA

KENYA

Equator

0°

EQUATORIAL
GUINEA

GABON

CONGO

SÃO TOME
AND PRINCIPE

RWANDA

Kigali •

INDIAN
OCEAN

BURUNDI

TANZANIA

DEMOCRATIC
REPUBLIC OF
THE CONGO

10°S

COMOROS

ATLANTIC OCEAN

ANGOLA

MALAWI

MOZAMBIQUE

ZAMBIA

MADAGASCAR

20°S

ZIMBABWE

NAMIBIA

Tropic of Capricorn

BOTSWANA

30°S

SOUTH
AFRICA

SWAZILAND

Durban •

LESOTHO

Cape Town •

30°W   20°W   10°W   0°   10°E   20°E   30°E   40°E   50°E   60°E

Lesson 6 Locating Continents and Oceans

WHAT YOU WILL LEARN

To locate major landmasses and bodies of water in many parts of the world

READING STRATEGY

Create a diagram like the one below to list the world's continents and oceans.

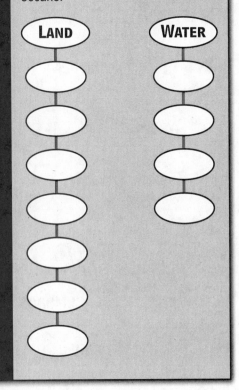

The surface of the earth is covered with land and water. The land is divided into seven continents: North America, South America, Europe, Asia, Africa, Australia, and Antarctica. The continents are divided into more than 190 countries. The water is divided into four oceans and a number of seas. The four oceans are the Atlantic, Pacific, Indian, and Arctic.

Before you proceed with this lesson, you should study the locations of the seven continents, major countries, and four oceans on a world map.

Using Your Skills

Ⓐ PRACTICING MAP SKILLS

The continents and oceans are labeled with letters on Map 1-9: The World: Physical. Write the name of each continent or ocean beside the correct letter below.

1. A _____
2. B _____
3. C _____
4. D _____
5. E _____
6. F _____
7. G _____
8. H _____
9. I _____
10. J _____
11. K _____
12. L _____
13. M _____

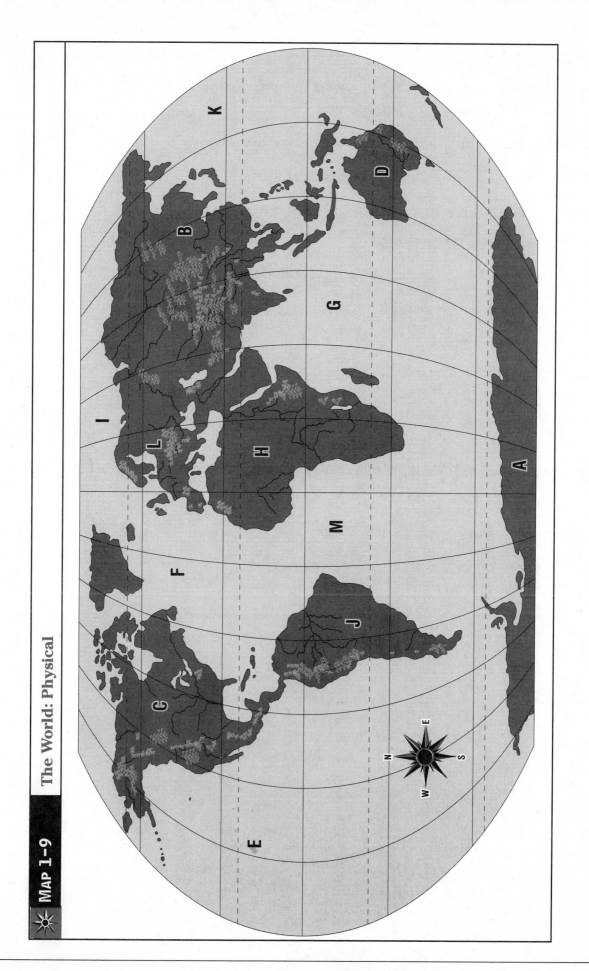

The World: Physical

MAP 1-9

❸ RECALLING FACTS

Fill in the blanks to complete the following sentences correctly.

1. South America is bordered by the _____ Ocean on the west and the _____ Ocean on the east.

2. Africa is _____ of Europe.

3. The most direct route from Australia to Africa is across the _____ Ocean.

4. North America is _____ of Europe.

5. Asia is bordered by the _____ Ocean on the east and the _____ Ocean on the south.

6. Africa is bordered by the _____ Ocean on the east and the _____ Ocean on the west.

7. Europe is _____ of the Arctic Ocean.

8. The most direct route from South America to Asia is across the _____ Ocean.

9. Asia is _____ of Europe.

10. Europe is _____ of South America.

Lesson 7 Understanding Map Symbols and Legends

What You Will Learn

To use map legends to interpret symbols commonly used on maps

Reading Strategy

Create a chart like the one below. Fill in examples of the kinds of information each type of map symbol is used to represent.

PICTURE SYMBOL	• • •
COLORS OR SHADING	• • •

Terms to Know

symbol, legend, key

Maps can be used to show many different kinds of information. One of the main uses of maps is to show the locations of towns and cities. However, maps can also show where cotton is grown, cattle are raised, and where different species of wild animals are found. The possibilities are almost endless.

Often one map shows more than one kind of information. This means that some way must be used to help the person reading the map understand several kinds of information shown on the map. For example, if a map shows the locations of towns, roads, and parks, there must be some way to know which is which.

Using Map Legends

Maps use **symbols** to help the reader distinguish different kinds of information. The meaning of each symbol is explained in the map's **legend,** or **key.** Each symbol used on the map is shown, along with an explanation of what the symbol means.

Look at Figure 1-8. What symbol is used to show the location of a city? What symbol is used to show the location of a city that is a state capital? What symbol is used to show the location of a park?

There can be many different symbols. Some maps show the kinds of products a state or country produces. Often these maps use picture symbols to show where goods are produced. For example, a small picture of an oil derrick ( ) may be used to show where oil is found. A picture of a sheep may be used to show where sheep are raised.

FIGURE 1-8 Map Legend 1

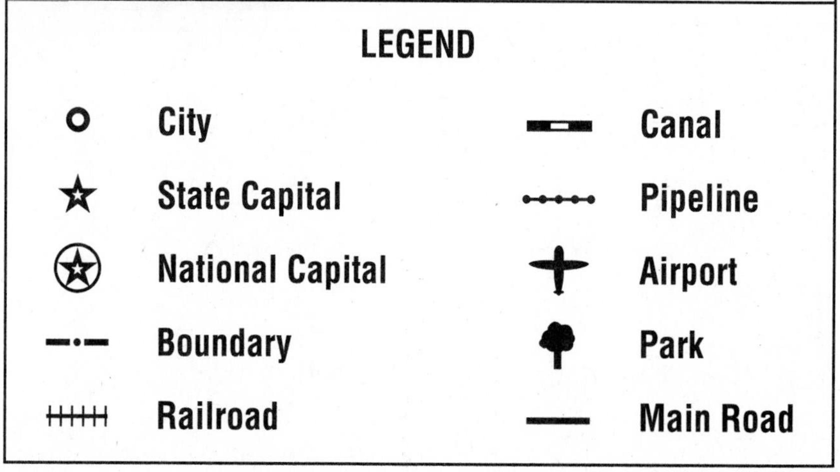
LEGEND
City
State Capital
National Capital
Boundary
Railroad
Canal
Pipeline
Airport
Park
Main Road

Look at Figure 1-9. What symbol shows where wheat is grown? What is grown where you see the symbol (●)?

Sometimes maps use colors or areas of shading as symbols. This is often used when the feature being shown covers a wide area. For example, Map 1-10 uses one color to show the area covered by the Amazon River basin. Population density maps use several colors to indicate different levels of population per square mile or kilometer. Here are some examples of shading: ▦ ▧ When you are reading a map that uses shading, you must be very careful to read the map correctly. It is easy to get shading like the following mixed up. ▨ ▩

If you have trouble telling such patterns apart, try this. Look at part of the map you wish to read. Then look at the legend and pick the pattern you

think is correct. Cover the others with your fingers or a piece of paper. Look at the legend and then at the map. This should help you decide if you have picked the correct pattern.

FIGURE 1-9 | **Map Legend 2**

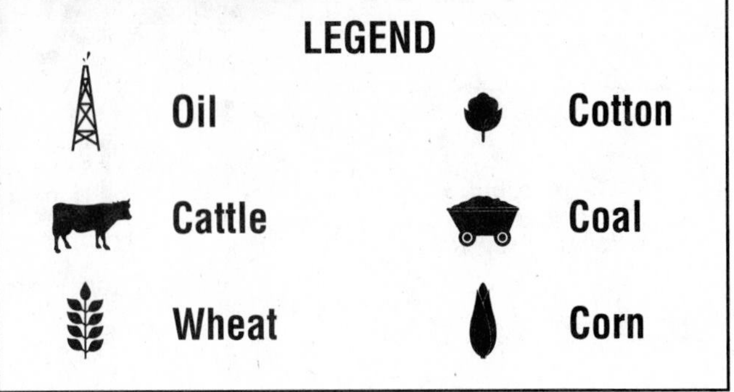

LEGEND

Oil   Cotton

Cattle   Coal

Wheat   Corn

Using Your Skills

Ⓐ PRACTICING MAP SKILLS

Use the map legends in Figures 1-8 and 1-9 to match each symbol below with its meaning.

_____ 1.    a. wheat

_____ 2.    b. airport

_____ 3. ★   c. corn

_____ 4.   d. oil

_____ 5.    e. railroad

_____ 6.   f. state capital

B PRACTICING MAP SKILLS

Use **Map 1-10: The Amazon Basin** and its legend to answer the questions that follow.

1. What covers most of the Amazon River basin?

   _____

2. In how many places in the Amazon River basin is gold found?

   _____

3. In what part of the Amazon River basin is coal found?

   _____

4. About how many miles apart are the deposits of tin in the Amazon River basin?

   _____

5. In what part of the Amazon River basin is oil found? Diamonds?

   _____

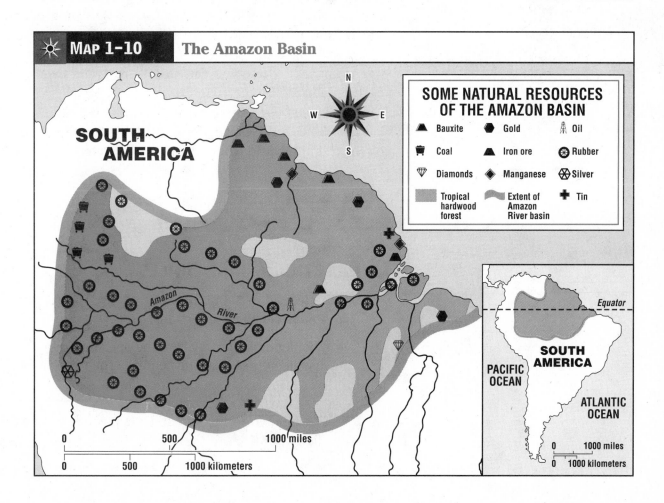

Reading a Road Map

WHAT YOU WILL LEARN

To use a road map to select routes and estimate distance and travel time, and plan a family trip

READING STRATEGY

Create a table like the one below listing four important uses for road maps.

HOW ROAD MAPS ARE USEFUL
1.
2.
3.
4.

A new thing from American carmakers is a car that doesn't need road maps. A special computer in the car "talks" to a satellite orbiting the earth. The computer and the satellite keep track of where the car is every minute. This information is displayed on a screen in the car. As you drive the car, its location is shown on a map on the screen. The new technology is called a Global Positioning System (GPS).

Using Road Maps

Even with this new technology, however, we will still need road maps. Road maps are useful for planning what route to take on a trip, finding the location of places that are new to us, and estimating how long it will take to drive to a particular place. Road maps can also give information about things to see and do.

Reading a road map requires many of the skills you have practiced in earlier lessons in this book. You need to know how to find direction and distance. Road maps have an index that uses a grid. Symbols are used on road maps to tell you such things as how large towns are, where you can stop to rest, and even points of interest along the way.

You will often use the index first when you read a road map. Find the name of the place you want to visit. The index will tell you the cell in the grid where the place is located.

Using Your Skills

Ⓐ PRACTICING MAP SKILLS

Use the legend of Map 1-11: Road Map of Part of New York State to answer these questions.

1. What kind of highways are the ones numbered 81 and 90 which cross near the center of the map?

   _____

2. What can you expect to find at a place marked with this symbol? **Ⱥ**

   _____

MAP 1-11   Road Map of Part of New York State

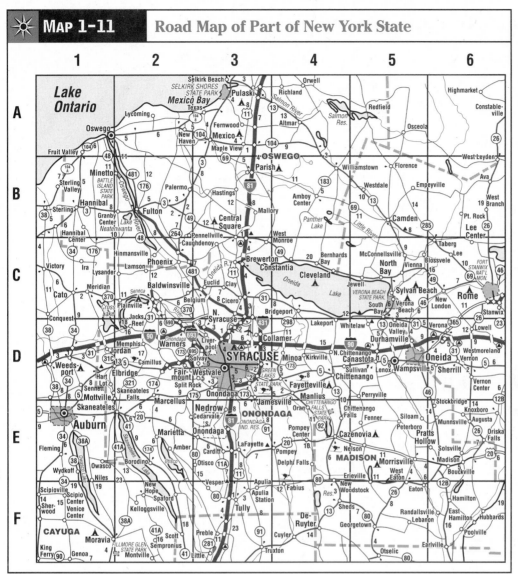

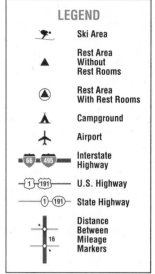

LEGEND

Ski Area
Rest Area Without Rest Rooms
Rest Area With Rest Rooms
Campground
Airport
Interstate Highway
U.S. Highway
State Highway
Distance Between Mileage Markers

3. What do the numbers between two marks like these ——+——+—— tell you?

_____

4. What is the difference in meaning between these two symbols? ⬤ ▲

_____

5. What could you expect to do at a place marked with this symbol? 🎿

_____

6. How many different kinds of highways are shown on the map?

_____

ⓑ PRACTICING MAP SKILLS

Use Map 1-11, its legend, and the map index to answer these questions.

1. In which cell in the grid is each of the following located?

   a. Parish _____

   b. Cleveland _____

   c. Texas _____

   d. Chittenango Falls State Park _____

2. What could you expect to do near Fabius (F-4) in January? _____

3. Plan a trip from Mexico to Weedsport using interstate highway as much

   as possible. About how far will you travel? _____

4. Suppose that you average about 50 miles per hour on interstate highways. About how long will it take you to travel from the farthest point
   north shown on the map to the farthest point south?

   _____

ⓒ PRACTICING MAP SKILLS

**Use a highway map of your own state to plan a vacation trip. Start at
your hometown and plot out a three-day trip of places you would like to
visit. What points of interest would you see? What towns would you go
through? How many miles would you travel over which highways? Think
about where you might stay overnight, stop for gasoline, and good places
to stop for food, too.**

_____

_____

_____

_____

_____

_____

_____

_____

_____

_____

_____

_____

_____

Earth-Sun Relationships

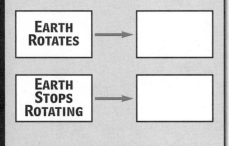
What is your favorite season of the year? Do you like summer more than winter? Do you know *why* we have seasons? Do you know that you can go from one season to another just by changing your location?

Our seasons are caused by the relationship between Earth and the sun. The sun plays a very important part in our lives. Life on Earth is supported by energy from the sun. Our language shows how important the sun is to our everyday lives. We have sun roofs, sunglasses, and sun suits. We need the Vitamin D that the sun provides to keep our bodies strong.

What Causes Seasons?

If all parts of the earth received the same amount of sunshine year-round, there would be no seasons. However, this is not the case. The difference in the amount of sunshine received is the result of two things: the movement of the earth around the sun, and the tilt of the earth on its **axis.** The earth's axis is an imaginary line drawn from the North Pole to the South Pole through the center of the earth.

Seasons in the Northern Hemisphere

Look at Figure 1-10 on page 38 of the earth's movement around the sun. This diagram shows the seasons for the **Northern Hemisphere,** the part of the earth north of the Equator. This is where the United States is located.

The earth rotates on its axis once in 24 hours. This is the length of our day. The earth also revolves around the sun. This trip takes a little over 365 days—one year. Notice that the earth's axis is tilted. As the earth travels around the sun, its axis always points in the same direction. This means that sometimes the North Pole is pointed toward the sun. At other times the North Pole is pointed away from the sun.

Find the position of the earth marked "summer" in Figure 1-10. Place a pencil on the drawing so that its ends line up with the North and South Poles. Notice that the upper end of the pencil is tilted toward the sun in the diagram. The North Pole points toward the sun when we are having our summer in the Northern Hemisphere.

Now find the position of the earth marked "winter." Without changing the angle at which your pencil is tilted, move the pencil to the earth's winter position. Notice that now the upper end of the pencil is tilted away from the sun. The North Pole points away

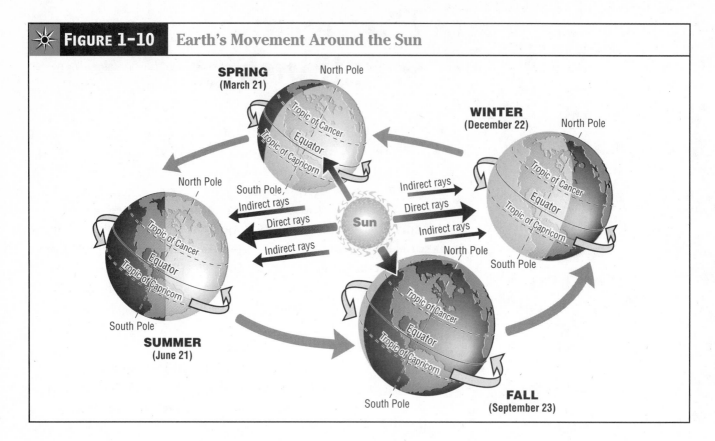

from the sun during winter in the Northern Hemisphere.

Seasons in the Southern Hemisphere

When it is summer in the Northern Hemisphere, it is winter south of the Equator in the **Southern Hemisphere.** For example, if you are baking in the heat and direct sun of an Arizona summer, you can fly to somewhere south of the Equator and enjoy cold winter weather.

Whether we are having summer or winter is due to how much heat our location on the earth is getting from the sun. When the northern half of the earth is pointing toward the sun, it gets more heat for two reasons. One reason is that there are more hours of daylight. The other reason is that the sun's rays fall more directly on the Northern Hemisphere. These direct rays are hotter than the sun's indirect rays in winter.

How the Sun Affects Seasons

You can use two pieces of paper, or two paper plates, to show why the direct rays of the sun are

hotter. Cut a circle about 1½ inches across in the first piece of paper. Hold this piece of paper up to the sun or a strong light. Hold the second piece of paper about 3 inches behind it so that light comes through the hole. This represents the light of the sun falling on the earth.

Now tilt the second piece of paper so that first it points straight up and down, and then so that its top points away from the first piece, and then toward it. What happens to the spot of light falling on the paper? It changes shape. When the top of the second piece of paper is tilted toward or away from the first piece of paper, the spot of light gets bigger.

The smaller the spot of light, the hotter it is. In summer the sun is almost directly overhead. Its rays fall on a smaller spot of Earth than in winter. That part of the earth gets more heat. In winter the sun is lower in the sky. Its rays are slanted and fall on a larger spot of Earth than in summer. That part of the earth gets less heat.

What happens if the sun is always almost directly overhead? There will be no seasons. The weather will always be warm. This happens near the Equator in places such as Latin America.

Ⓐ RECALLING FACTS

Use Figure 1-10: Earth's Movement Around the Sun to help you label
Figure 1-11: Seasons in the Northern Hemisphere correctly.

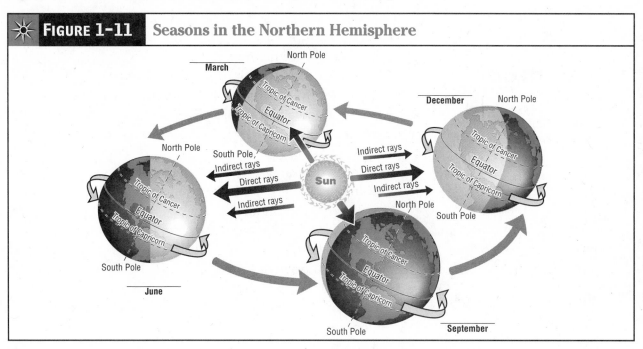

☀ **FIGURE 1-11** Seasons in the Northern Hemisphere

Ⓑ RECALLING FACTS

Seasons in the Southern Hemisphere are opposite those in the Northern
Hemisphere. Label Figure 1-12: Seasons in the Southern Hemisphere.

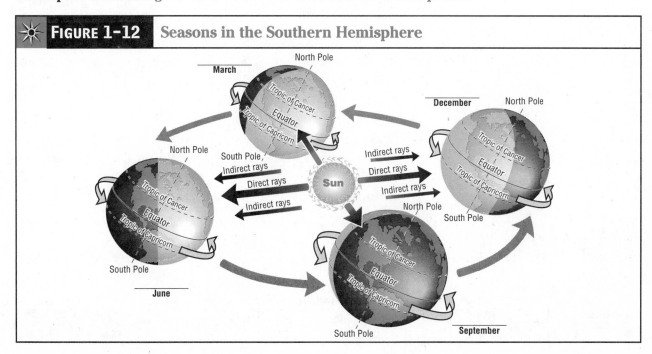

☀ **FIGURE 1-12** Seasons in the Southern Hemisphere

Lesson 10 Understanding Time Zones

WHAT YOU WILL LEARN

To understand the relationship between time, the rotation of the earth, and time zones

READING STRATEGY

Draw a diagram like the one below. Label the four time zones of the continental United States in order from east to west.

Pacific Ocean | | | | | Atlantic Ocean

TERMS TO KNOW

time zone

Would you like to be able to fly through space at over 1,000 miles per hour? Well, you are—right this minute. The earth rotates on its axis at about 1,000 miles per hour at the Equator, carrying you with it. Each hour your spot on the earth travels 15 degrees of longitude toward the east.

You may think you do not notice any sign of your speedy trip, but you do. Every day you see the sun march across the sky. The sun is not actually moving, of course. The earth is turning from west to east. That is why the sun comes up in the east and sets in the west.

It takes the earth 24 hours to rotate on its axis once. Imagine that the sun has just come up. In one hour the sun will be higher in the sky. With each hour that passes, the sun will rise higher, until noon. Then it will become lower, until finally it sinks out of sight.

Imagine that you have a friend who lives 1,000 miles west of you. When the sun has been up for one hour where you live, it will just be coming up where your friend lives. You have another friend who lives 1,000 miles east of you. When the sun has been up for one hour where you live, it will have been up for two hours at your friend's house to the east.

Using the Sun to Tell Time

People have used the sun to tell time for many years. How high the sun is in the sky can tell us how long it has been since sunrise, and how long it is until sunset. When the sun is at its highest point in the sky, it is noon. Remember your two friends to the east and the west of you? When it is noon where you are, it is an hour past noon where your friend to the east lives. It is an hour before noon at your friend's house to the west.

Look at Figure 1-13. It shows the 24 hours in a day. The sun is at 12 noon. Each division of the bar stands for the distance the earth turns in one hour. As you move east on the bar, times become later in the day. As you move west, times become earlier. For example, one division east of 12 noon, the time is 1:00 P.M. while

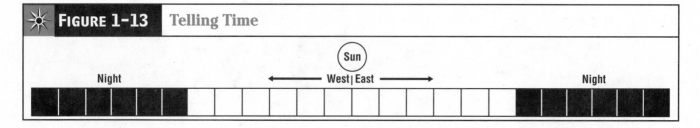

☀ **FIGURE 1-13** | **Telling Time**

Night   ← West | East →   Sun   Night

one division west of 12 noon, the time is 11:00 A.M. Fill in the blanks on the bar to show the correct times. Cut the bar out and tape it around a tennis ball. This shows you how time changes as you travel around the world. Notice that when it is 12 noon on one side of the world, it is 12 midnight on the other.

Time Zones

The earth is divided into 24 parts for keeping time, just like the bar in Figure 1-13. We call each division of the earth a **time zone.** Every place on the earth within a time zone has the same time as every other place in that zone.

Before we had time zones, every town kept its own time. Because of the earth's rotation, noon came at different times for towns even 40 or 50 miles east or west of each other. As long as travel was slow, this was not a problem. But with the coming of railroads the differing times became a big problem. Trying to tell people when trains would arrive and leave was almost impossible when the clocks in every town were set at a different local time.

Time zones were set up to solve this problem. Time zones are about 1,000 miles across from east to west at the Equator. Time zones become narrower as you move toward the Poles. Only four time zones are needed to cover the entire continental United States. (Alaska and Hawaii are in other time zones because they are farther west.) These four time zones are called the Eastern Time Zone, the Central Time Zone, the Mountain Time Zone, and the Pacific Time Zone. In some cases the time zones follow the boundaries of states or countries rather than lines of longitude. Find these zones on Map 1-12 below.

People who travel across time zones must keep track of time. Whenever you cross a time zone going east, the time becomes one hour *later*. You must set your watch ahead one hour. Whenever you cross a time zone going west, the time becomes one hour *earlier*. You must set your watch back one hour.

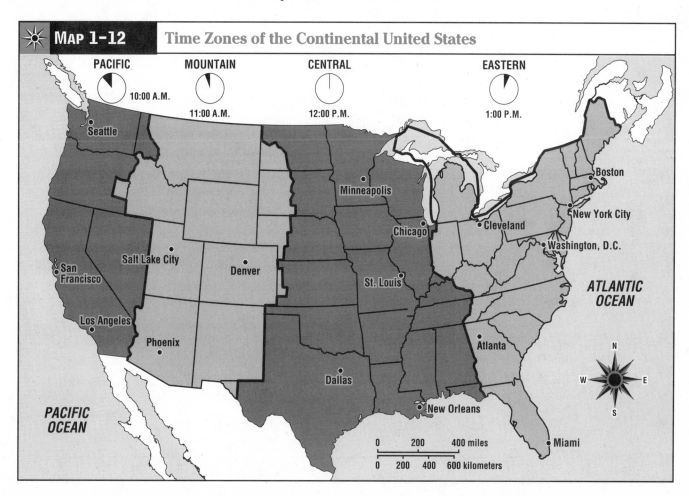

MAP 1-12 Time Zones of the Continental United States

ⓐ PRACTICING MAP SKILLS

Use Map 1-12: Time Zones of the Continental United States to answer the questions.

1. Which time zone is farthest east? _____

2. Which time zone is farthest west? _____

3. When it is 12 noon in Dallas, what time is it in New York City? _____

4. When it is 4:00 P.M. in Denver, what time is it in San Francisco? _____

5. Suppose that you live in Atlanta. Your grandparents in Seattle want to call you on your birthday. They go to sleep at 10:00 P.M. What is the latest Atlanta time you can expect to hear from them?

   _____

6. Suppose you live in St. Louis. You have a computer made by a company near Los Angeles. You want to call people at the company about a problem you are having with your computer. They go to work at 9:00 A.M. What is the earliest St. Louis time you can call them?

   _____

7. Imagine that you are flying from Boston to San Francisco. You leave Boston at 8:00 A.M. What time is it in San Francisco?

   _____

8. The plane trip from Boston to San Francisco takes six hours. You leave Boston at 8:00 A.M. What time will it be in Boston when you land?

   _____

   What time will it be in San Francisco when you land? Why?

   _____

   _____

9. You have to fly from San Francisco to Chicago. You leave San Francisco at 5:30 P.M. What time is it in Chicago?

   _____

10. The plane trip from San Francisco to Chicago lasts four hours. You leave San Francisco at 5:30 P.M. What time will it be in Chicago when you land? Why?

   _____

   _____

Comparing Types of Maps

WHAT YOU WILL LEARN
To use maps with different themes

READING STRATEGY
Create a diagram like the one below. In each of the outer circles, write an example of a feature you would find on a typical physical map.

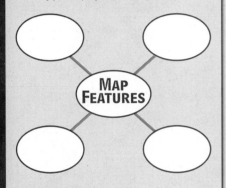

MAP FEATURES

TERMS TO KNOW
physical map, relief map, political map, special-purpose map

Suppose you are planning a trip to another country. What would you like to know about that country before you leave home? What language is spoken there? Where are the country's interesting places to visit located? Should you take clothes for warm weather, or cold?

These are just a few of the things you can learn from maps. In fact, there are almost as many kinds of maps as there are kinds of information to show on them. Let's look at some of the different kinds of maps and what they can tell us about our world.

Using Physical Maps

A **physical map** shows how the land looks. Mountains, rivers, plains, and lakes—the physical features of the land—are shown on a physical map. Sometimes a physical map shows the height of the land above sea level. It may use colors and shading to show *relief*—or how flat or rugged the land surface is. This kind of physical map is called a **relief map.**

Look at Map 1-13: United States: Physical on page 44. Find the Rocky Mountains. What physical feature lies just east of the Rocky Mountains? Into what river do the Ohio and Missouri rivers flow? Into what body of water does the Mississippi River flow? What ocean lies east of the United States? These are all kinds of information you can find on physical maps.

Using Political Maps

A **political map** shows how humans have divided the surface of the earth into countries, states, and other political divisions. Often, a political map will show some physical features, such as lakes and rivers, because these are sometimes used as political boundaries. A political map will show where the boundaries between countries, states, or counties are located. It may also show the locations of cities. Unlike physical maps, which remain fairly constant over time, political maps change as political relationships shift.

Look at Map 1-14: Australia and New Zealand: Political on page 45. Notice the dashed lines on the map. These show the boundaries between states. The letters in SMALL CAPITALS are the names of the states. Queensland is the name of one state. Can you name

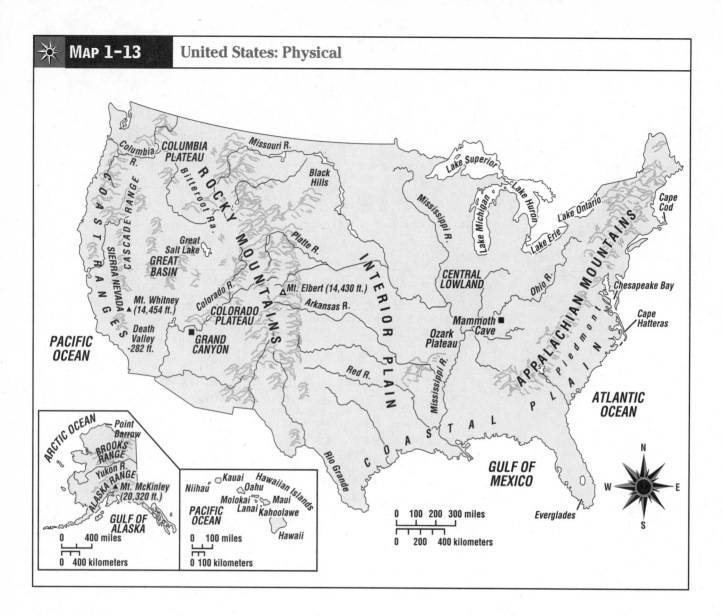

the others? What is the capital of Australia? What tells you it is the capital? What are some other cities shown on the map?

Using Special-Purpose Maps

Maps that emphasize a single idea or a particular kind of information about an area are called **special-purpose maps.** There are many kinds of special-purpose maps, each designed to serve a different need. Population density maps, time zone maps, and climate maps are among the different kinds of special-purpose maps. You will learn to read these and other kinds of special-purpose maps later in this book.

Some special-purpose maps—such as economic activity maps and natural resource maps—show the distribution of particular activities, resources, or products in a given area. Colors and symbols represent the location or distribution of activities and resources.

Many times maps will be a combination of physical, political, and special-purpose. For example, a special-purpose map that shows what products are produced in the United States will usually have state boundaries shown. What kind of map shows boundaries? A land-use map may also show major rivers. What kind of map shows rivers?

When you read a map, what should you look at first? In order to know what the map is about, you must first look at the map's title. The title may be at the top or bottom of the map, or it may be in a box with the legend.

MAP 1-14   **Australia and New Zealand: Political**

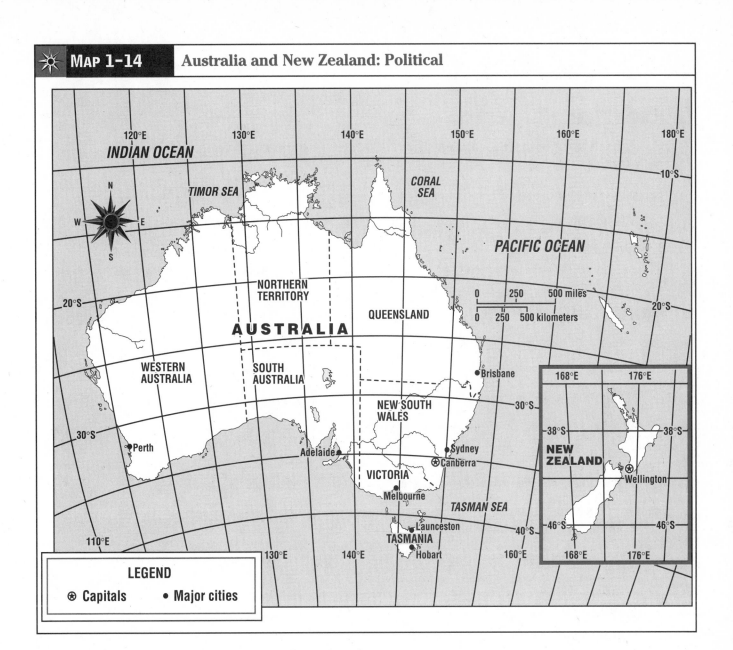

INDIAN OCEAN

TIMOR SEA

CORAL SEA

PACIFIC OCEAN

NORTHERN TERRITORY

AUSTRALIA

QUEENSLAND

WESTERN AUSTRALIA

SOUTH AUSTRALIA

• Brisbane

NEW SOUTH WALES

• Perth

Adelaide •

• Sydney
⊗ Canberra

VICTORIA

• Melbourne

TASMAN SEA

• Launceston
TASMANIA
• Hobart

0   250   500 miles
0   250   500 kilometers

NEW ZEALAND

⊗ Wellington

LEGEND

⊗ Capitals   • Major cities

Using Your Skills

Ⓐ REVIEWING KEY TERMS

Match each term with its meaning. Draw a line from each term to its definition.

1. political map
2. physical map
3. special-purpose map

a. a kind of map that shows features of the land

b. a kind of map that gives one particular kind of information

c. a kind of map that shows how humans have divided the earth into countries and states

Ⓑ PRACTICING MAP SKILLS

Use Map 1-15: Ethiopia, 2001 below to answer the questions.

1. What is the title of this map? _____

2. What part of the map tells you what the symbols on the map mean? _____

3. What do the solid black lines on the map stand for? _____

4. What does ▨▨▨▨▨▨ on the map stand for? _____

5. What does ▪▪▪▪▪▪▪▪ on the map stand for? _____

6. Would you call this a physical map, a political map, a special-purpose map, or a combination of all three? Why?

_____

_____

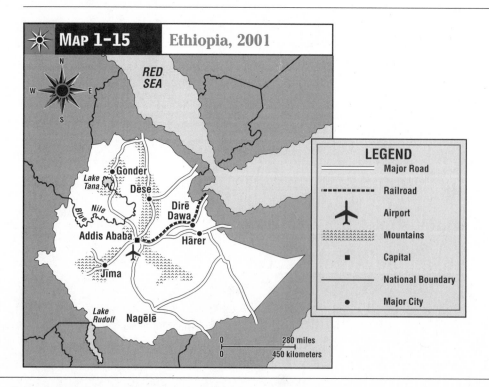

LEGEND
— Major Road
▪▪▪▪▪ Railroad
✈ Airport
▨▨▨ Mountains
■ Capital
— National Boundary
● Major City

Comparing Map Projections

WHAT YOU WILL LEARN

To compare and contrast different map projections

READING STRATEGY

Create a chart like the one below. On the left, list three words or phrases that describe globes. On the right, do the same for maps.

GLOBES	MAPS

TERMS TO KNOW

map projection, Mercator projection, cylindrical projection, planar projection, conic projection, Winkel Tripel projection

Have you ever heard the saying, "You can't have your cake and eat it, too"? It's a way of saying that when we get one thing, often we must give up something else.

Choosing a map sometimes means giving up one thing in order to get another. Maps show four things: *direction, distance, shape,* and *size.* Only a globe can show all four with accuracy at the same time. Maps, however, cannot. A map may show direction well, but the shapes of landmasses may be quite inaccurate. Or, if shapes are shown correctly, distances may not be.

You might think that the way to get around this problem would just be to use globes all the time. However, think how hard it would be to get a globe in your pocket or inside the covers of a book.

Understanding Map Projections

There are many different kinds of **map projections.** A map projection is a way of showing the rounded earth on a flat piece of paper. Where does the word "projection" come from? Imagine a clear globe with latitude and longitude lines and the outlines of the landmasses on it. Suppose there was a lightbulb inside the globe. If you wrapped a piece of paper around the globe and turned on the lightbulb, the outlines of the grid and landmasses would be projected onto the paper. The three basic categories of map projections are cylindrical, planar, and conic.

Cylindrical Projections

Look at Figure 1-14 of a **Mercator projection.** This type of projection is a **cylindrical projection.** It shows how the earth would look if a piece of paper were wrapped to form a tube or cylinder around the globe. You will recall that lines of latitude are the same distance apart on a globe. But look at what happened to lines of latitude on a Mercator projection. The lines get farther apart as you move away from the Equator. This means that distances are not true. It also means that the sizes of landmasses near the North and South Poles are greatly exaggerated in size.

Planar Projections

Some maps are round; they look like a flattened disk of the earth's surface. Longitude lines on these maps are straight and meet in the center of the circle. Latitude lines form a series of circles that get smaller as they reach the center of this kind of map.

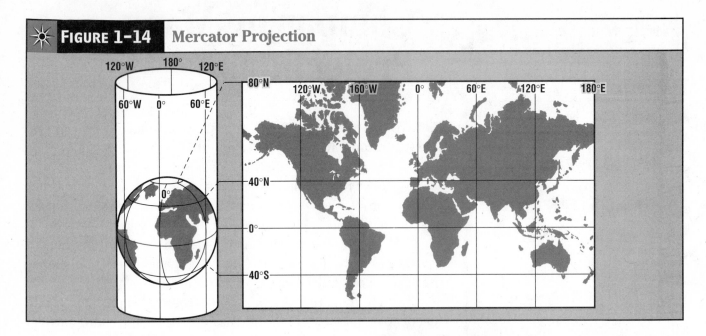

☀ **FIGURE 1-14** | **Mercator Projection**

This is called a **planar projection.** Also known as an *azimuthal projection,* it comes from the idea of projecting the globe onto a plane that is touching the globe at one point. A common form of planar projection is a polar projection. Polar projections show the North Pole or the South Pole as the center of the map.

Although size and shape are distorted on planar projections, distances and directions are accurate when the line of travel passes through the center of the map.

☀ **FIGURE 1-15** | **Planar Projection**

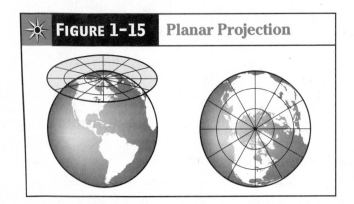

Conic Projections

Often you will see maps on which the longitude lines are straight and get closer together toward the north, or top of the map. Latitude lines are curved on this kind of map. It is called a **conic pro-\
jection.** It comes from the idea of placing a cone \
r part of a globe.

☀ **FIGURE 1-16** | **Conic Projection**

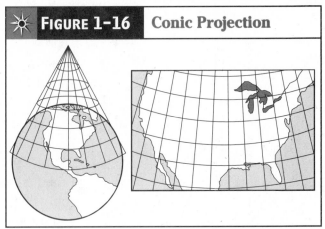

A conic projection is good for showing small areas midway between the Equator and the Poles. Size, distance, and direction are fairly accurate.

There are a number of other kinds of projections that show the sizes of landmasses fairly

☀ **FIGURE 1-17** | **Robinson Projection**

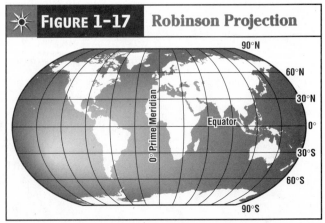

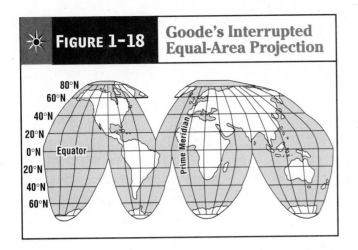

FIGURE 1-18 Goode's Interrupted Equal-Area Projection

the shapes and sizes of landmasses to be depicted with a high degree of accuracy.

Remember that no map can show direction, distance, shape, and size at the same time as accurately as a globe. Every kind of map has a special use, but none is perfect. When you look at a map, keep in mind that the sizes of landmasses may not be correct, or distances or directions may not be true. Be careful not to make judgments about the world based only on maps.

Winkel Tripel Projection

The **Winkel Tripel projection,** Figure 1-19, is used in most general reference maps today. It provides a balance between the size and shape of land areas as they are shown on the map. Even the polar areas are shown with little distortion of size and shape.

accurately. Look at Figures 1-17 through 1-19. Notice that each has a particular shape. The Robinson projection shows only minor distortions in true size, distance, and shape of landmasses. Goode's Interrupted Equal-Area projection allows

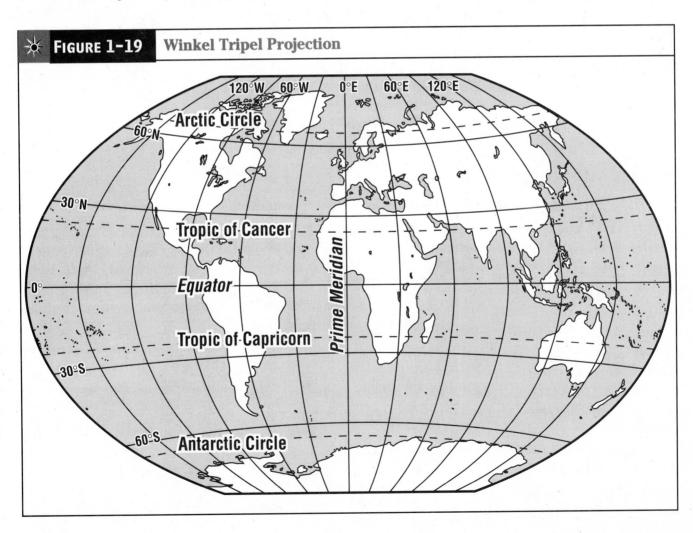

FIGURE 1-19 Winkel Tripel Projection

Ⓐ REVIEWING KEY TERMS

Match each term at left with its meaning.

_____ 1. planar projection   **a.** based on the projection of the globe onto a cone

_____ 2. conic projection   **b.** based on the projection of the globe onto a cylinder

_____ 3. cylindrical projection   **c.** based on the projection of the globe onto a plane

Ⓑ RECALLING FACTS

Decide whether each statement is true or false. Write _T_ if the statement is true. Write _F_ if the statement is false.

_____ 1. Only globes can show true distance, direction, size, and shape of landmasses all at the same time.

_____ 2. No map can show true distance and direction.

_____ 3. All maps show the surface of the earth in the same way.

_____ 4. All maps can show accurate size, but inaccurate distance.

_____ 5. A map can show that a landmass is much larger than it really is.

Ⓒ RECALLING FACTS

Fill in the blanks to correctly complete the following sentences.

1. On a Mercator projection, the sizes of landmasses near the North and South Poles are greatly exaggerated in _____.

2. On a planar projection, the size and shape of the landmasses are _____, but distance and direction are _____.

3. A conic projection is good for showing _____ areas midway between the _____ and the Poles.

4. A planar projection is also known as a(n) _____ projection.

5. A _____ projection provides a balance between size and shape of land areas as shown on the map.

Lesson 13 Mental Mapping

WHAT YOU WILL LEARN

To create mental maps of familiar areas

READING STRATEGY

Create a chart like the one below, listing uses for mental maps.

USES FOR MENTAL MAPS
•
•
•
•

TERMS TO KNOW

mental map

Have you ever asked someone for directions when you were in an unfamiliar place? Often the person will think for a moment and then provide a set of directions to help you find the location. People respond in different ways when you ask them for directions. Some people give directions using landmarks; others detail the number of streets, traffic lights, or stop signs between turns. Whatever method people use to give directions, they can only give them if they first have a mental map of the area.

Developing Mental Maps

A **mental map** is a person's internal image of a place. Without even thinking about it, you have developed mental maps that allow you to travel from place to place. For example, you use a mental map to get from home to school each day. Using this mental map, you could draw a sketch of the route you take.

As you read about places you have never visited, you can use the descriptions about the physical features of the place or region to develop a mental map of the area. Consider the following description:

> We hired a car for the day. The driver headed north and the road climbed steadily as we left Beijing. In about an hour, the wall loomed in front of us. Tall and winding, it followed the landscape for as far as the eye could see. We ascended the steep stairs and walked east for about a mile. We could see places ahead where the wall had collapsed, but it was still a spectacular site—one that I will never forget.

From this description of the Great Wall of China, how would you describe the location? While the passage does not give an exact location, you have learned that it lies about one hour by car north of Beijing. You also know that it follows the physical features of the land as far as the eye can see. You have formed a mental map of the wall's location from one brief passage. As you learn more about the Great Wall, you will add to this mental map.

Each person's mental maps are unique. They combine specific knowledge such as the names of streets and landmarks with individual feelings or impressions of a location. For example, you may consider the buildings in your community very tall, until you visit a skyscraper in another city. Based on this new information, you may revise your impressions of your own community. The actual height of its buildings has not changed, but your impressions about the buildings have.

Uses of Mental Maps

Mental maps help you understand the world around you. They help you organize and remember information about a place or a region. From the mental map, you can draw a sketch of a place or region. You can provide details such as highways, important landmarks, and bodies of water.

When you read about a place, consider drawing a sketch showing various geographic or human features. As you continue to learn about a place, review your sketch and add more details or redraw the sketch based on the new information you have learned.

Some sketches show a great deal of detail. For example, Map 1-16 shows a sketch of a neighborhood including details such as the names of streets, and the locations of businesses, the school, and parking lots.

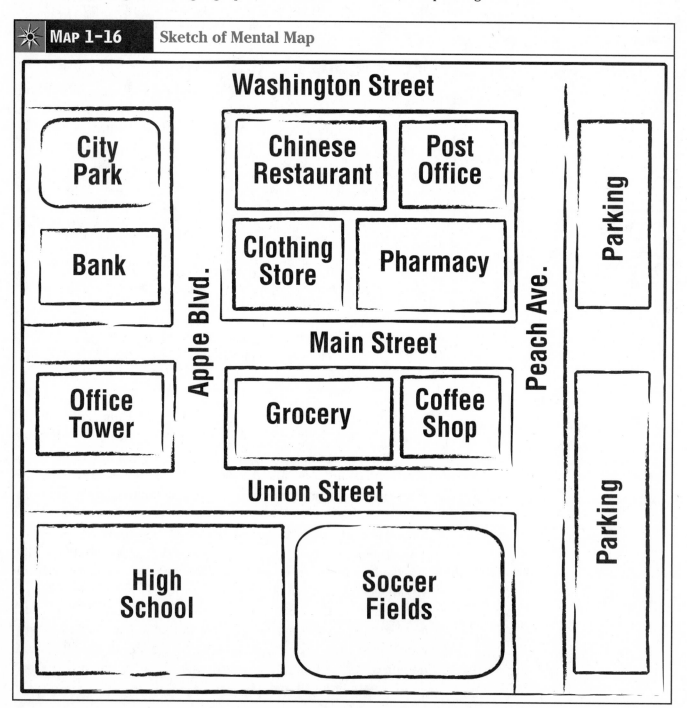

MAP 1-16   Sketch of Mental Map

Sketches of entire regions show fewer details, but allow the reader to see how parts of the region fit together. Map 1-17 shows a sketch created from a mental map of the original thirteen colonies of the United States. The exact shape of the states is less important than the relative positions of the states to one another. For example, it is important to know that Pennsylvania is south of New York.

Geographers are interested in mental maps and how people develop them. Understanding the way people think of different places and regions helps geographers gain knowledge about people's perceptions of places. Are some places perceived as dangerous, while others are not? Understanding people's mental maps also helps experts predict several things. They may be able to predict how the land may be used, and what patterns of migration may occur. This type of information is useful for urban planners and developers trying to establish new apartment complexes and industrial parks.

MAP 1-17 Sketch of the Thirteen Colonies

Using Your Skills

Ⓐ PRACTICING MAP SKILLS

Use Map 1-16 to answer the following questions. Circle the choice that best completes the sentence or answers the question.

1. You are at the high school. Which of the following buildings is closest to you?

   A. the bank

   B. the post office

   C. the grocery

   D. the pharmacy

2. You need to walk from the soccer fields to the bank. What is the shortest route?

   A. west on Union Street, then north on Apple Blvd.

   B. west on Union Street, north on Peach Ave., and west on Main Street

   C. east on Union Street, then north on Apple Blvd.

   D. east on Union Street, north on Peach Ave., and west on Main Street

3. You are leaving the post office and are standing on Washington Street. Someone asks you for directions to the coffee shop. Which of the following directions is the most direct route?

A. At the end of the street turn left onto Peach Ave. You will find the coffee shop at the corner of Peach and Main.

C. Take Washington to Apple. Turn left on Apple and go one block to Main. Turn left on Main. You will find the coffee shop at the corner of Peach and Main.

B. At the intersection of Washington and Peach, turn right. You will find the coffee shop at the corner of Peach and Main.

D. Walk west on Washington to Peach. Turn south, or right, onto Peach. Go one block to Peach and Main. The coffee shop will be on the corner.

4. You park in the south parking area. You need to make stops at the bank, post office, pharmacy, and grocery. You need to pick up two items at the pharmacy, and you expect to purchase food to fill two bags of groceries. In which order should you make your stops in order to walk the shortest distance, carrying the fewest things?

A. pharmacy, post office, grocery, bank

C. grocery, bank, post office, pharmacy

B. bank, pharmacy, post office, grocery

D. bank, post office, pharmacy, grocery

❸ PRACTICING MAP SKILLS

Use Map 1-16 to answer the following questions.

1. The Chinese restaurant is at the intersection of what two streets?

_____

2. What do the north/south streets share in common?

_____

3. What buildings are located the farthest west on the map?

_____

4. Which direction do you travel to get from the soccer fields to the post office?

_____

❹ PRACTICING MAP SKILLS

Think about your neighborhood. Then, on a separate piece of paper, draw a sketch map of it from your mental map. Which neighborhood streets or roads did you include? What are the three most important features on your map?

Understanding GPS and GIS

WHAT YOU WILL LEARN

To understand how a Global Positioning System and geographic information systems work

READING STRATEGY

Draw a diagram like the one below. In the left circle list facts about a GPS. In the right circle list facts about GIS. In the overlapping area write facts that are true about both.

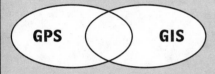

TERMS TO KNOW

Global Positioning System (GPS), geographic information system (GIS)

Millions of salmon return to Bristol Bay in Alaska to spawn each July. Hundreds of fishermen with boats and long nets wait for them. To ensure that there will be future generations of salmon, the Alaska Department of Fish and Game (ADFG) monitors the fishing grounds and sets limits on when and where the fishermen can fish. As Map 1-18 shows, ADFG has drawn two boundary lines in the water, one at each end of the bay. The Alaska Department of Fish and Game imposes heavy fines on fishermen who fish outside those boundary lines.

Fishermen cannot see the lines with their eyes. They know, however, where the lines are. They use Global Positioning System (GPS) receivers to monitor their positions, allowing them to stay within the limits set by the Alaska Department of Fish and Game.

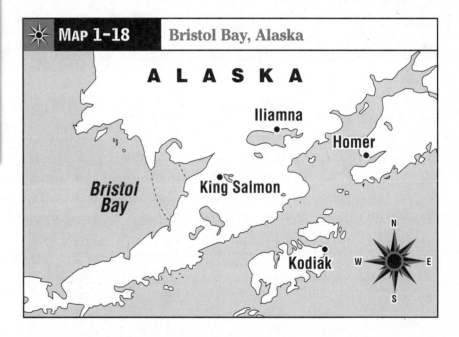

✳ MAP 1-18   Bristol Bay, Alaska

How GPS Works

The **Global Positioning System (GPS)** consists of three elements: the *satellites, receivers,* and *ground stations*. There are 24 satellites in fixed orbit around the earth. Over 11 nautical miles out in space, these giant "eyes in the sky" complete an orbit of the earth every 12 hours. The satellites transmit data at the speed of light continually, regardless of weather conditions, to the receivers.

Receivers, located anywhere on Earth, receive signals from at least six satellites at any one time. Even though the satellites send

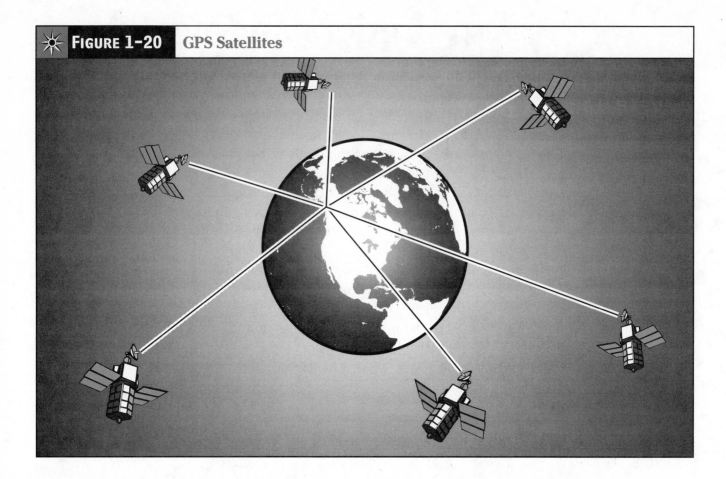

the signals at the speed of light, it still takes a measurable amount of time for the signals to reach the receivers. To give an accurate reading of a location, the receivers first calculate the distance to the satellites by measuring the difference between the time the signal was sent from the satellite and the time it was received, multiplied by the speed of light. Using data received from the satellites, the receiver can determine its exact location on the earth.

Originally developed by the U.S. military, GPS receivers now come in all shapes and sizes; most are the size of a cellular phone. Some are handheld; others are installed in cars, trucks, ships, and planes. Their job is to receive and decode signals from the satellites and present the results on a screen.

The third element of the GPS is the five large control stations and many unmanned ground stations located around the world. Their job is to stay in constant contact with the satellites. They track their courses and monitor their output.

Uses of Geographic Information Systems (GIS)

A **geographic information system (GIS)** is sophisticated software that combines and analyzes different types of information relevant to a specific geographic location. After information about an area is entered into the GIS database, the computer can create maps showing any combination of the data. Each type of data is stored as a separate "layer" of the map. So numerous combinations of data can be combined to build a very specialized map.

Farmers use GIS when they combine various types of data about their fields. Traditionally, farmers find out too late when pests damage their crops. Since they do not know how deep the pests have penetrated their fields, they often over-spray with expensive pesticides. Maps produced by GIS analysis can be used to pinpoint problem areas in the farmers' fields. Instead of treating the whole field, farmers are able to spot treat the problem.

Using Your Skills

Ⓐ REVIEWING KEY TERMS

Match each term with its meaning.

_____ 1. receiver

_____ 2. GPS

_____ 3. ground station

_____ 4. GIS

_____ 5. satellites

a. geographic information system

b. place that tracks the orbits and monitors the output of satellites

c. machines in space that transmit data to Earth

d. Global Positioning System

e. small device that decodes and processes data from satellites

Ⓑ RECALLING FACTS

Use the reading and Figure 1-20 to answer these questions.

1. At what speed does the satellite transmit data?

   _____

   _____

2. How many times does a GPS satellite orbit the earth in a week?

   _____

   _____

3. How many satellites broadcast to receivers at any one time?

   _____

   _____

4. How many satellites make up the GPS?

   _____

   _____

5. How many nautical miles are the GPS satellites out in space?

   _____

   _____

6. Describe one use of data from a geographic information system.

   _____

   _____

   _____

Unit 1 Review — The World In Spatial Terms

Ⓐ REVIEWING KEY TERMS

Underline the term in parentheses in each sentence which will complete the statement correctly.

1. Map makers use a (compass rose, legend) to show direction on a map.

2. Maps usually have a (grid, scale) to show what distance on the earth is represented by a certain distance on the map.

3. The location of a place on the earth as compared to some other place is called (absolute location, relative location).

4. Depending on other people is called (interdependence, socialism).

5. Distance north and south of the Equator is measured in degrees of (latitude, longitude).

6. Distance east or west of the Prime Meridian is measured in degrees of (latitude, longitude).

7. Another name for the Prime Meridian is (0° latitude, 0° longitude).

8. The legend of a map tells what the (symbols, cells) on the map mean.

9. When it is winter in the Northern Hemisphere, it is (spring, summer) in the Southern Hemisphere.

10. When it is 12 noon where you are, it is 2:00 P.M. two time zones to the (east, west).

11. A map that shows how the land looks is called a (physical, political) map.

12. A land-use map is an example of a (relief, special-purpose) map.

13. Direction, distance, shape, and size can all be shown correctly at the same time only on a (globe, map).

14. A person's internal image of a place is called a (physical map, mental map).

15. The tracking system composed of satellites, receivers, and ground stations is called the (Global Positioning System, geographic information system).

B PRACTICING MAP SKILLS

Follow the instructions below as you label Map 1-19: The World: Physical.

1. Find the Prime Meridian. Label it 0° longitude.

2. Find the Equator. Label it 0° latitude.

3. Label the continents.

4. Label the Atlantic, Pacific, Indian, and Arctic Oceans.

C PRACTICING MAP SKILLS

Use Map 1-19 **below to answer these questions.**

1. Name the two continents located entirely south of the Equator.

   _____

2. Name the continents crossed by the Prime Meridian.

   _____

3. Much of Europe and Asia are at the same latitude as _____.

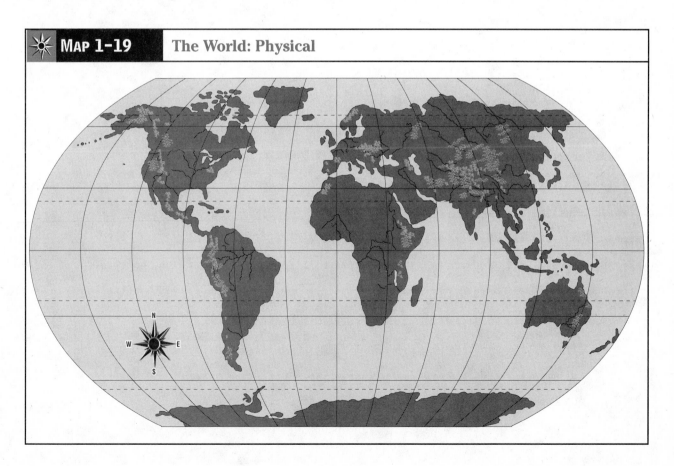

MAP 1-19   The World: Physical

Unit 2

Places and Regions

The Greek island of Symi, in the Aegean Sea, shows physical features that humans have adapted to.

Objectives

After completing this unit, you will be able to:

- read a variety of maps, charts, tables, and graphs;
- construct maps, charts, tables, and graphs from given data;
- explain how regions may be defined by physical, political, or cultural features;
- name different kinds of regions.

Unlucky Thirteen

How many times have you heard that the number thirteen is unlucky? This is a fear that is common all over the world, and one that many people take seriously. Many buildings in the United States label the floor that follows twelve as "fourteen" because they have found that people don't want to live or work on the thirteenth floor. The French never issue the house number thirteen, and in Italy, they leave the number out of the national lottery.

Not all countries and cultures share the belief that the number thirteen is unlucky. In Korea, for example, you can find a thirteenth floor but not a fourth floor. Since the Korean word for the number four is the same as the Korean word for death, four is considered unlucky in that country.

Whatever the location, there are certain things about a place that make it what it is. Every location has certain physical and human features that make it different from any other. This is what geographers mean when they talk about place. They do not mean *where* a place is (location). Instead, they mean what a place is *like*.

Places on Earth have physical features, such as mountains, deserts, lakes, rivers, plants, and animals. Places on Earth also have human features. Do many people live there, or only a few? Geographers often present information about places in visual formats such as maps, graphs, and tables. These formats allow the reader to gather information at a glance. They also allow geographers to easily compare and contrast spatial information.

Geographers attempt to understand and explain how these places are the same and how they are different. To do so, they often group places into regions—areas that have similar characteristics. *Physical regions* are areas that have one main physical feature in common, such as landforms and vegetation. *Political regions* usually have a common political system, such as democracy, socialism, or communism.

Geographers identify three types of regions. *Formal regions* have a common feature that sets them apart. For example, the Corn Belt of the United States is a formal region in which corn is the main crop. *Functional regions* focus on a central area and the surrounding territory linked to

them. Metropolitan areas such as Tokyo and New York City are functional regions. *Perceptual regions* are defined by feelings and images. "America's heartland" refers to a central region in which traditional values are believed to rule.

Places and regions is one of the six essential elements of geography. Once we know about the weather, the land, and how people live, work, and play, we know a great deal about a place. Geographers use regions to organize the study of geography. However, it would be too confusing to divide the world into too many regions for study. So geographers usually divide the world into eight to ten major regions based on features such as land, climate, and culture. In this unit, you will learn how to read and create several kinds of maps, graphs, and tables to describe a place. You will also come to understand how regions are formed and how regions change.

Landforms and Bodies of Water

WHAT YOU WILL LEARN

To distinguish between types of landforms and bodies of water

READING STRATEGY

Create a table like the one below. Give three examples of each item listed in the table.

Landforms			
Bodies of Water			

TERMS TO KNOW

landform

The earth is a very interesting place. There are millions of miles of land and thousands of cultures you have never seen before. Humans seem to have a need to explore, to go places they have never been before. In fact, the travel industry is one of the largest in the world.

The earth would not be so interesting if all places on it looked the same. Your family probably would not travel hundreds of miles to visit a place exactly like your hometown. The earth does not look the same everywhere because it has many different landforms. **Landforms** are the physical features of the earth's surface, such as mountains and plains.

Using Your Skills

Ⓐ REVIEWING KEY TERMS

Read each description of a landform or body of water. Then write the term in the correct place on Map 2-1: Landforms and Bodies of Water.

bay—part of a large body of water that extends into a shoreline

canyon—a deep, narrow valley with steep walls

cape—point of land that extends into a river, lake, or ocean

coast—land along a sea or an ocean

delta—flat, low land built up from soil carried downstream by a river and deposited at its mouth

gulf—part of a body of water that extends into a shoreline; larger and deeper than a bay

island—body of land completely surrounded by water

isthmus—narrow stretch of land connecting two larger land areas

lake—body of water completely surrounded by land; usually freshwater

mountain—land with steep sides that rise sharply from the surrounding land

mouth of a river—place where a river empties into a larger body of water

peninsula—body of land jutting into a lake or ocean, surrounded on three sides by water

plain—area of level land, usually at low elevation and often covered with grasses

plateau—area of flat or rolling land at high elevation, about 300 to 3,000 feet high

river—large natural stream of water that flows through land

tributary—small stream or river that flows into a large river or stream

valley—low land between hills or mountains

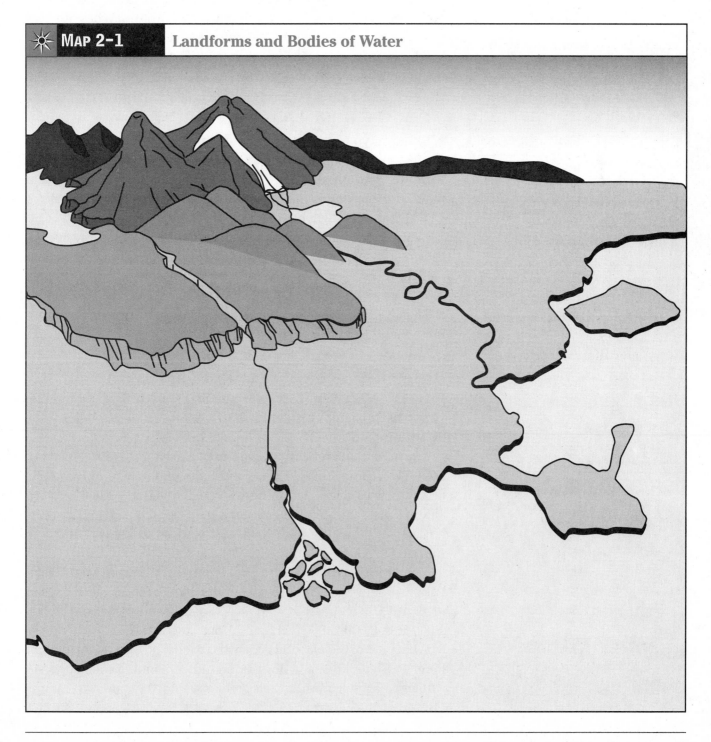

☼ **MAP 2-1**   **Landforms and Bodies of Water**

Lesson ② Reading Elevation Maps

WHAT YOU WILL LEARN

To use elevation maps to gain information about the physical characteristics of a place

READING STRATEGY

Create a chart like the one below by writing the meaning of each of the terms listed.

elevation	
sea level	
relief	
elevation map	

TERMS TO KNOW

elevation, sea level, altitude, relief, elevation map

When you are standing on the top rung of a ladder, you may be four feet above the ground. However, your elevation will not be four feet, unless you happen to be standing on a ladder at the beach. It is important to remember that all **elevation,** or height, is measured from sea level. **Sea level** is the average level of the water in the world's oceans, or 0 feet. You may be four feet above the ground, but your elevation may be 2,000 feet above sea level. Or, in a few spots on the earth's surface, your elevation could be 100 feet or more below sea level.

The Importance of Elevation

Knowing your elevation can sometimes be a matter of life and death. Suppose you are flying a plane at an altitude of 10,000 feet. **Altitude** is another word for elevation. Ahead of you is a mountain. Your map says the elevation of the top of the mountain is 12,500 feet. What will happen unless you do something?

Elevation is an important characteristic of a place. In general, the greater the elevation, the cooler the climate. The difference in elevation between points on the earth, or **relief,** is also important. If moisture-bearing winds blow from a low area to a higher area, more rain will fall at the higher elevation. Streams flow from higher land to lower land.

Showing Elevation on Maps

Look at Map 2-2 of East Asia. Shading is used to show the elevation of the land. This kind if map is often called a relief map or **elevation map.**

A map cannot show the elevation of every single spot. Instead, areas are grouped together. For example, on the map of East Asia, all areas with an elevation between sea level and 1,000 feet are shaded the same. Within that area may be hills and valleys, but no hill will be higher than 1,000 feet, and no valley will be lower than sea level.

Elevations on this map are grouped in the following way. All elevations below sea level are shaded the same. Elevations from sea level to 1,000 feet are shaded alike. So are elevations from 1,000–2,000 feet, 2,000–5,000 feet, and so on.

What part of the map tells you what each kind of shading means? Read the legend. What does this kind of shading mean ■ ? Above what elevation are all areas shaded the same no matter how great the elevation?

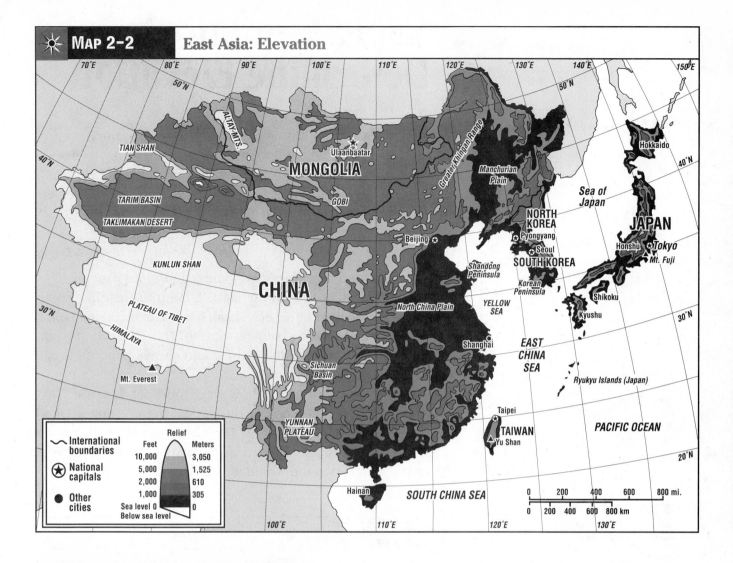

MAP 2-2 East Asia: Elevation

Relief

International boundaries	Feet		Meters
National capitals	10,000		3,050
	5,000		1,525
	2,000		610
Other cities	1,000		305
	Sea level 0		0
	Below sea level		

Using Your Skills

Ⓐ PRACTICING MAP SKILLS

Use Map 2-2: East Asia: Elevation above to answer these questions.

1. What is the elevation of the Plateau of Tibet? _____

2. Look at the part of the legend on the map that shows relief.

    a. Where is the shading for low elevations located? _____

    b. Where is the shading for high elevations located? _____

3. Find the North China Plain on the map. What is its elevation? _____

4. What is the elevation of the land around the Sichuan Basin? _____

5. One area on the map has an elevation below sea level. Give the location

    of that area using latitude and longitude. _____

Lesson ③ Using Contours to Determine Elevation

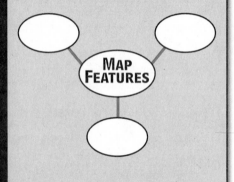
You read in Lesson 2 how elevation maps show the height of land over large areas. But suppose you are trying to decide where to build a new road. You need to know the exact elevation of particular places in order to choose the best route. An elevation map would not be very helpful.

Contour Maps

There is a map that does show elevation more exactly. This kind of map is called a **contour map.** A contour map has many lines on it. These lines show elevation. Each line on the map joins all the places that have the same elevation. This means that if you walked along one contour line, you would always be at the same height above sea level.

Look at Figure 2-1. It shows how a contour map is made. This drawing is of an island. Look at the part of the drawing marked "Top View." This shows you how the island would look from an airplane. Look at the part of the drawing marked "Side View." This shows you how the island would look from a boat on the water.

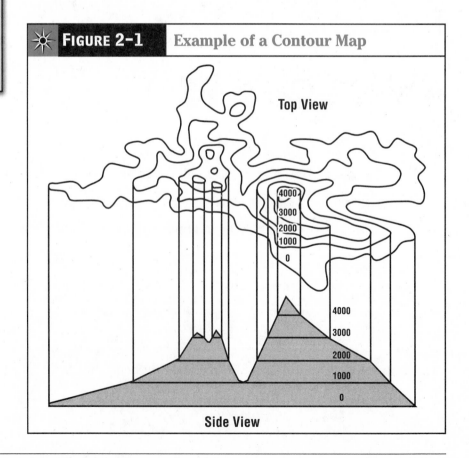

FIGURE 2-1   **Example of a Contour Map**

Top View

4000
3000
2000
1000
0

4000
3000
2000
1000
0

Side View

Notice the lines on the drawing marked "Side View." These imaginary lines cut through the island at different elevations. The elevations are marked on the drawing. The first line is at sea level, or 0 feet. At what elevation is the next higher line? The highest?

Now look at the top view. Imagine yourself in an airplane high above the island, looking down. Imagine that you could see where all the lines that cut through the island come out. The lines would look like the top view. Each line is called a **contour line,** because it follows the shape, or contour, of the land. Each contour line joins points with the same elevation. Each line is numbered to show the height above sea level of the points joined by that line. Notice how these lines form circles or ovals—one inside the other.

By reading the numbers on contour lines, you can tell how high each line is above sea level. How high above sea level is the highest line labeled in the drawing?

In the side view of the drawing, the lines are all the same distance apart. Why is this not true on the top view? The lines are not the same distance apart because they follow the shape of the land. Look at the left-hand side of both the top view and the side view. In the side view, you can see that the island slopes up gently from the sea on the left. In the top view, you can see that the contour lines are far apart on the left side. Now look at the middle of both views. The island rises steeply in the middle, as you can see in the side view. In the top view, the contour lines are close together in the middle of the drawing.

This is one of the most important things you need to remember about the contour maps. When the lines on a contour map are close together, the land is steep. When the lines are far apart, the land is flat.

Reading Contour Maps

To read a contour map, first identify the area shown on the map. Then look for the legend. The legend will tell you whether the contour lines are numbered in feet or meters. It will also tell you

how much elevation there is between contour lines. This is called the **contour interval.** Locate the highest and lowest numbers, which indicate the highest and lowest elevations. Finally, notice the amount of space between the lines. This will tell you whether the land is steep or flat.

Look at Map 2-3. It is part of a contour map of Death Valley, California. Part of Death Valley is below sea level. Can you find the dark contour line that runs across the middle of the map from top to bottom? Near the bottom of the map the line is marked "sea level." That contour line joins the points on the map that are at 0 feet.

Now look directly to the right of the words *sea level.* Near the edge of the map you will find another contour line that is darker than the others. It is marked "400." That line joins points on the map that are 400 feet above sea level. Now look to the left of the words *sea level.* Near the edge of the map on the left you will find a contour line marked "–240." Notice the minus sign in front of the numbers. This means that the line joins points that are below sea level.

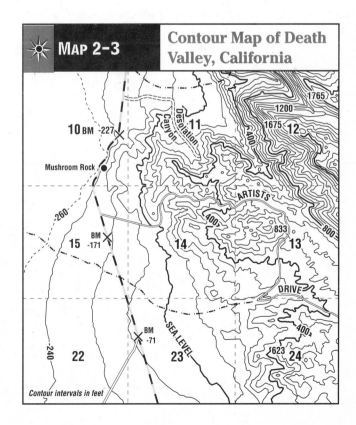

Ⓐ REVIEWING KEY TERMS

Fill in the blanks with the correct words to complete the following sentences.

1. Each line on a _____ map is called a contour line.

2. Each contour line connects points with the same _____.

3. When the lines on a contour map are close together, the land is

    _____.

4. When the lines on a contour map are far apart, the land is

    _____.

5. The amount of elevation between contour lines is called the

    _____.

6. On a contour map numbered in meters, a contour line marked "150"

    connects all points on that map that are 150 meters _____ sea level.

7. On a contour map numbered in feet, a contour line marked "–100"

    connects all points on that map that are 100 feet _____ sea level.

Ⓑ PRACTICING MAP SKILLS

Use Map 2-4: Contour Map of Ithaca, New York to answer these questions.

1. Is the land around the Newman Golf Course (in cell B-5) flat or steep?

    How do you know? _____

    _____

2. What is the land like just to the west of the Ithaca Municipal Airport? How do you know? (Remember that if there is no compass rose on a

    map, north is at the top.) _____

    _____

3. Find the numbered contour line in the flat area of cell D-4. What does

    the number on that line mean? _____

    _____

Contour intervals in feet

Lesson ④ Reading Climographs

WHAT YOU WILL LEARN

To obtain information about places from climographs

READING STRATEGY

Create a flowchart like the one below and describe each step in analyzing a climograph.

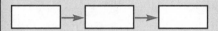

TERMS TO KNOW

temperature, precipitation, climograph

When you are making plans to do something outdoors, what are the two things about the weather you are most interested in knowing? You will want to know how hot or cold it will be. You will also want to know if it will be wet or dry.

Temperature (how hot or cold it is) and **precipitation** (rainfall or other moisture) are the two most important things to know about the weather and climate.

Using Temperature and Rainfall Graphs

Information about temperature and precipitation can be shown on graphs. Look at Figure 2-2 below. The title tells you that this graph shows the average monthly rainfall for Brasília, Brazil.

Read the label to find out what the numbers on the left side of the graph represent. It is very important to notice whether temperatures are given in degrees Fahrenheit (°F) or degrees Celsius (°C). You should also note whether rainfall amounts are given in inches (in.) or centimeters (cm). Some graphs give both.

The letters across the bottom of the graph stand for the months of the year. The first letter on the left is *J*. It stands for January, the first month.

Notice that the names of several months begin with the same letter—*J, M,* or *A.* If you are not sure which month a letter stands for, begin with January at the left and say the names of the months in order, pointing to each in turn. Stop when you get to the name of the month you are interested in reading.

In which month does Brasília receive the most rainfall? In which months does it receive no rainfall?

Information about the average monthly temperature in Irkutsk, Russia, is shown on Figure 2-3 at the bottom of the next page.

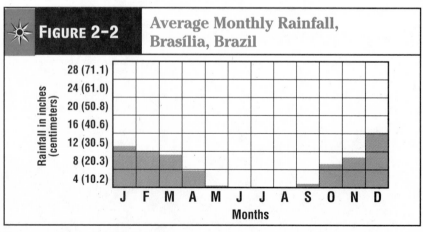

Source: www.worldclimate.com

Notice that this graph also shows the months of the year beginning with January on the left and ending with December on the right. What is the warmest month in Irkutsk? What is the average temperature in Irkutsk in October?

Using Climographs

Information about both temperature and precipitation can be combined on one graph. This kind of graph is called a **climograph.** A climograph combines a line graph and a bar graph to show average variation in temperature and precipitation.

Look at Figure 2-4. The bars across the bottom of the graph show the average monthly rainfall. The numbers on the *right* side of the graph are used to read the amounts represented by the bars. Do the bars stand for inches of rainfall, or centimeters? What is the average monthly rainfall in Jacksonville in June? In which month does the most rain fall?

Temperature on the climograph is shown by the line on the graph above the rainfall bars. The numbers on the *left* side of the graph are used to read the temperature line. Are temperatures given in degrees Fahrenheit, or Celsius? What is the average monthly temperature in Jacksonville in December? In which month is the temperature highest?

To analyze information in a climograph, first identify the highest and lowest temperatures. Then determine the variation in annual precipitation. Which months of the year have high amounts of rainfall? Low amounts of rainfall?

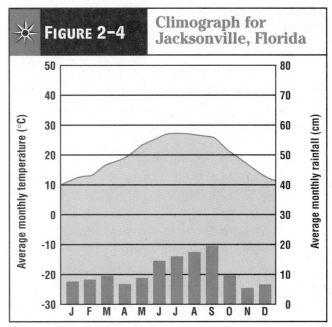

Source: www.worldclimate.com

Finally, draw a conclusion about the place based on the information.

Many characteristics of a place can be inferred by analyzing the climograph. For example, suppose a climograph shows that a place has high temperatures throughout much of the year, as well as large amounts of rainfall throughout the year. This information tells you several things about the place. First, the place is located in a warm, rainy climate, probably a tropical rain forest. Second, as a rain forest, the place has natural vegetation that includes hardwood trees like teak and mahogany. And third, because of the climate, little continued agricultural activity occurs. Periods of heavy rainfall can ruin crops.

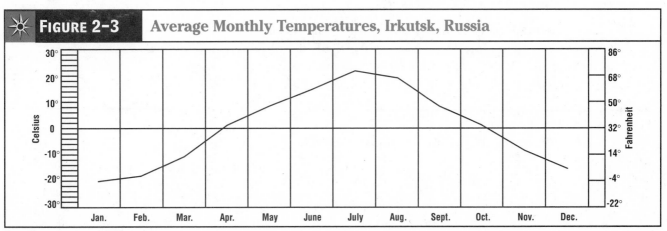

Source: www.worldclimate.com

Using Your Skills

Ⓐ USING GRAPHICS

Use **Figure 2-5: Climograph for Khartoum, Sudan** to answer these
questions.

1. What is the highest average monthly rainfall for Khartoum? In which
    month(s) does it occur?

    _____

2. What is the lowest average monthly rainfall for Khartoum? In which
    month(s) does it occur?

    _____

3. What is the lowest average monthly temperature in Khartoum? The
    highest?

    _____

4. Using information about rainfall and temperature from the climograph,
    how would you describe the climate of Khartoum in words?

    _____

    _____

    _____

    _____

    _____

    _____

    _____

Ⓑ USING GRAPHICS

**Construct a climograph for Cherrapunji, India, using the information
below and the blank graph on page 73.**

Rainfall in Cherrapunji amounts to about 1 inch in January, 2 inches in
February, 7 inches in March, 24 inches in April, 67 inches in May, 115 inches
in June, 96 inches in July, 71 inches in August, 46 inches in September,
17 inches in October, 2 inches in November, and 1 inch in December.

The average temperature in January is 53°F.

For the rest of the months of the year in order, the figures are 58°, 62°, 66°,
67°, 68°, 69°, 67°, 61°, 55°.

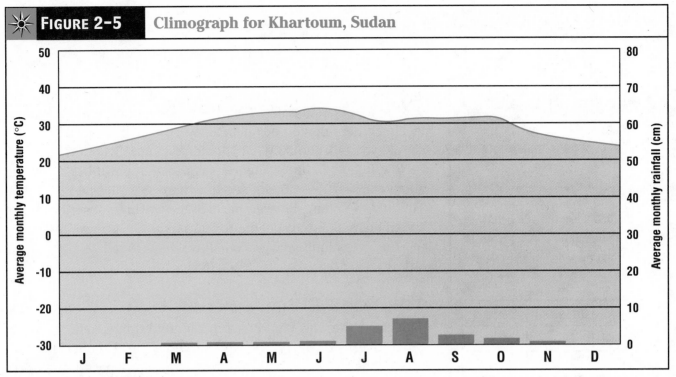

FIGURE 2-5   Climograph for Khartoum, Sudan

Source: www.worldclimate.com

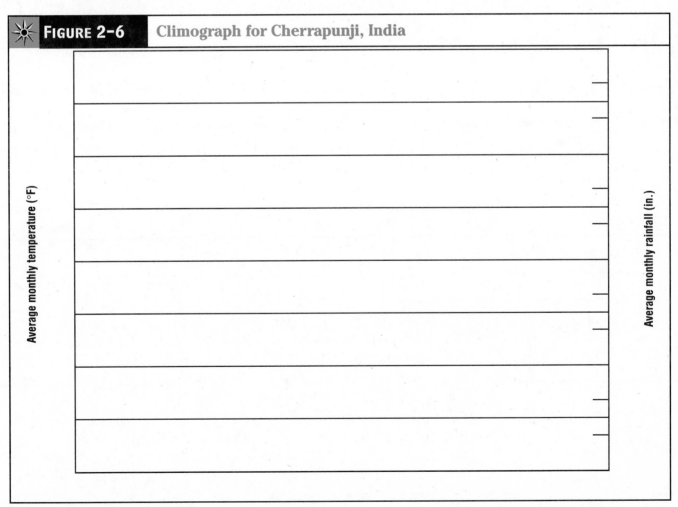

FIGURE 2-6   Climograph for Cherrapunji, India

Source: www.worldclimate.com

Lesson 5 Regions

WHAT YOU WILL LEARN

To understand that regions are basic units of geographic study

READING STRATEGY

Create a table like the one below. Fill in the definition of each type of region, and provide an example of each.

REGION	DEFINITION	EXAMPLE
functional		
formal		
perceptual		

TERMS TO KNOW

region, functional region, formal region, perceptual region

Has someone ever said to you, "Can you tell me all about yourself?" A question like this leaves most people with a helpless feeling. Where do you begin an answer to such a question? What should you talk about? What should you not talk about?

Now imagine that someone says to a geographer, "Tell me about the world." You can see how hard it would be to do this. There are so many different parts of the world to describe. There are so many different people to learn about. A geographer could talk for a very long time and still have more to tell.

Your Community—A Region

Because the world has so many different things to learn about, geographers do not try to study the whole world at once. Instead, they divide the world into **regions.** A region is a part of the world that has at least one characteristic in common. Dividing the world into regions makes the study of geography easier. Geographers sometimes choose to focus their study on just one region of the world. That way they can learn much about one region, rather than a little about many regions.

There is one region of the world that you probably already know a great deal about. That region is the community where you live. Your community may be a kind of region called a **functional region.** A large city and all the area around it where people live, work, and shop is a functional region. Such large areas are often called *Metropolitan Statistical Areas* (MSAs).

Geographers also identify **formal regions.** Formal regions feature a common human trait, such as the existence of people who share a particular language or religion. Physical features can also characterize formal regions. The presence of a particular type of climate or vegetation defines a formal region. In addition, political units such as counties, states, countries, and provinces are classified as formal regions.

Perceptual regions are not as structured as the functional and formal regions described above. Perceptual regions reflect people's feelings and attitudes about an area. They also tend to reflect the elements and features of people's mental maps. However, mental maps are not always appropriate or accurate. For example, one person's mental map of the Midwest may include Ohio and Kentucky, while another person's mental map of the Midwest does not include these states. As a result, perceptual regions may not have precise borders.

Most people are aware of spatial relationships, and use regions to distinguish between different parts of the earth. For example, people individually and collectively agree on where they live. They may call their home "Dixie," rather than referring to it as the southeastern United States. The regions they recognize are reflected in the names used in businesses, by sports teams, and in advertising. Regions help people understand spatial relationships and interpret their world.

Using Your Skills

Ⓐ PRACTICING MAP SKILLS

Use the directions and questions below and the map form on page 76 to make a map of a region—your community.

1. Choose the boundaries of your region. If you live in a Metropolitan Statistical Area, you may use the boundaries of the MSA. If you base the boundaries of your region on political boundaries, you could choose to include the county or town in which you live. Or, you could include only part of your county or town, such as a ward, precinct, or district used to elect government leaders. If you base the boundaries on physical features of the land, you might include only the low or high areas of your community, or the land within a certain distance of a river or highway. If you choose to base your boundaries on cultural features, you might draw your boundary based on how different ethnic groups are distributed in the area. For example, your region might include the part of town where most of the people are Italians. Draw the boundary on the map form on the next page.

2. Show the locations of the following features on your map: your home, your best friend's home, the stores where your family shops, your school, and parks.

3. Use shading to show on your map any large areas of land that are used for the same purpose, such as farming, airports, factories, apartments, or stores. Make a legend to show the meaning of the shading.

4. Use the grid on the map to make an index for the map.

5. On your own paper describe the region you have mapped. What are its boundaries? Why did you choose those boundaries? What are features that make this region different from others you could have chosen?

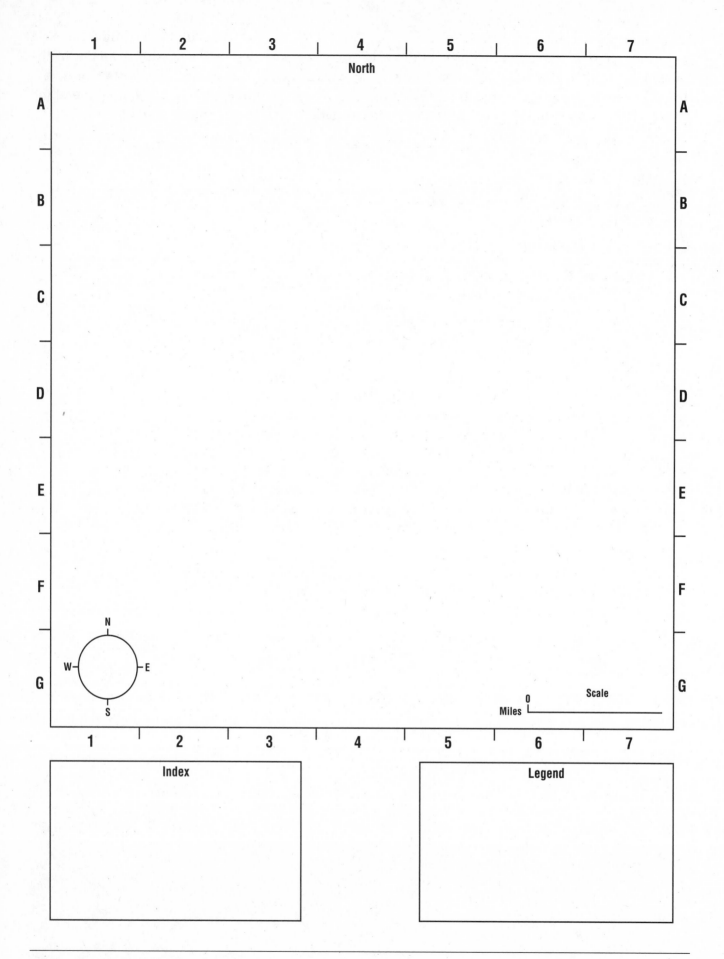

Lesson 6 Physical Regions

WHAT YOU WILL LEARN

To explain how regions may be defined by physical features

READING STRATEGY

Create a diagram like the one below. In the outer circles, fill in examples of physical regions.

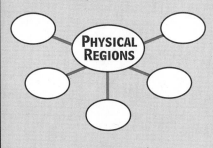

TERMS TO KNOW

continent, landform

Have you seen a picture of Earth taken from far out in space? From a great distance, only broad features of the earth stand out. You can see oceans and the shape of the largest landmasses, called **continents.**

Of course, the earth has more features than just oceans and continents. The features of the earth's surface are called **landforms.** You learned about landforms in Lesson 1 of this unit. The surface of the earth can be divided into regions based on landforms. Three of the main landforms are mountains, plateaus, and plains. Map 2-5 on page 78 shows some of the major mountain ranges, plateaus, and plains areas of the earth.

Physical Regions

You have read that a region is a part of the earth that has similar characteristics. Think of where you live. Is most of the land flat and not too far above sea level? If so, you may live in a plains area. If the land is flat and high above sea level, you may live on a plateau. And of course, if the land around you is very high with many peaks and valleys, you may live in the mountains.

Physical features such as plains, plateaus, and mountains can be used to divide the earth's surface into regions based on physical features. Map 2-6 on page 80 shows the seven physical regions of North America. The boundaries of countries are shown only to help you understand where the regions are in relation to where you live.

From space you can see the earth's oceans and continents.

MAP 2-5

The World: Physical

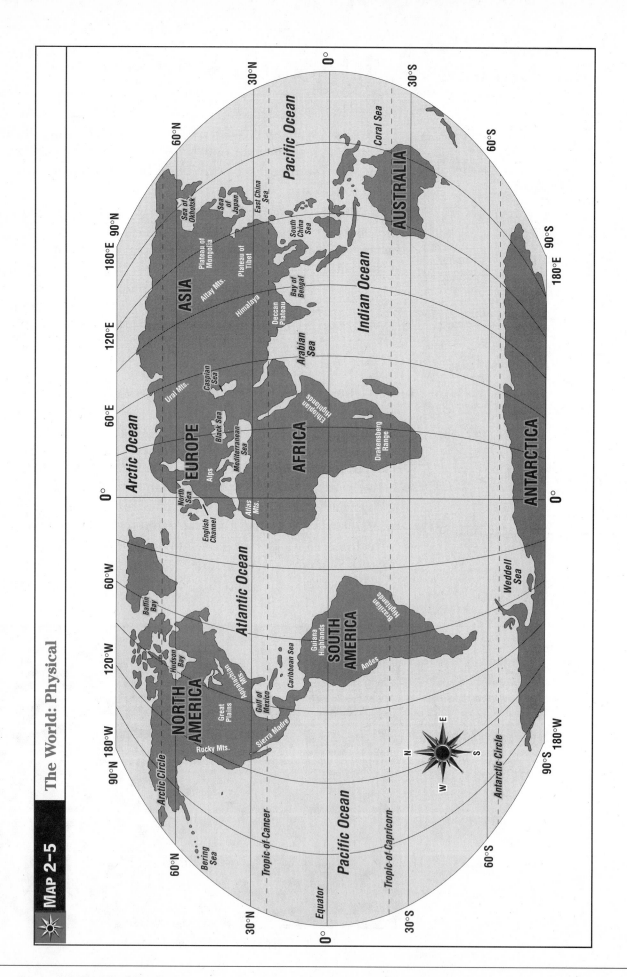

Ⓐ PRACTICING MAP SKILLS

Use what you have learned in this book about reading maps to answer these questions using Map 2-5: The World: Physical and Map 2-6: Physical Regions of North America on page 80.

1. What continent is located at latitude 30°S and longitude 120°E?

   _____

2. What continent is located directly north of the continent of Africa?

   _____

3. What body of water is located at latitude 20°N and longitude 60°E?

   _____

4. North America is not directly north of South America. What term best describes the direction you would travel in going from the Brazilian Highlands to the Great Plains?

   _____

5. Which physical region of North America runs the greatest distance from north to south?

   _____

   _____

6. Which physical region of North America is located immediately to the east of the Western Interior Mountains and Basins in the United States?

   _____

   _____

7. Based on the map of physical regions of North America, where would you expect to find more low, flat land: along the east coast of the United States, or along the west coast? Why?

   _____

   _____

   _____

   _____

   _____

   _____

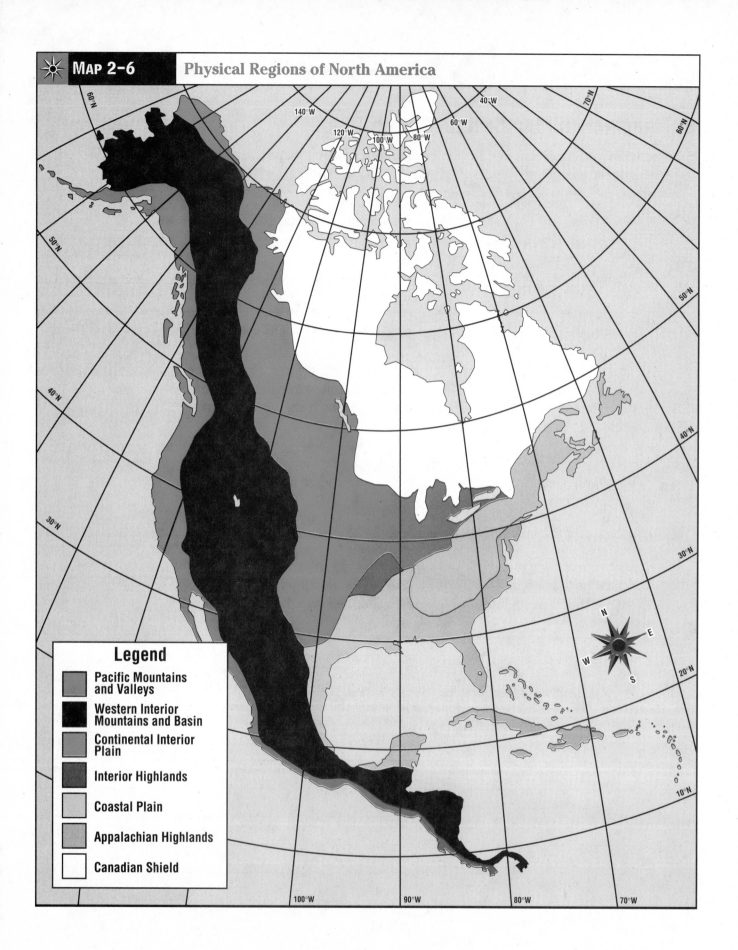

MAP 2-6 Physical Regions of North America

Legend

Pacific Mountains and Valleys

Western Interior Mountains and Basin

Continental Interior Plain

Interior Highlands

Coastal Plain

Appalachian Highlands

Canadian Shield

Lesson 7 Political Regions

WHAT YOU WILL LEARN

To explain how regions may be defined by political systems and political boundaries

READING STRATEGY

Create a chart like the one below. List three facts about political regions.

POLITICAL REGIONS
1.
2.
3.

TERMS TO KNOW

democracy, political region, political boundary

Do you know what kind of government the United States has? In the United States, laws are made by leaders elected by the people. We call this kind of government a **democracy.** Some other democracies are Canada, the United Kingdom, India, and Australia.

Defining Political Regions

One way to define a region is by the kind of government a country has. For example, the United States is a **political region.** A political region is an area that has a particular kind of government. Remember from Lesson 5 in this unit, that political regions are a type of formal region. Each country in the world is a political region. The boundary around each political region is called a **political boundary.** Political regions are one of the most rigidly defined types of regions. This is because political boundaries are carefully surveyed, discussed, and marked by governments. Each state in the United States has a political boundary around it. Each state is also a political region. Each county within each state is a political region. And each voting district within each county is a still smaller political region.

As you can see, the same area can be part of several different political regions. A voting district can be part of a county, a state, and a country all at the same time. In the same way, a country can be a political region all by itself, or it may be part of a region that includes other countries. For example, the European Union (EU) is a political region that includes many of the countries in Europe.

The Kremlin in Moscow, Russia, is the symbol of that country's government.

Using Your Skills

Ⓐ RECALLING FACTS

Use the reading to help you answer these questions.

1. What is a political region?

    _____

2. Name all the political regions of which your city or town is a part.

    _____

Ⓑ PRACTICING MAP SKILLS

The Arab League was formed to help unify the Arab world. It tries to strengthen cultural ties in the region, which are based on a common Islamic cultural heritage. The countries of the Arab League form a political region. A list of Arab League countries follows. Write the name of each country in the proper place on Map 2-7: The Arab League.

Algeria	Bahrain	Comoros	Egypt
Iraq	Djibouti	Kuwait	Lebanon
Jordan	Mauritania	Morocco	Libya
Oman	Qatar	Saudi Arabia	Somalia
Yemen	Sudan	Syria	Tunisia
United Arab Emirates			

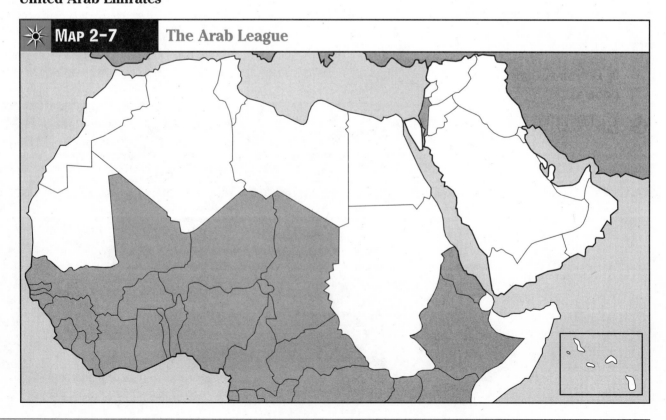

☀ MAP 2-7   The Arab League

Lesson **8** Culture Regions

WHAT YOU WILL LEARN

To explain how regions may be defined by cultural features

READING STRATEGY

Create a diagram like the one below. In each section, write one element of culture and give an example of it from the United States.

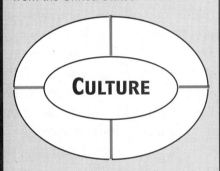

TERMS TO KNOW

industrialization, developed country, developing country, economic system, free enterprise, socialism, culture region

Have you ever traveled to a place where the people were very different from you? What made them different? Was it the language they spoke? The clothes they wore? Did they use money that was strange to you?

A people's way of life is called culture. Culture includes many things, however, some of the most important elements of culture are language, religion, government, the use of technology, and type of economic system.

Elements of Culture

Language is an important element of culture. People who speak the same language feel that they are part of the same group. Think about how you feel when you hear people speaking a language you cannot understand. Speaking different languages keeps people apart. Speaking the same language draws people together. Geographers sometimes divide the world into regions based on the languages that people speak.

Another element of culture is religion. There are many different religions in the world. In some countries, most of the people follow one religion. In other countries there are several religions that different groups of people practice. The world can be divided into regions based on the religions that people follow.

The type of government a people has is an important part of culture. In some countries, people make their own laws. In other countries the rulers make the laws. In Lesson 7 of this unit you saw an example of how the world can be divided into political regions based on the kind of government people have. In the past, there were many countries in Europe that had communist forms of government. Together these countries were called the Communist World. However, great changes took place in the 1980s and 1990s and communist governments ceased to exist in some countries. As a result, there is no longer a region called the Communist World.

You have read that technology is the use of tools and skills to make life easier. In some parts of the world, people use a great deal of technology, which has led to industrialization. **Industrialization** is the process in which countries shift from agriculture to manufacturing. The United States, Canada, and Japan are examples of such countries. Countries that use a great deal of technology and are very industrialized are often grouped in a region called **developed countries.** Countries that use little technology and have experienced little industrialization are called **developing countries.** Guatemala, Ethiopia, and Cambodia are examples of developing countries.

The Pyramids at Giza in Egypt symbolize the North African culture for many people.

mostly free to decide for themselves what kind of work they will do. In such countries, a person can own a business and keep the profits from that business. This kind of economic system is called **free enterprise.** The United States is one of the leading free enterprise countries.

In other countries, the government decides what kind of work people will do. In such countries, the government owns most businesses. This kind of economic system is called **socialism.**

Culture Regions

It is possible to divide the world into regions based on any of the elements discussed in this lesson, plus many others. Any one country could fit into many different regions. However, the study of the world would be very confusing if regions kept changing all the time. One way to make things simpler is to group the countries of the world into broad regions based on a combination of many elements. **Culture regions** are based on the elements discussed in this lesson. Using these elements, it is possible to group the countries of the world into 10 major culture regions.

The way in which people use their resources to satisfy their needs and wants is called their **economic system.** In some countries, people are

Using Your Skills

Ⓐ REVIEWING KEY TERMS

Choose the correct term from the pair in parentheses in each sentence. Underline the correct term.

1. A country that uses little technology and has low levels of industrialization is called a (culture region, developing country).

2. A country with an economy based more on industry than agriculture is called a (developed country, developing country).

3. The way in which a country uses its resources to satisfy its people's wants and needs is called its (culture region, economic system).

4. In a free enterprise system, businesses are owned by the (people, government).

5. The United States is one of the leading countries with a (free enterprise, communist) system.

ⓑ PRACTICING MAP SKILLS

Map 2-8: World Culture Regions on page 86 shows the world divided into 10 culture regions. Below is a list of countries. Write the name of each country on the list in the correct place on the map.

Argentina	Brazil	Canada
Venezuela	Colombia	United States
France	Ireland	Italy
Spain	United Kingdom	Ukraine
Germany	Poland	Russia
Egypt	Iran	Iraq
Israel	Saudi Arabia	Ethiopia
Kenya	Nigeria	South Africa
Democratic Republic of the Congo	India	Pakistan
China	Japan	Taiwan
Philippines	Vietnam	Australia

ⓒ RECALLING FACTS

Answer the following questions about Map 2-8.

1. Japan is a part of what culture region?

    _____

2. Germany is a part of what culture region?

    _____

3. Russia is a part of what culture region?

    _____

4. Mexico is a part of what culture region?

    _____

5. Iraq is a part of what culture region?

    _____

6. This map shows three continents each of which include only one culture region. What are the names of these three continents? Of what culture region is each continent a part?

    _____

    _____

    _____

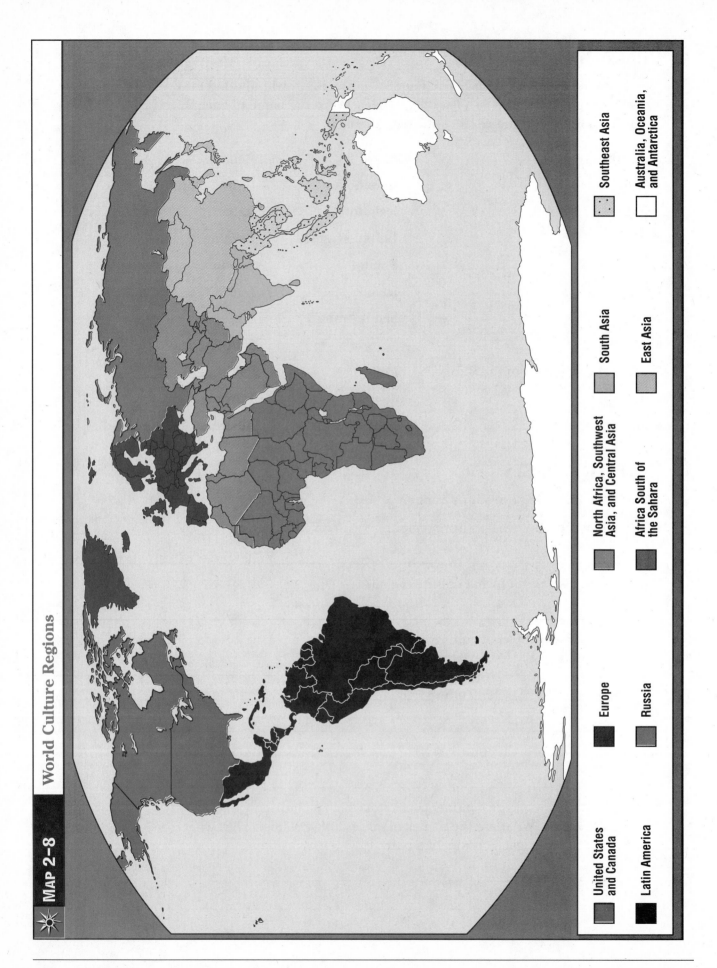

MAP 2-8   World Culture Regions

Legend:
- United States and Canada
- Latin America
- Europe
- Russia
- North Africa, Southwest Asia, and Central Asia
- Africa South of the Sahara
- South Asia
- East Asia
- Southeast Asia
- Australia, Oceania, and Antarctica

Lesson 9 Formal Regions

WHAT YOU WILL LEARN

To give examples of formal regions

READING STRATEGY

Create a diagram like the one below. In the outer ovals, write examples of formal regions.

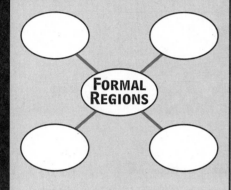

FORMAL REGIONS

TERMS TO KNOW

formal region

Have you ever walked or driven through a part of a town where most of the people were from Italy, or Greece, or some other country? Perhaps you have been on a trip that took you through mile after mile of desert. Or perhaps you have been to a place where wheat or corn grew in all directions as far as you could see. If you have been to any such place, you know what a **formal region** is. A formal region is an area that has one feature that sets it apart.

A formal region can be based on almost any feature. For example, the Cotton Belt is a part of the United States where cotton is the main crop. The Sun Belt is the part of the United States where temperatures are warm most of the year. Miami's "Little Havana" is where many people of Cuban descent live.

Using Your Skills

❶ PRACTICING MAP SKILLS

Use Map 2-9 and Map 2-10 to answer these questions.

1. What formal region is shown on Map 2-9?

   _____

2. What would you expect to see growing on most farms in Iowa, Illinois, and Indiana? _____

3. What formal region is shown on Map 2-10?

   _____

4. What would you expect to see growing on most farms in Kansas and North Dakota? _____

5. About how many miles does the Corn Belt stretch from east to west? _____

6. What is the southernmost state in the Wheat Belt?

   _____

7. How far west does the Wheat Belt extend?

   _____

8. Which states are included in both the Corn Belt and the Wheat Belt?

   _____

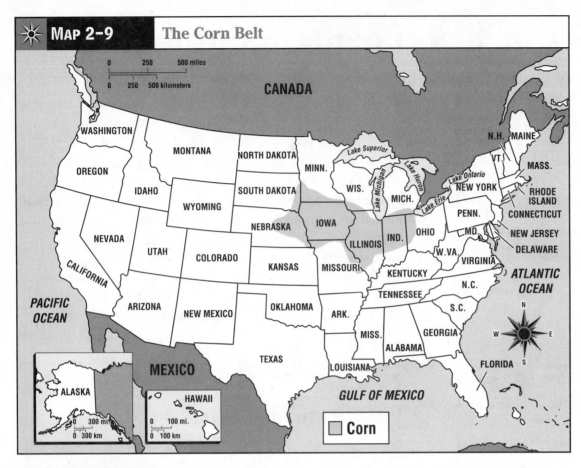

MAP 2-9   The Corn Belt

☐ Corn

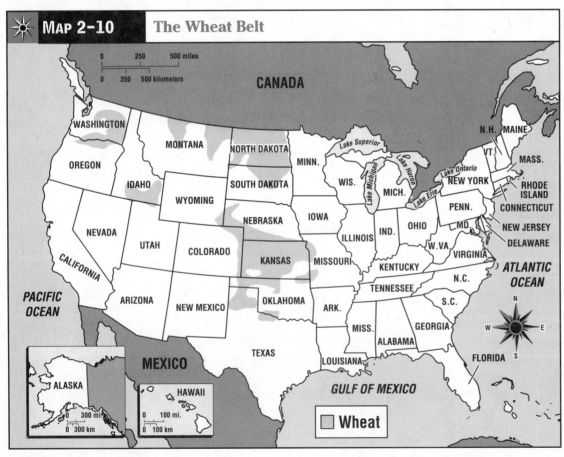

MAP 2-10   The Wheat Belt

☐ Wheat

❸ PRACTICING MAP SKILLS

Some countries depend on one product for most of the money they earn from exports. These countries can be grouped into formal regions according to the product upon which they depend. Below is a list of such countries in Africa. Choose a color or shading to represent each product. Then color or shade each country on Map 2-11: One-Product Countries. Complete the legend to identify the formal regions.

Oil		Diamonds	Coffee	Iron Ore
Algeria	Libya	Botswana	Burundi	Liberia
Angola	Nigeria	Guinea	Rwanda	Mauritania
Congo	Tunisia	South Africa	Uganda	Morocco
Gabon	Egypt	Democratic Republic of the Congo		

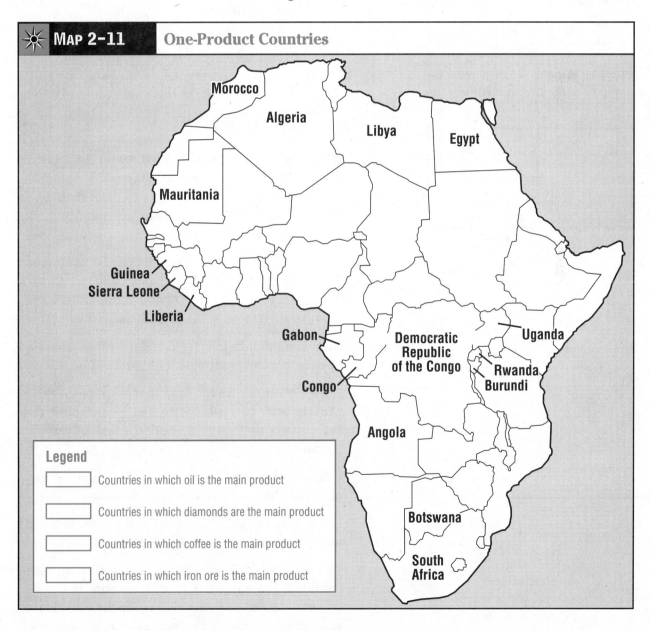

MAP 2-11   One-Product Countries

Morocco
Algeria
Libya
Egypt
Mauritania
Guinea
Sierra Leone
Liberia
Gabon
Democratic Republic of the Congo
Uganda
Congo
Rwanda
Burundi
Angola
Botswana
South Africa

Legend
- ☐ Countries in which oil is the main product
- ☐ Countries in which diamonds are the main product
- ☐ Countries in which coffee is the main product
- ☐ Countries in which iron ore is the main product

Lesson 10 Making Your Own Map

This lesson will challenge you to use the skills you have studied in Units 1 and 2. If you are not sure how to complete any of the tasks, look back at the lesson or lessons that deal with the skill you need.

WHAT YOU WILL LEARN

To demonstrate mastery of map and graph skills

READING STRATEGY

Create a chart like the one below. In the left column, list the types of maps or graphs discussed in this unit. In the right column, list what each type of map or graph is useful for showing.

TYPE OF MAPS AND GRAPHS	USEFUL FOR SHOWING

Using Your Skills

Ⓐ PRACTICING MAP SKILLS

Follow the instructions below to complete Map 2-12 on page 92.

1. Read all the instructions before beginning work. What you do in one step may affect a later step, so you need to be aware of all parts of the project before you begin. Draw *lightly* in pencil in case you need to change something later.

2. Draw in a coastline with Metro City on the west side of a bay. The coastline has been started for you at the top and bottom of the map. Be sure to draw the bay so that Metro City will be on the shore. Name your bay, and label it on the map.

3. Put a small town on the coast 225 miles southeast of Metro City. Put another small town 150 miles northwest of the center of the first town. Use the correct symbol to show the towns. Name the towns and label them.

4. Draw a small lake in cell F-3 and a swamp in cell E-12. Use the correct symbols for each.

5. Draw a river across the land that empties into the bay. Draw at least two tributaries that feed into the river. Draw rivers that lead into both the lake in cell F-3 and the swamp in cell E-12.

6. Place the symbol for a gold mine 100 miles southwest of the center of Metro City.

7. Locate the capital city in the exact center of the map with the correct symbol. Name the city and label it.

8. The land in cells C-9, C-10, and D-9 is used for farming. Outline this area with a heavy line. Choose a good color to represent farms, and color the area. Place the same color in the correct place in the legend.

9. Use the correct symbol to locate a small town near the center of the farming area. Name the town and label it.

10. Draw highways to connect the farming town, the capital city, and Metro City. Use the map scale to determine the distances between the towns. Measure from the center of one town to the center of the other town. Write the distances in miles between cities along the highways.

11. Connect the gold mine to the nearest city with a railroad. Then connect this city to Metro City with a railroad. Use the map scale to measure the distances between these places, and write the distances along the railroad.

12. Choose a resource that might be found in the northern part of your country, and a resource that might be found in the southern part of your country. Design a symbol for each resource. Draw the symbols on the map. Then draw the symbols in the blank boxes in the legend. Label the symbols in the legend.

❶ Using Graphics

Using the information below and the blank graphs on page 93, draw two climographs for the country depicted in Map 2-12.

The country shown on this map has a cold, dry climate in the south, where most precipitation falls in the winter months, and a warm, wet climate in the north, where rain falls mostly in the spring. *This country is south of the Equator. Remember that seasons in the Northern and Southern Hemispheres are reversed.* Draw a climograph for each part of the country.

MAP 2-12

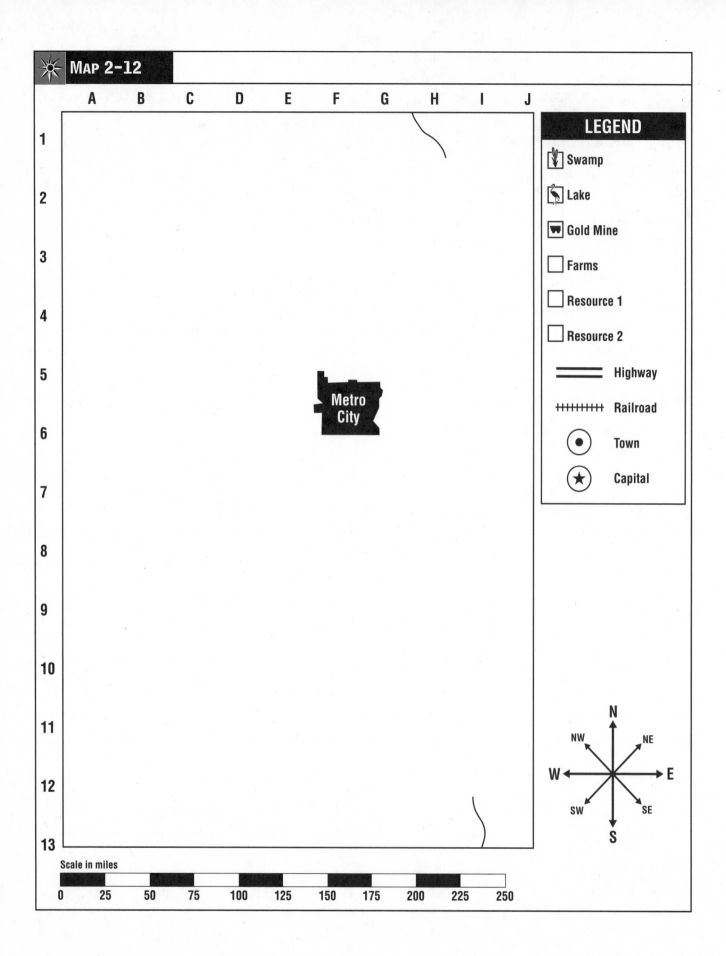

LEGEND

Swamp

Lake

Gold Mine

Farms

Resource 1

Resource 2

Highway

Railroad

Town

Capital

Metro City

Scale in miles

0   25   50   75   100   125   150   175   200   225   250

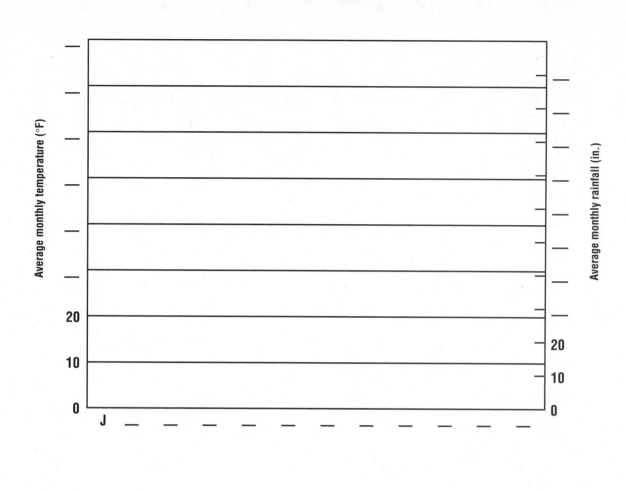

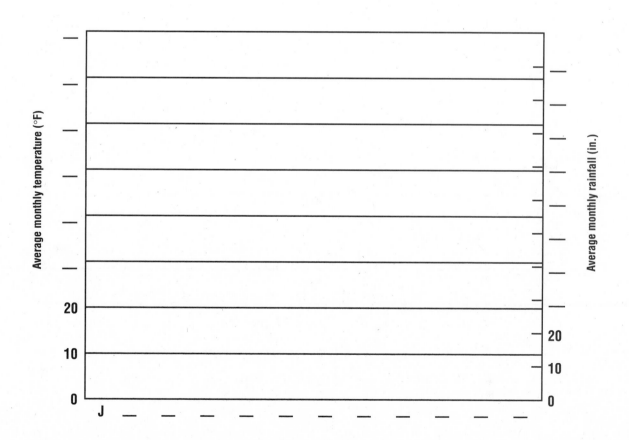

Unit 2 Review

Places and Regions

Ⓐ REVIEWING KEY TERMS

Match each term in Column A with its definition in Column B.

Column A

_____ 1. valley

_____ 2. functional region

_____ 3. peninsula

_____ 4. political region

_____ 5. plain

_____ 6. physical region

_____ 7. plateau

_____ 8. island

_____ 9. formal region

_____ 10. mountain

Column B

a. area of level land, usually at low elevation

b. a region that is based on a common feature

c. a region that is based on the kind of government a country has

d. land with steep sides that rise sharply from the surrounding land

e. land completely surrounded by water

f. low land between hills or mountains

g. a region that is based on physical features

h. body of land jutting into a lake or ocean, surrounded by water on three sides

i. area of flat or rolling land at high elevation

j. a region that focuses on a central area and its surrounding territory

Ⓑ RECALLING FACTS

Write the letter of the word or words that completes each statement correctly.

_____ 1. Elevation is measured from

   a. contours.   b. sea level.   c. mountain peaks.

_____ 2. A region that is based on the languages that people speak is a

   a. culture region.   b. political region.   c. functional region.

_____ 3. A graph that shows both temperature and rainfall is called a

   a. line graph.   b. circle graph.   c. climograph.

_____ 4. Countries with little use of technology and low levels of industrialization are called

      a. developing countries.   **b.** culture regions.   **c.** developed countries.

_____ 5. The amount of elevation between contour lines on a contour map is
called the

      a. contour measure.   **b.** contour interval.   **c.** interval measure.

_____ 6. Part of a large body of water that extends into a shoreline is called

      a. a bay.   **b.** an isthmus.   **c.** a delta.

_____ 7. Culture regions are based on

      a. many elements.   **b.** one element.   **c.** physical features.

_____ 8. Another word for rainfall is

      a. temperature.   **b.** humidity.   **c.** precipitation.

_____ 9. A climograph is two types of graphs put together. These two types of
graphs are a line graph and a

      a. population pyramid.   **b.** circle graph.   **c.** bar graph.

_____ 10. A narrow stretch of land that connects two larger land areas is

      a. a peninsula.   **b.** an isthmus.   **c.** a cape.

_____ 11. Regions that are based on people's feelings and attitudes are called
_____ regions.

      a. perceptual   **b.** formal   **c.** functional

_____ 12. The type of economic system in which businesses are owned by the
people is called

      a. socialism.   **b.** industrialization.   **c.** free enterprise.

ⓒ PRACTICING MAP SKILLS

**Look at Maps 2-13, 2-14, and 2-15 on pages 92 and 93. Write the kind
of region shown by each map.**

1. _____

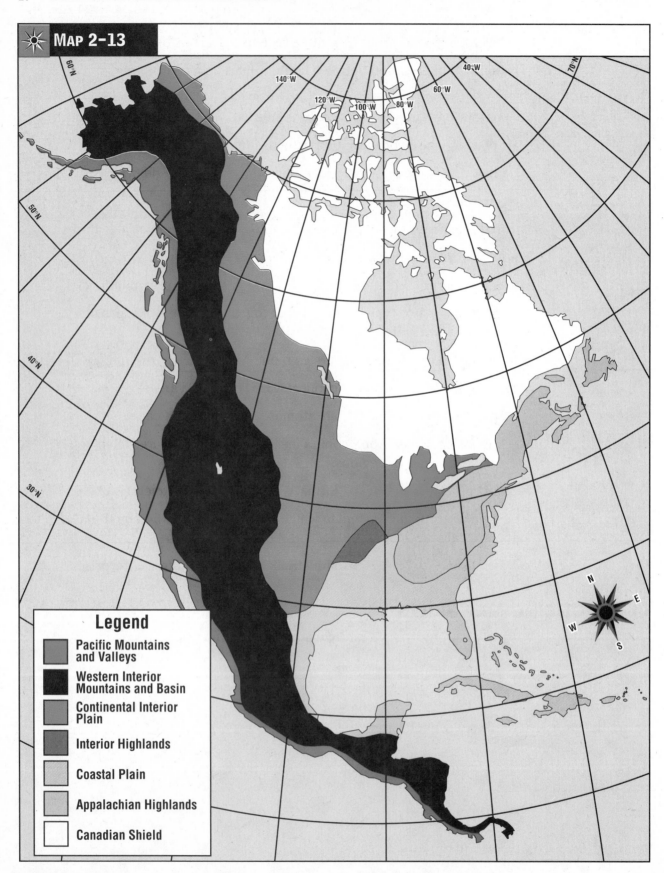

MAP 2-13

Legend

- Pacific Mountains and Valleys
- Western Interior Mountains and Basin
- Continental Interior Plain
- Interior Highlands
- Coastal Plain
- Appalachian Highlands
- Canadian Shield

2. _____

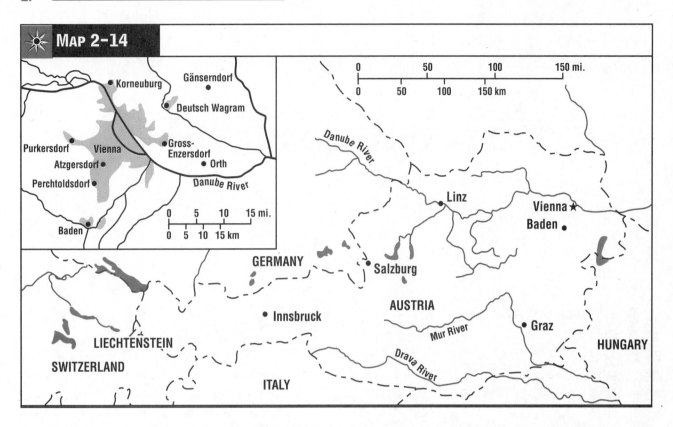

MAP 2-14

Korneuburg
Gänserndorf
Deutsch Wagram
Purkersdorf   Vienna
Gross-Enzersdorf
Atzgersdorf
Orth
Perchtoldsdorf
Danube River
Baden

0   5   10   15 mi.
0   5   10   15 km

0   50   100   150 mi.
0   50   100   150 km

Danube River

Linz
Vienna ★
Baden

GERMANY

Salzburg

AUSTRIA

Innsbruck

Mur River

Graz

LIECHTENSTEIN

HUNGARY

SWITZERLAND

Drava River

ITALY

3. _____

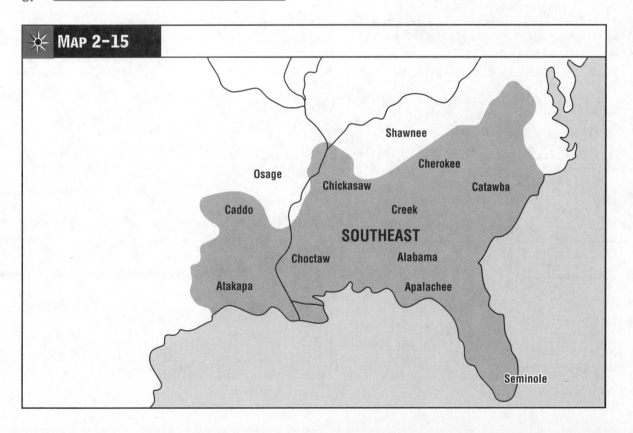

MAP 2-15

Shawnee

Osage

Cherokee

Chickasaw

Catawba

Caddo

Creek

SOUTHEAST

Choctaw

Alabama

Atakapa

Apalachee

Seminole

Unit 3

Physical Systems

Mt. Fuji, a dormant volcano on the island of Honshu, is Japan's tallest peak.

Objectives

After completing this unit, you will be able to:

- give examples of how physical processes help shape the earth's surface;
- describe the characteristics of ecosystems;
- explain how human activities affect ecosystems.

Geographers study how physical processes shape the surface of the earth. They use the theory of *plate tectonics,* which states that the surface of the earth is made up of huge plates that move relative to each other. As they move, plates may crash into each other, pull apart, or grind and slide past each other. Geographers use plate tectonics to explain how the features of the earth's surface, such as mountains and seas, were formed. They also use the theory to understand why earthquakes happen where they do.

Geographers also study the earth's *climates.* These are the weather patterns typical for an area over long periods of time. These patterns are affected by winds and by ocean currents. The kinds of winds a place experiences or the kind of ocean currents that flow near it can affect the climate of that particular place.

Geographers look at how physical features interact with plant and animal life to create, sustain, and modify an *ecosystem.* An ecosystem is a community of plants and animals that depend upon one another and their surroundings for their survival. The relationships in an ecosystem are very complex, and changes in one part of it affect all the other parts.

Physical systems is one of the six essential elements of geography. Geographers study physical systems to explain why the earth's surface looks the way it does. They study physical systems to understand how the plants and animals of an ecosystem depend on one another and their surroundings for survival. Geographers study how all the physical systems interact with one another.

DID YOU KNOW ?

What Are the Horse Latitudes?

Have you ever heard the term "horse latitudes?" These latitudes are located at the edge of the Tropics at about 30° N and 30° S latitudes. In these bands of calm air winds are not constant.

Sailors were most likely the first to call these latitudes the "horse latitudes." In the days of wind-powered sailing ships, crews often feared being stranded in the windless areas. When ships reached the band of calm air at the edge of the Tropics, the lack of wind made them immobile, sometimes for days. To lighten the load so the ships could take advantage of the slightest breeze, sailors would toss excess cargo and supplies overboard. This included livestock being carried to colonial settlements. This practice gave rise to the name "horse latitudes."

The Tallest Trees Alive

The coastal redwood tree *(Sequoia sempervirens)* flourishes in the marine west coast climate of the Pacific coast of the United States. These trees, which typically grow taller than 300 feet (91 m), are the tallest trees alive today. The trees need several hundred years to mature. Some have been known to live as long as 1,500 years.

In this unit you will learn what processes helped to shape the oceans and the continents. You will learn what factors help to determine the climate of a particular place. You will also learn what things make up an ecosystem and how humans can affect an ecosystem.

Plate Tectonics

Did you ever wonder how mountains were formed or why they are located where they are? Why do earthquakes happen?

The earth's surface is not the same everywhere, and it keeps changing. One cause of these changes has to do with what's happening inside the earth.

Inside the Earth

Look at Figure 3-1. It shows that the earth is made up of three layers—the core, the mantle, and the crust. The **core** is located about 4,000 miles (6,430 km) below the earth's surface. It is made up of iron and nickel. The middle layer is the **mantle.** This is a layer of hot, molten rock. The outer layer is the earth's **crust.** This layer of rock ranges from about 2 miles (3 km) thick under the oceans to about 75 miles (121 km) thick under mountains.

The crust is broken into more than a dozen great slabs of rock called **tectonic plates.** These plates float on a partially melted layer of the mantle. The plates carry the earth's continents and oceans. Map 3-1 shows the earth's major tectonic plates and their boundaries.

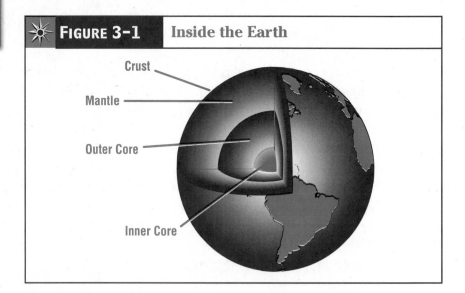

FIGURE 3-1 — **Inside the Earth**

Crust

Mantle

Outer Core

Inner Core

How Do the Tectonic Plates Move?

The theory of **plate tectonics** explains how most of the major features of the earth's surface were formed. According to this theory, tectonic plates have been moving and shaping the surface of the earth for 2.5 to 4 billion years. Map 3-1 shows the direction in which the plates are moving. Most of the time, plate movement is so gradual—only about 4 inches (10 cm) a year—that it cannot be

MAP 3-1   Plates and Plate Movement

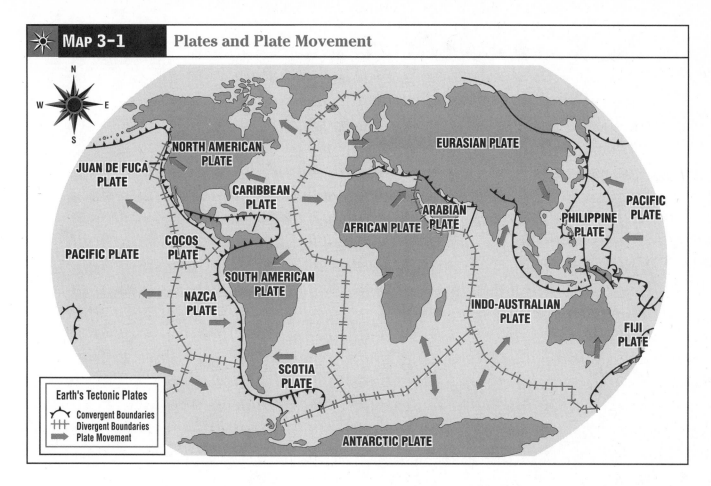

Earth's Tectonic Plates
- Convergent Boundaries
- Divergent Boundaries
- Plate Movement

felt. The way the plates move determines the kinds of landforms that are formed. It also determines where earthquakes occur.

There are three kinds of movement that happen at the boundaries between the plates. At **divergent boundaries,** tectonic plates move apart, or rift, from each other. When a rift occurs on a continent, it creates a gap into which water flows. This creates lakes and when the gap continues to widen, it creates seas. The Red Sea, for example, was formed when a rift occurred between the African and Indo-Australian tectonic plates.

When a rift occurs in the ocean, liquefied rock, called **magma,** rises up to fill the gap between the separating plates. The magma creates new crust on the edges of the two plates. The separation of the plates and the new crust helps to enlarge the ocean floor. The built-up crust forms long underwater mountain ranges called ocean ridges.

At **transform boundaries,** plates slide past each other along what are called faults. This movement does not create landforms, but it does create earthquakes along the boundary of the two plates. Look at Map 3-1. Find the North American Plate and the Pacific Plate. The North American Plate moves in a northwest direction. The Pacific Plate moves in a westward direction. The San Andreas Fault in California is a boundary between the two plates. Many earthquakes occur along this boundary.

At **convergent boundaries,** two tectonic plates move toward each other and collide. One plate is often forced below the other. When an ocean plate collides with a continental plate, the ocean plate slides under the continental plate and forms a deep ocean trench. The Mariana Trench in the north Pacific Ocean is an example of such activity. When continental plates collide, they form major mountain ranges, such as the Himalaya. Look at Map 3-1. What two plates collided to form the Himalaya?

Sometimes a plate that is forced beneath another reaches into the deeper regions of the earth where it is hot enough to melt part of the plate. The melted rock, or lava, rises back toward the surface where it forms volcanoes and islands. The Hawaiian Islands were formed in this way.

A REVIEWING KEY TERMS

Match each term with its meaning. Draw a line from each term to its definition.

1. tectonic plates

2. mantle

3. divergent boundaries

4. transform boundaries

5. convergent boundaries

6. crust

7. magma

8. core

a. boundaries where tectonic plates move toward each other

b. a layer of hot, dense rock inside the earth

c. boundaries where tectonic plates slide past each other

d. slabs of rock that are part of the earth's crust

e. boundaries where tectonic plates move away from each other

f. innermost layer of the earth

g. outer layer of the earth

h. liquefied rock

B RECALLING FACTS

Fill in the blanks to correctly complete the following sentences.

1. The earth's _____ is made up of iron and nickel.

2. According to the theory of plate tectonics, plates have been moving for

   _____ years.

3. The way that _____ move determines the kinds of landforms that are created on the earth's surface.

4. The Himalaya were formed at a _____ boundary of two tectonic plates.

5. Earthquakes in California often occur at the

   _____ boundary of two tectonic plates.

6. The Red Sea was formed at the _____ boundary of two tectonic plates.

7. When a rift occurs in the ocean, _____ rises up to fill in the gap between the two plates.

8. The _____ was formed at a convergent boundary of a continental plate and an ocean plate.

ⓒ PRACTICING MAP SKILLS

Use Map 3-1 on page 101 to answer the following questions.

1. On which tectonic plate is the United States located?

   _____

2. On which tectonic plate is Panama located?

   _____

3. On which tectonic plate is India located?

   _____

4. Which two plates make up a convergent boundary near South America?

   _____

5. Which two plates make up a convergent boundary near Southeast Asia?

   _____

6. Which three plates make up a divergent boundary near the Atlantic Ocean?

   _____

7. Which two plates are responsible for the creation of the Himalaya mountain ranges?

   _____

8. Which two plates are responsible for the creation of the Andes mountain ranges?

   _____

Lesson ② Winds and Ocean Currents

WHAT YOU WILL LEARN

To describe the world's winds and ocean currents

READING STRATEGY

Create a table like the one below. List the location of each type of wind next to the correct heading.

WIND	LOCATION
trade winds	
westerlies	
polar easterlies	
doldrums	

TERMS TO KNOW

wind, low latitudes, middle latitudes, high latitudes, prevailing winds, trade winds, westerlies, polar easterlies, front, doldrums, ocean currents

Do you enjoy a windy day? Did you ever wonder what happens to make winds occur?

What Is Wind?

Wind is air that moves across the earth's surface. Winds occur because the sun heats up the earth's atmosphere and surface unevenly. When the sun heats the air over the Equator, the warm air becomes lighter, rises, and creates areas of low pressure. Cool air from the Poles is heavy, tends to sink, and creates areas of high pressure. The cool air blows in to replace the rising warm air at the Equator. These movements over the earth's surface cause winds, which distribute the sun's heat around the planet.

Winds and Latitude

In Unit 1, Lesson 4, you learned about lines of latitude. Lines of latitude can be divided into three zones, or belts. Look carefully at Figure 3-2. Find the Tropic of Cancer and the Tropic of Capricorn. These lines, at $23\frac{1}{2}°$N and $23\frac{1}{2}°$S latitude, mark the boundaries of the **low latitudes.** This zone includes the Equator. Find the lines of latitude from the Tropic of Cancer to $66\frac{1}{2}°$N and the Tropic of Capricorn to $66\frac{1}{2}°$S. This area is the **middle latitudes.** Find the **high latitudes.** It includes the area from $66\frac{1}{2}°$N to the North Pole and from $66\frac{1}{2}°$S to the South Pole.

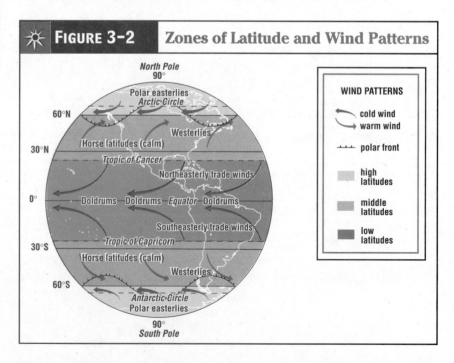

☀ **FIGURE 3-2**   **Zones of Latitude and Wind Patterns**

Global winds blow in fairly constant patterns called **prevailing winds.** The direction of prevailing winds is determined by latitude and is affected by the movement of the earth. As you have learned, cooler air from the Poles sinks and blows toward the Equator. These are **trade winds.** Look at Figure 3-2. What kind of trade winds blow toward the Equator from the north?

The winds of the middle latitudes are called **westerlies.** They generally blow from west to east. Winds in the high latitudes are known as **polar easterlies.** These winds generally blow from east to west. The polar easterlies bring cold conditions to the middle latitudes. When the cold air of the polar easterlies meet the warmer air of the westerlies, they form a **front.** Stormy weather usually occurs when two different types of air meet.

Near the Equator global winds are diverted north and south, leaving a generally windless band called the **doldrums.** Located between about 10°N and 10°S latitudes, the doldrums are calm; winds almost disappear. How do you think the doldrums might affect wind-powered ships attempting to travel through the area?

Ocean Currents

The world's winds also help move the **ocean currents.** These are the cold and warm streams of water that move through the oceans. Look at Map 3-2. It shows the direction and location of the world's major ocean currents. As you can see, they flow in a circular pattern. They generally flow in a clockwise direction in the Northern Hemisphere and in a counterclockwise direction in the Southern Hemisphere.

As ocean currents circulate, cold water from the Poles moves slowly toward the Equator. This water warms as it moves through the low latitudes, forming warm ocean currents. The warm water, in turn, moves away from the Equator. As it moves, it cools to become a cold ocean current.

Ocean currents affect climate in the coastal lands along which they flow. Cold ocean currents help to cool the lands they pass. Warm ocean currents bring warmer temperatures. For example, the warm North Atlantic Drift, shown in Map 3-2, gives Europe a mild climate in spite of its location in the higher latitudes.

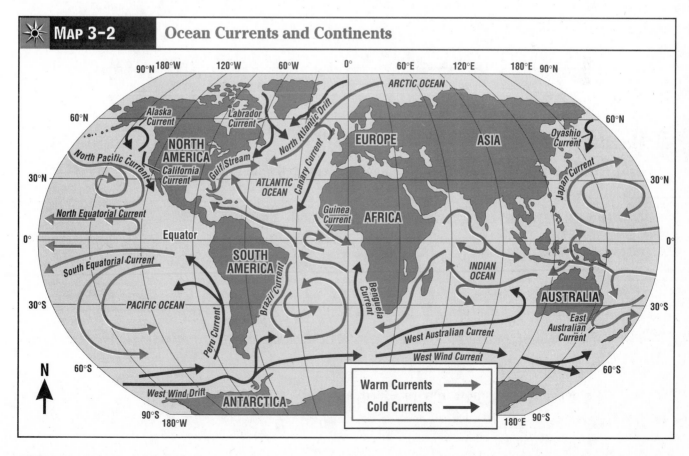

MAP 3-2 **Ocean Currents and Continents**

Using Your Skills

Ⓐ RECALLING FACTS

Answer these questions about winds and ocean currents.

1. How does the sun affect the movement of air?

   _____

   _____

   _____

2. What determines the direction of prevailing winds?

   _____

   _____

   _____

3. Describe the locations of the three zones, or belts of latitude.

   _____

   _____

   _____

4. In what direction do ocean currents flow?

   _____

   _____

   _____

Ⓑ USING GRAPHICS

Use Figure 3-2 and Map 3-2. Fill in the blanks to correctly complete the following sentences.

1. The _____ blow across most of the United States.

2. The _____ blow across the central part of South America.

3. The polar easterlies are _____ winds.

4. The ocean current that flows near the southeastern coast of the United States is the _____.

5. Cold ocean currents flow from the north and south toward the

   _____.

Lesson ③ The World's Climates

WHAT YOU WILL LEARN

To describe and locate the world's major climate zones

READING STRATEGY

Draw a globe like the one below. Label the three climate zones that are based on latitude. Then identify the lines of latitude that separate the climate zones.

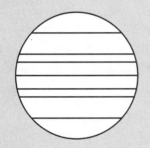

TERMS TO KNOW

weather, climate

It is the weekend and you have plans to go to the beach. You will probably be interested in knowing what the **weather** will be like that day. You will want to know if it will be wet or dry, cool or warm. If you were planning to move to another part of the world to live, you would want to know more about the place than its weather. You would want to know about its **climate.** Climate refers to the weather patterns in a place over a long period of time.

Why Are Climates Different?

Why is it always cold at the North Pole? Why is it warm year-round in cities near the Equator? The climate of a place depends on the amount of direct sunlight it receives. Places near the Equator receive direct sunlight year-round. In contrast, the North Pole never receives direct sunlight.

The sun is not the only factor that affects climate. Wind, ocean currents, and landforms also determine the climate of an area.

The World's Climate Zones

Geographers often divide the earth into climate zones—tropical, dry, middle latitude, high latitude, and highlands. Because climates vary within these broad regions, geographers further divide the major regions into smaller ones. Figure 3-3 describes the temperatures and precipitation that are generally found in each of the major climate zones.

Look at Map 3-3. The map shows where the climate zones of the world are located. Find the five major climate zones on the map. Near what lines of latitude can you find the tropical climate zone? How does sunlight help to make places in this area hot year-round? What part of the United States has a dry climate?

☀ **FIGURE 3-3**	**World Climate Zones**	
CLIMATE ZONE	**Temperature**	**Precipitation**
Tropical	Hot year-round	Large amounts of precipitation
Dry	Hot summers and cool winters; hot days and cold nights	Little or no precipitation
Middle Latitude	Range of temperatures; warm to hot summers and cool to cold winters	Moderate amounts of precipitation
High Latitude	Freezing temperatures common much of the year; cold summers and very cold winters	Very little precipitation
Highlands	Depends on elevation; the higher the elevation, the cooler the temperatures	Precipitation varies widely

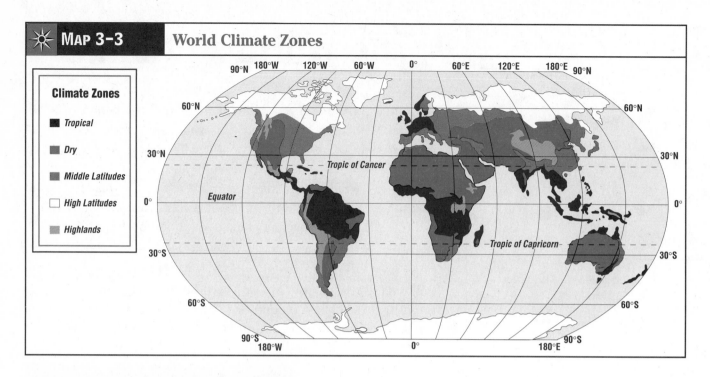

MAP 3-3   **World Climate Zones**

Climate Zones

- ■ *Tropical*
- ■ *Dry*
- ■ *Middle Latitudes*
- □ *High Latitudes*
- ▨ *Highlands*

Using Your Skills

Ⓐ RECALLING FACTS

Use the reading, Figure 3-3, and Map 3-3 to answer these questions.

1. What is the difference between weather and climate?

   _____

   _____

2. What four factors help to determine the climate of a given area?

   _____

3. What kinds of temperature and precipitation are found in the high latitude climate zone?

   _____

4. How does elevation affect temperature in highlands climate zones?

   _____

5. What climate zone has hot temperatures year-round? _____

6. In what climate zone is much of eastern Europe located? _____

7. What climate zone is located near the Equator? _____

8. Name three areas of the world in which highlands climate zones are found.

   _____

   _____

Lesson 4 — The World's Biomes and Ecosystems

WHAT YOU WILL LEARN

To describe a biome and an ecosystem

READING STRATEGY

Draw a table like the one below. In the right column, write a result of the fact listed in the left column.

FACT	RESULT
The sun provides energy.	
Secondary consumers are predators.	
Decomposers break down dead plants and animals.	

TERMS TO KNOW

biome, ecosystem, food chain

What kinds of plants and animals live near your community? Have you ever observed how they depend on each other?

This savannah in Kenya is an example of a grasslands biome.

What Is a Biome?

A plant and animal community that covers a large geographical area is called a **biome.** A biome has certain kinds of plants and animals. It is located in a specific climate and generally has a specific kind of soil. For example, a desert biome is located in a climate that is very dry. Cacti and shrubs are among the plants that grow there. Lizards and snakes are some of the animals that live there. A desert biome anywhere in the world will have a similar climate, as well as similar plants and animals.

Some of the major land biomes of the world include forest, grasslands, desert, and tundra. The ocean is another major biome. Look at Figure 3-4. It shows you the characteristics of some of the major world land biomes.

What Is an Ecosystem?

A biome can include several ecosystems. An **ecosystem** refers to all the living things and nonliving things within a certain area and the relationships among them. Living things include the plants, animals, and microbes (such as bacteria and fungi). The nonliving environment includes air, soil, water, and sunlight. An ecosystem contains everything that is needed for the plants and animals living there to survive.

☀ FIGURE 3-4   World Land Biomes

Biome	Kinds of Plants	Kinds of Animals	Kind of Climate
Tundra	Lichens, mosses, and sometimes dwarf trees	Polar bears, reindeer, caribou, arctic foxes, hares, hawks, falcons	Very cold, dry
Tropical rain forest	Tall, closely spaced evergreen trees, vines, flowers	Monkeys, apes, gorillas, leopards, lizards, tree frogs, black panthers, colorful birds, snakes	Warm, often hot, and wet
Temperate forest	Broadleaf or needleleaf trees, climbing vines, flowers	Birds, raccoons, lynx, cougars, bears, foxes, squirrels, deer, snakes, insects, spiders	Temperatures and precipitation vary; warm to hot summers and cold winters
Desert	Cacti, low shrubs	Lizards, snakes, jackrabbits, kangaroo rats, insects	Very dry
Grasslands	Grasses, trees, flowers	Antelope, bison, coyotes	Mild, moderate temperatures and rainfall

The relationship of living and nonliving things in an ecosystem can be seen in the food chain. Look at Figure 3-5.

The **food chain** shows how the living and nonliving parts of an ecosystem are interrelated. The sun provides the energy that the primary producers need to make food. Primary producers are mainly green plants. Plants also need things such as water and minerals from the soil to grow. Primary consumers include animals that eat plants, such as rabbits and grasshoppers. Secondary consumers are predators, or animals that eat other animals. Finally, decomposers, such as bacteria, break down dead animals and plants into nutrients that go back into the soil. The nutrients are used again by plants.

☀ FIGURE 3-5   The Food Chain

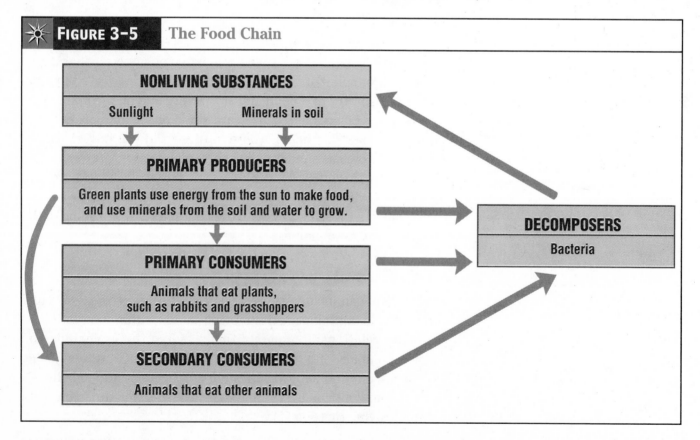

Using Your Skills

A RECALLING FACTS

Answer the following questions about biomes and ecosystems.

1. What characteristics make up a biome?

   _____

   _____

2. What are five major land biomes of the world?

   _____

   _____

3. What things make up the living and nonliving parts of an ecosystem?

   _____

   _____

4. What part of an ecosystem provides the energy needed for primary

   producers to make food? _____

5. What role do decomposers play in the food chain?

   _____

   _____

   _____

B USING GRAPHICS

Use Figures 3-4 and 3-5 to answer the questions.

1. What kinds of plants grow in the tundra?

   _____

2. What kinds of animals could you expect to find in a grasslands biome?

   _____

3. What living things in the food chain are producers? _____

4. What do producers use to make food?

   _____

5. What is the difference between primary and secondary consumers?

   _____

   _____

   _____

Lesson 5 The Water Cycle

WHAT YOU WILL LEARN

To describe the water cycle and human effects on it

READING STRATEGY

Create a diagram like the one below. Starting at the top, write the steps of the water cycle—each in a separate square—in the correct sequence.

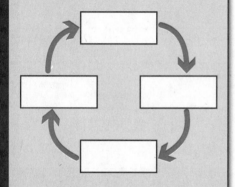

TERMS TO KNOW

water cycle, evaporation, condensation, precipitation, transpiration, groundwater, surface runoff, water table, pollution, deep-well injection, acid rain

What do you have in common with King Tut, George Washington, and dinosaurs? The rain and snow that falls on you today may once have fallen on them.

How is this possible? The answer lies in what we call the **water cycle,** the movement of water from the oceans to the air to the ground and finally back to the oceans. The total amount of water on Earth does not change, but the Earth's water is constantly moving. As water moves through the water cycle, it becomes mixed with water from all over the earth—and sooner or later, water that once fell on a dinosaur falls on you.

The Water Cycle

Figure 3-6 shows how the water cycle works. The water cycle really has no beginning or ending point. It is an endless cycle. However, the sun drives the cycle by evaporating water from the surfaces of oceans, lakes, and streams. **Evaporation** is the changing of liquid water into vapor, or gas. The sun's heat causes evaporation. The amount of water vapor the air holds depends on its temperature. Warm, less dense air holds more water vapor than does cool air.

When warm air cools, it cannot retain all of its water vapor, so the excess water vapor changes into liquid water—a process called **condensation.** Tiny droplets of water come together to form clouds. When clouds gather more water than they can hold, they release moisture, which falls to the earth as **precipitation—**rain, snow, sleet, or hail, depending on the air temperature and wind conditions. Some of the precipitation is absorbed by plants, which "breathe" the water vapor back into the air through their leaves. This process is called **transpiration.** Other precipitation sinks into the ground to become **groundwater,** and is eventually pumped from wells or flows from springs. **Surface runoff** collects in streams and lakes to return to the oceans. Soon most of it evaporates, and the cycle begins again.

The amount of water that evaporates is approximately the same amount that falls back to the earth. This amount varies little from year to year. As a result, the total volume of water in the water cycle is more or less constant.

Precipitation falls in various forms—rain, snow, sleet, or hail. Some precipitation immediately evaporates and returns to the atmosphere. On a hot summer day, you may see steam rising from a sidewalk after a sudden rain shower. The water in the steam will turn to water vapor and return to the atmosphere.

Some precipitation is collected in rivers, lakes, and streams. However, the amount collected in these bodies of water is actually quite small. Most of the precipitation seeps into the ground to become groundwater. This is a vital source of water; there is 10 times more groundwater than there is water in rivers, lakes, and streams.

Some groundwater stays near the surface in the *zone of aeration.* In this zone, both air and water collect in gaps in the soil. Groundwater that seeps farther into the ground will reach a *zone of saturation.* In this zone, all gaps in the soil and rocks are filled with water. The actual point below ground that marks these two zones varies as the amount of water in the soil changes. The boundary between the two zones is known as the **water table.** The water table rises as the amount of groundwater increases. The water table falls as the amount of groundwater decreases.

Human Effects on the Water Cycle

Let's look at how humans affect the water cycle. Humans create a great deal of **pollution.** Pollution is the existence of impure, unclean, or poisonous substances in the environment. We dump sewage into lakes and rivers. Factories billow smoke into the air and gush harmful chemicals into our rivers. Other wastes from factories are pumped into wells drilled deep into the ground.

Look again at Figure 3-6 of the water cycle. Find the part of the diagram labeled "groundwater." Some factories use the process of **deep-well injection.** In this process, wells are drilled deeper than the groundwater level, and harmful chemicals are deposited where they can be contained in the subsurface rock. In fact, over half the dangerous wastes produced in the United States are pumped down deep wells. Some of these wastes, unfortunately, leak into the groundwater. Once the dangerous wastes enter the water cycle, it may be years before they are removed—if ever.

Surface runoff provides another way for wastes to enter the water cycle. Rain or snow falling on the ground picks up pollution from streets and garbage dumps and then carries it into streams.

Chemicals that farmers use to kill weeds and insects also become part of surface runoff.

Wastes also enter the water cycle through the air. Each year in the United States alone, billions of pounds of poisons enter the air from factories, trash burning, garbage dumps, cars, and agricultural spraying. Some of these poisons fall directly into lakes and streams. Others are washed out of the air by rain or snow. In either case, the poisons enter the water cycle.

Acid rain is rain or snow that carries pollution. Most of the pollution in acid rain comes from the burning of fossil fuels such as coal and oil. Acidic chemicals created by the burning of fossil fuels combine with precipitation to form acid rain. Acid rain eats away at the surfaces of buildings, kills fish, and can even destroy entire forests.

A number of years ago, a seventh-grade student working on a class project in Austin, Texas, came up with a slogan: "You're the solution to water pollution." The Texas Department of Parks and Wildlife used that slogan to make people realize this important fact: People cause pollution, and people can stop it.

This forest in the eastern United States shows the damaging effects of acid rain.

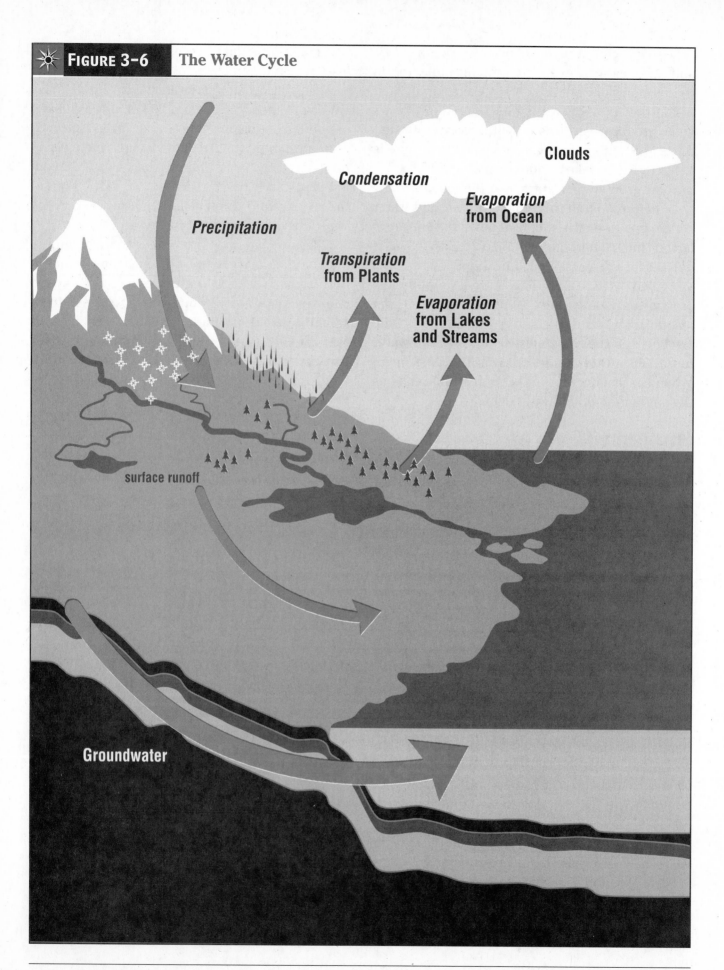

Using Your Skills

Ⓐ REVIEWING KEY TERMS

Write the meaning of each term.

1. water cycle

_____

_____

_____

2. water table

_____

_____

_____

3. pollution

_____

_____

4. acid rain

_____

_____

Ⓑ RECALLING FACTS

Answer the questions.

1. Where is groundwater collected and stored?

_____

_____

2. What are the ways in which people are causing pollution?

_____

_____

_____

_____

3. On Figure 3-6 of the water cycle on page 114, draw and label pictures to show how pollution enters the water cycle. Include deep-well injection, wind-carried pollution, and acid rain.

Physical Systems

Ⓐ REVIEWING KEY TERMS

Match each term in Column A with its definition in Column B.

Column A

_____ 1. divergent boundary

_____ 2. convergent boundary

_____ 3. prevailing winds

_____ 4. trade winds

_____ 5. doldrums

_____ 6. climate

_____ 7. biome

_____ 8. ecosystem

_____ 9. water cycle

_____ 10. precipitation

Column B

a.   global winds that blow in fairly constant patterns

b.   the movement of water from the oceans to the air to the ground and back to the oceans

c.   calm, windless areas near the Equator

d.   a plant and animal community that covers a large geographical area

e.   moisture that falls to Earth in the form of rain, snow, sleet, or hail

f.   boundary where tectonic plates move apart

g.   the living and nonliving things in a certain area and the relationships among them

h.   winds that bring cooler air toward the Equator

i.   weather patterns over a long period of time

j.   boundary where tectonic plates move toward each other

Ⓑ RECALLING FACTS

In each sentence underline the term in the parentheses that will complete the statement correctly.

1.   The (mantle, core) is a layer of hot, dense rock inside the earth.

2.   The (tectonic plates, core) carry Earth's continents and oceans.

3.   Mountains are formed at the (convergent, divergent) boundaries of tectonic plates.

4.   California's San Andreas Fault is located on a (divergent, transform) boundary.

5.   A (front, ecosystem) is created when two different types of air meet.

6. (Prevailing winds, Ocean currents) flow in a clockwise direction in the Northern Hemisphere.

7. The winds of the middle latitudes are called (westerlies, trade winds).

8. (Climate, Pollution) is influenced by how much direct sunlight a place receives during the year.

9. The coldest climate zone on the earth is the (tropical, high latitude) climate zone.

10. The climate in a (tundra, grasslands) biome is one that has mild temperatures and moderate rainfall.

11. In the food chain, (primary, secondary) consumers are animals that eat other animals.

12. The burning of fossil fuels can result in (transpiration, acid rain).

❻ Using Graphics

Use **Figure 3-7** to answer these questions.

1. What are the steps in the water cycle?

_____

2. How does water get from the ground to the oceans?

_____

_____

3. In which part of the water cycle does water return to Earth? _____

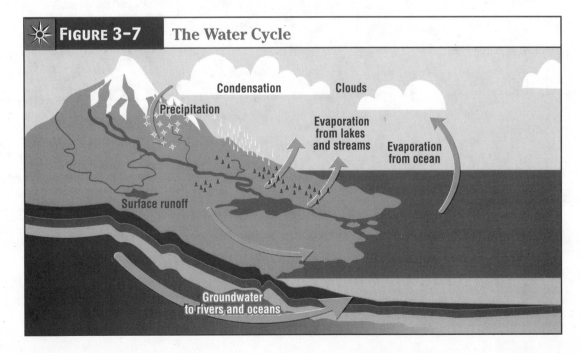

☀ **FIGURE 3-7** The Water Cycle

Condensation
Clouds
Precipitation
Evaporation from lakes and streams
Evaporation from ocean
Surface runoff
Groundwater to rivers and oceans

Human Systems

Hong Kong, a city of over 6,000,000 people, has a very high population density.

Objectives

After completing this unit, you will be able to:

- learn about population characteristics by using maps, charts, and graphs;
- demonstrate how humans interact within and among countries;
- discuss how peoples of the world are linked by trade and transportation;
- analyze how the United States is interdependent with other countries.

Every day each of us interacts with people around the world, even though we may not realize it. When you wake up in the morning and punch your pillow before going back to sleep, you may be touching cloth made from cotton grown in Egypt. Your breakfast may include bananas from Latin America. Your ride to school or work may take place in a car from Japan, Germany, or South Korea. Even if the car was made in the United States, chances are that it was put together in Canada. Your jeans my have been sewn in Mexico.

Transportation—the movement of goods and people—makes our interactions with people around the world possible. Imagine how different your life would be if the only goods you could buy were ones produced within your immediate area. Imagine how you would feel if you had to live out your life without ever traveling more than a few miles from where you were born.

Human systems is one of the six essential elements of geography. Geographers study how people shape the earth's surface. They examine how people move from place to place, how they settle the earth, and how they form societies. Although the human population is scattered unevenly across the earth, we all interact with each other. Some people travel from place to place. Others talk to people around the world by telephone, mail, and e-mail. The Internet, radio, television, and books spread different ideas and ways of life.

DID YOU KNOW ?

Fairy Tales From Around the World

Growing up, all of us have listened to and read many fairy tales, such as those collected and retold by the Brothers Grimm. Did you know that these fairy tales came from all over the world and were told and retold many times before anyone began writing them down?

The earliest records of these tales can help us understand where they came from. "Sleeping Beauty" came from Italy, "Little Red Riding Hood" came from France, "Hansel and Gretel," and "Snow White and the Seven Dwarfs" were told in Germany, and "Goldilocks and the Three Bears" was first told in England. Over twelve hundred years ago, Chinese parents and grandparents entertained their children by telling them the story we know as "Cinderella." Through communication, these stories have survived the years and spanned the globe to be told, read, watched, and enjoyed by children today.

Goods and services are also exchanged around the world. Some of the clothes we wear comes from other countries. In turn, we send other countries things they need that we produce.

In short, we need other countries, and they need us. No country in the world today can survive strictly on its own. The word we use to describe this relationship is *interdependence*.

In this unit you will study some of the ways people interact with each other in the world today. You will learn how people in the United States interact with each other and with people around the world. You will see how a culture can spread across a large part of the earth. And you will gain a greater appreciation for the complexity and interdependence of our modern world.

Reading Population Density Maps

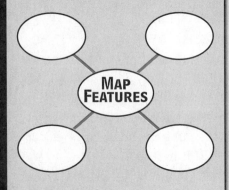
Think about where you live. Do many other people live nearby? If you were to count all the people who live within half a mile of you in all directions, how many would there be? Ten? Four hundred? Two thousand? Ten thousand?

Human population is not spread evenly over the surface of the earth. Some parts of the earth are home to only a few people, living very far apart. In other places, such as New York City, a great many people live very close together.

Population Density Maps

Population density is the number of people living in a unit area of land. Maps can show where on the earth's surface clusters of people live. This kind of map is called a **population density map.** A population density map uses shading or colors to show how many people live in each square mile or square kilometer of a given area. Population density maps use lighter shading or colors for areas of low density, or areas where few people live. Darker shading or colors are used for areas of high density, or areas where many people live. The legend tells you what each shading or color on the map represents.

Cities that are shown by dots or squares also represent different population sizes. For example, an open circle indicates that a city's population is between 500,000 and 1,000,000 people. A dot may represent a city with a population of 1,000,000 to 5,000,000 people. A square can show that a city has a population of over 5,000,000 people. Population density maps usually have a second map legend to show city information.

Comparing Population Density Maps

People tend to live closer together in places where there are more resources to support life. For example, look at Maps 4-1 and 4-2 of Egypt. Map 4-1 shows major farming areas in Egypt. As you can see, farming takes place along the Nile River.

Now look at Map 4-2. What is the title of the map? The legend shows you the persons per square mile represented by each category of shading. How many people per square mile live in areas with this shading ? ███ Where are the large cities located?

Compare the two maps of Egypt. What conclusion can you draw about the importance of agriculture to the people of Egypt? What conclusion can you draw about the importance of the Nile River to the lives of the Egyptian people?

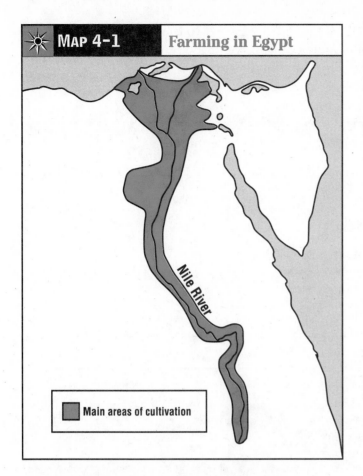

MAP 4-1 Farming in Egypt

Nile River

Main areas of cultivation

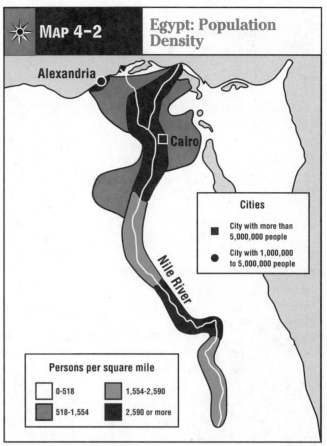

MAP 4-2 Egypt: Population Density

Alexandria

Cairo

Nile River

Cities

■ City with more than 5,000,000 people

● City with 1,000,000 to 5,000,000 people

Persons per square mile

☐ 0-518

☐ 1,554-2,590

☐ 518-1,554

☐ 2,590 or more

Using Your Skills

④ PRACTICING MAP SKILLS

Use Map 4-3: East Asia: Population Density on page 122 to answer the questions.

1. What part of East Asia has the highest population density (the greatest number of people per square mile)? _____

2. What happens to population density in China as one travels from east to west? _____

3. China has more people than any other country. Are there parts of China where no people live? How do you know?

    _____

4. How many people per square mile live in the area around the city of

    a. Wuhan? _____

    b. Ulaanbaatar? _____

    c. Guangzho? _____

5. Look back at Map 2-2: East Asia: Elevation on page 65. Compare it to the population density map of East Asia. What conclusion can you draw about the relationship between elevation and population density in East Asia?

_____

6. Which Chinese cities have populations of more than 5 million people?

_____

7. What do the locations of the cities listed in question 6 have in common?

_____

8. Which cities in the region have populations of 500,000 to 1,000,000

people? _____

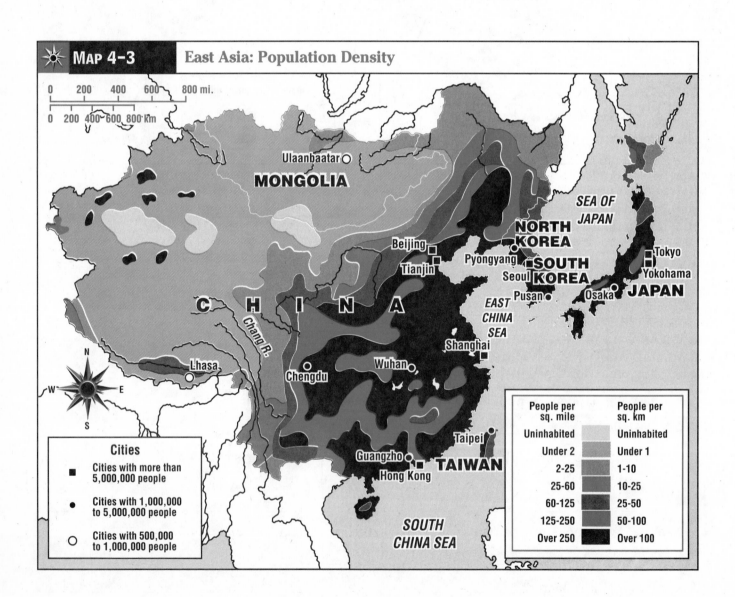

MAP 4-3 **East Asia: Population Density**

Cities
- ■ Cities with more than 5,000,000 people
- ● Cities with 1,000,000 to 5,000,000 people
- ○ Cities with 500,000 to 1,000,000 people

People per sq. mile	People per sq. km
Uninhabited	Uninhabited
Under 2	Under 1
2-25	1-10
25-60	10-25
60-125	25-50
125-250	50-100
Over 250	Over 100

Human population increases as babies are born, and decreases as people die. For most of human history, births have only slightly exceeded deaths each year. As a result, human population grew slowly. About the time of the Industrial Revolution, human population began to increase rapidly.

Exponential Growth

Let's examine how human population has grown. Figure 4-1 shows this rapid population growth as a J-shaped curve. This illustrates the exponential growth of population. **Exponential growth** (1, 2, 4, 8) rather than arithmetic growth (1, 2, 3, 4), results in large numbers. To explain this type of growth consider the following family trees:

Family 1: A and B have only one child. And the succeeding generations each have only one child. If all members of the family are alive, the two (A and B) have grown to five people.

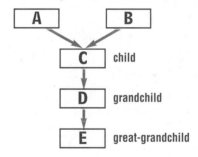

Family 2: A and B have two children and each succeeding generation has two children. In three generations this family has grown to 16 people.

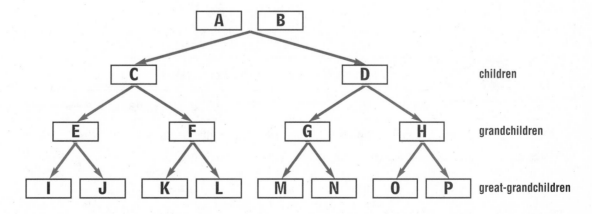

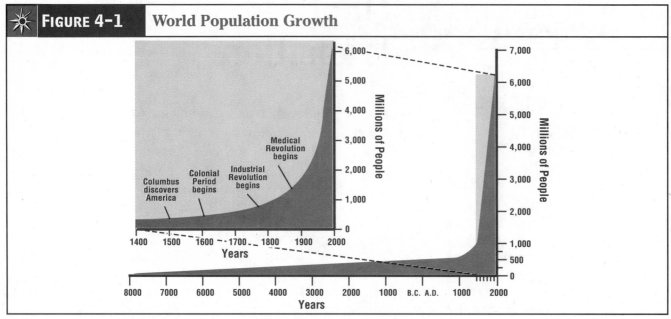

FIGURE 4-1 World Population Growth

Source: *Human Geography: Landscapes of Human Activities,* 1997.

If you assume that in Family 3 there are three children in each of the three generations, the family will grow to 41 people. If you were to graph this growth, you would see that high birthrates result in a large population growth rate.

Of course, some of these people will die and the population will decrease. The death rate in many countries has declined sharply since the Industrial Revolution. **Life expectancy,** the number of years that an average person lives, has increased as a result of improved diets and hygiene, and better medical practices.

Stages of the Demographic Transition

Although world population growth has been exponential, there are some signs that the growth is slowing. This pattern can be seen in the **demo-graphic transition,** a model used to explain the population history of a country or region.

There are four stages of the demographic transition. As shown in Figure 4-2 below, the population of each country can be categorized by stage. Today, there are few countries in Stage 1. Many countries in Latin America and Asia are said to be in Stage 2. In order to slow world population growth, researchers look for ways to move countries' populations from Stage 2 to Stage 3. As countries industrialize their birthrates tend to decrease. In agricultural economies, more children means more farm workers. In an urban setting, however, large families are not needed for work. Families in industrialized countries tend to have fewer children. As a result, many developed countries are in Stage 3, while several, such as Sweden and Germany, have moved into Stage 4. Such countries have little increase in their populations.

FIGURE 4-2 Stages of the Demographic Transition

Stage	Characteristics	Effect on Population Growth
Stage 1	High birthrates and high death rates	Little change in population
Stage 2	High birthrates and declining death rates	Life expectancy increases significantly and population grows explosively
Stage 3	Birthrates decline and low death rates	Population growth slows
Stage 4	Very low birth and death rates	Little population increase

Using Your Skills

Ⓐ RECALLING FACTS

Circle the choice that best completes the sentence or answers the question.

1. Which of the following is the best definition of life expectancy?
    A. the number of years until you have a child
    B. the exact number of years that you will live
    C. the number of years that an average person will live
    D. a country's birth rate divided by its death rate

2. What type of growth best describes the world's population since the Industrial Revolution?
    A. exponential   B. linear   C. declining   D. inclining

3. Which of the following best characterizes Stage 3 of the demographic transition?
    A. high birth rates and low death rates
    B. declining birth rates and low death rates
    C. declining birth rates and high death rates
    D. very low birth and death rates

Ⓑ USING GRAPHICS

Use the space below to draw a family tree. First write the number of brothers and sisters you have. Next, assume that each of you has the same number of children, grandchildren, and great grandchildren.

1. How many people, beginning with you and your brothers and sisters are in your family tree? _____

2. If you added one more generation using the same assumptions and if everyone on the tree is still living, how many people are in your family tree? _____

WHAT YOU WILL LEARN

To obtain and use information about human systems from line graphs

READING STRATEGY

Create a diagram like the one below. In each oval, list features of a line graph.

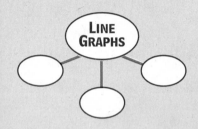

TERMS TO KNOW

line graph, trend, rate of change

We often need to show changes over a period of time. For example, you may wish to show how you grew taller as you got older. This kind of information is best shown on a **line graph.**

A line graph is made up of a grid. The amounts being measured are plotted on the grid and connected by a line. The amount is usually shown on the vertical, or Y-axis of the graph. Time is usually shown on the horizontal, or X-axis of the graph.

Using Line Graphs to Show Trends

Line graphs are useful for showing how an amount changes over time. How the amount changes is called the **trend.** If a line on the graph goes up, we say the trend is up, or increasing. If a line on the graph goes down, we say the trend is down, or decreasing. If a line shows little change up or down, we say the trend is flat.

Use the steps below to read Figure 4-3.

1. Find out what kind of information is shown on the graph. Look for the title of the graph. It will tell you what the graph is about. Often the title will also tell you what period of time the graph covers. What is the title of this graph? What period of time does the graph cover?

Notice the graph's legend. This explains the meaning of the three lines shown on the graph. If only one line is shown on a graph, no legend is needed. What does the legend tell you the red line on the graph means? What does the dashed blue line represent? The solid blue line?

2. Study the labels on the graph. The labels tell you what the numbers on the graph stand for. Look at the numbers on the left vertical axis of the graph. The number 0 is at the bottom of the graph. Above it are numbers up to 1,300. What does the label say these numbers stand for? What do the numbers on the right vertical axis represent? Now look at the numbers on the horizontal axis of the graph. Next to 0 on the left side is the number 1949. At the far right is the number 1995. What do these numbers stand for?

3. Read the line graph. Begin reading the graph from the left. Read across the graph to the right. Notice that there is a symbol on each line above each year. To find out how much the symbol stands for, read across to the left and use the vertical scale. For example, the diamond for the year 1973 is at 200 on the left vertical axis. This tells you that about how many million people died in China in 1973. About how many million people were born in China in 1990?

4. Draw conclusions from the graph. Observe the lines on the graph. Line graphs are useful because a glance at one can tell you not only the trend, but also the **rate of change.** The rate of change is the speed with which change is taking place. A line which slopes gently up or down shows that change is taking place slowly. A line that shoots up or down steeply shows that change is taking place rapidly. Is the trend of the total population of China up or down? Is the birthrate increasing or decreasing? What was the rate of change in the death rate in China between 1983 and 1995? What was the rate of change between 1949 and 1958?

FIGURE 4-3 Population Growth and Birth and Death Rates in China, 1949–1995

Source: International Institute of Applied Systems Analysis.

Using Your Skills

ⓐ REVIEWING KEY TERMS

Explain the meaning of each term below.

1. trend _____

2. rate of change _____

   _____

ⓑ USING GRAPHICS

Use the graph in Figure 4-3 on page 127 to answer the following questions.

1. In what years did the birthrate in China show the largest decline?

    A. 1954–1956   B. 1957–1961   C. 1961–1963   D. 1963–1966

2. What has been the general trend in China's birthrate since 1963?

    A. downward   B. upward   C. flat

3. What has been the general trend in China's death rate since 1963?

    A. downward   B. upward   C. flat

4. If the birth and death rates for the 1990s continue, what will happen to China's total population?

    A. It will rise sharply.

    B. It will decline sharply.

    C. It will gradually level off.

    D. It will rise gradually.

5. Explain the reason for the choice you made in Question 4.

ⓒ USING GRAPHICS

Use the information in the paragraph below to complete the line graph (Figure 4-4) which has been started for you.

The estimated world population in 1850 was 1.5 billion. In 1930 it was 2 billion. By 1960 there were 3 billion people in the world. As of 1987 there were 5 billion. The number reached 6 billion in 2000 and should reach around 8 billion by 2025.

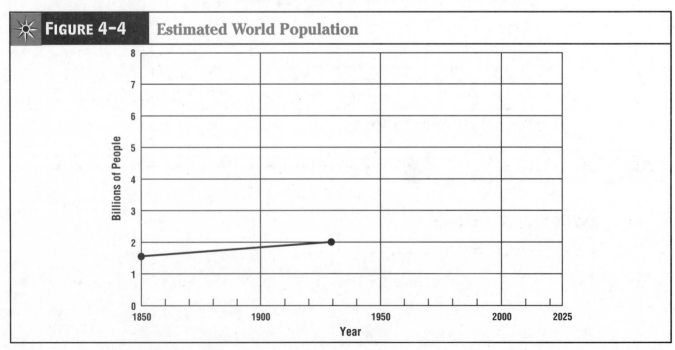

FIGURE 4-4 **Estimated World Population**

Lesson 4 Migration

Lesson ④

Have you ever considered why and how people move from one continent to another? Since the last Ice Age, humans have moved in large numbers from one continent or region to another. These large-scale permanent movements of people, as well as smaller permanent flows of people from place to place, are known as **migration.**

Modern Migration

Since 1700, there have been both voluntary and forced movements of people from one continent to another. Map 4-4 shows the major movements of large groups of people from one continent to another. As you can also see from this map, all of Australia and New Zealand, and large portions of North America, South America, and Asia are inhabited by people who are descended from immigrants.

Types of Migration

There are three types of migrations: voluntary, reluctant, and forced. Voluntary migration occurs when people move from one place to another because they believe that life's circumstances will be improved in the new location. In the United States today, the populations of southern states are increasing largely due to migration of people from northern states. In general, these people believe that a better economic situation and a milder climate will improve their living conditions.

Reluctant migration often occurs when living conditions become intolerable in the current location. For example, people in Afghanistan have left the country to escape the harsh rule of the Taliban government. Many of these people become **refugees,** or people who flee their country because of persecution or danger. Although most refugees plan to return home after the danger has passed, many are never able to return to their homeland.

Migrations that occur as the result of force leave the migrants with no choice. The decision to relocate is made solely by people other than the migrants themselves. The migration of Africans to the Americas during the 1500s to the 1800s is an example of forced migration. During that period, 10 to 12 million Africans were forcibly moved to the Western Hemisphere. During the Soviet era, the government forcibly relocated millions of people to Siberia. In 1996, the African country of Tanzania expelled ethnic Hutus who had sought refuge from fighting in their own country of Rwanda.

MAP 4-4 | Principal Migrations of Recent Centuries

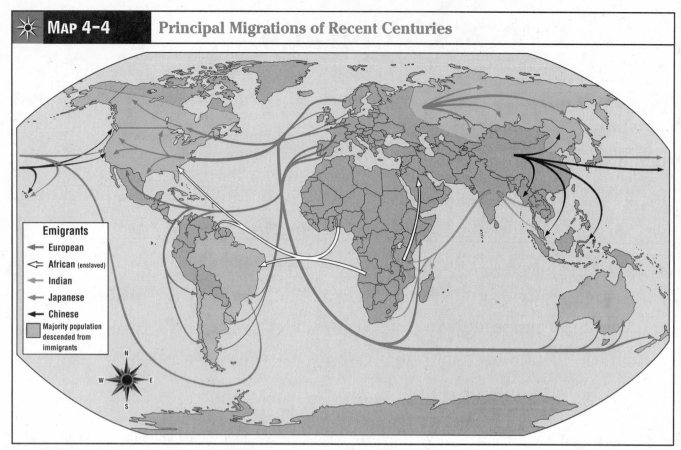

Emigrants
- ← European
- ⇐ African (enslaved)
- ← Indian
- ← Japanese
- ← Chinese
- ▨ Majority population descended from immigrants

Source: Daniel Noin, *Geographie de la Population* (Paris: Masson, 1979).

Using Your Skills

A RECALLING FACTS

Use the reading and Map 4-4 to complete the sentences.

1. The permanent movement of people from place to place is called

   _____.

2. A person who moves to a new city to take a job is participating in

   _____ migration.

3. _____ leave their country to find safety in another
   place.

4. According to Map 4-4, people migrated from _____ to all
   other inhabited continents.

5. According to Map 4-4, people have migrated from Japan to

   _____ and _____.

ⓑ PRACTICING MAP SKILLS

Use Map 4-5: Westward Shift of Population, 1790–2000 below to answer the following questions in the space provided.

1. In which general direction is the population of the United States moving?

   _____

2. During which decade did the largest shift occur? _____

3. During which decade did the population move south more rapidly than

   it moved west? _____

4. Why does the symbol for the population center change in 1960?

   _____

   _____

5. Why do you think mapmakers needed to indicate this change with a
   symbol?

   _____

   _____

   _____

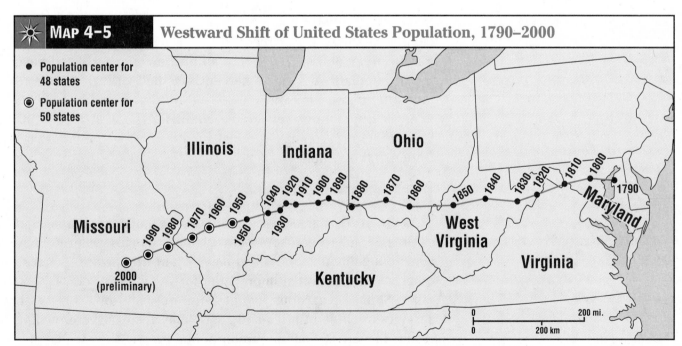

| ☀ MAP 4-5 | Westward Shift of United States Population, 1790–2000 |

● Population center for 48 states

◉ Population center for 50 states

Illinois   Indiana   Ohio

Missouri   West Virginia   Virginia   Maryland

2000 (preliminary)   Kentucky

1790 1800 1810 1820 1830 1840 1850 1860 1870 1880 1890 1900 1910 1920 1930 1940 1950 1960 1970 1980 1990 2000

0 ——— 200 mi.
0 ——— 200 km

The center of population is defined as the point at which a rigid map of the United States would balance, reflecting the identical weights of all residents on the census date.

Source: *Human Geography: Landscapes of Human Activities,* **2001.**

Lesson 5 Urbanization

WHAT YOU WILL LEARN

To explain the reasons for urbanization

READING STRATEGY

Create a diagram like the one below. List three causes of urbanization.

CAUSES ──→ URBANIZATION

TERMS TO KNOW

urban areas, rural areas, urbanization

In developed, or industrialized countries the number of people living in **urban areas,** or cities and towns, is high. In fact, more people live in urban areas than in the countryside. Cities and towns attract people looking for jobs and for better services such as health care and transportation systems. In developing countries, or countries in the process of industrializing, more people tend to live in **rural areas,** often on farms. However, the number of people moving to, and living in urban areas is on the rise.

Urban Migration

The worldwide trend toward **urbanization,** or the movement to cities, has two basic causes. In some areas, people are *pushed* from rural areas to urban areas for survival. In the Sahel countries, for example, where desertification makes the land unable to sustain life, people are forced into cities and towns to look for food, work, and shelter. In other cases, people are *pulled* to urban areas by the opportunities that exist. Such opportunities may include safety, food, job prospects, better schools and health care, and so on.

Most industrialized parts of the world—North America, Europe, and East Asia—are the most urbanized. They have the highest percentage of their total populations living in cities. For example, Figure 4-5 shows the percent of urban population for selected European countries. Notice that all of the countries listed have urban populations over 50 percent. As the world continues to industrialize, we can expect increases in urban populations. This is especially true of developing countries. Look at Figure 4-6. What generalization can you make about the level of industrialization in this region?

Effects of Urbanization

As urban areas grow and spread out, the amount of arable land declines. Some researchers fear that such changes will eventually lead to significant food shortages. When urbanization occurs quickly, cities are often unprepared for the influx of new inhabitants. Slums, hazardous living conditions, and problems with services such as utilities and roads may result. Overcrowding results in increased air and water pollution.

As technology continues to become a part of our everyday lives, some researchers predict that the trend of urbanization in industrialized countries may slow. When people can work from remote locations, more people may chose to live in rural areas, rather than crowded urban areas.

☀ FIGURE 4-5	Urbanization in Europe (selected countries)
Country	Percent of Urban Population
Austria	65
Belgium	97
France	74
Germany	86
Luxembourg	88
Netherlands	62
Switzerland	68

☀ FIGURE 4-6	Urbanization in Southeast Asia (selected countries)
Country	Percent of Urban Population
Cambodia	16
Indonesia	39
Laos	17
Malaysia	57
Myanmar	27
Philippines	47
Thailand	30

Source: Population Reference Bureau, 2000–2002.

Using Your Skills

Ⓐ RECALLING FACTS

Use the reading and Figures 4-5 and 4-6 to answer the questions.

1. Which types of countries have a larger percentage of urban population—developed or developing? _____

2. Which European country in Figure 4-5, has the highest percentage of urban population? _____

3. Which Southeast Asian country in Figure 4-6, has the highest percentage of urban population? _____

4. What often occurs when urban areas grow rapidly?

   _____

5. How do large urban areas affect the environment? _____

Ⓑ RECALLING FACTS

Imagine that you live in a rural village in Southeast Asia and that you are considering moving to the country's capital city. In the spaces below list the push and pull factors that may contribute to your decision.

Push Urbanization	Pull Urbanization

Lesson 6 Reading Population Pyramids

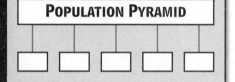
Have you ever been to a place where there was no one else around the same age as you? Were most of the people younger than you? Were most of the people older?

The age structure of a country's population is very important. For example, if a country has a population made up mostly of very young people and very old people, there will be few people of working age. If there are not enough people to work in agriculture or manufacturing, this can cause food shortages as well as other issues, such as the need to import more goods. If a country has a great many young children, there may be a need for more schools and teachers when those children reach school age.

Population Pyramids

People who study population have developed a special kind of bar graph to show how the population of an area is divided by age and by sex. This kind of graph is called a **population pyramid.**

The term *pyramid* describes the graph's shape for many countries in the 1800s, when the population pyramid graph was created. At that time many countries had large numbers of young people and small numbers of older people. Some countries today still fit this description, or are currently moving away from it. Look at Figure 4-7, the population pyramid for South Korea.

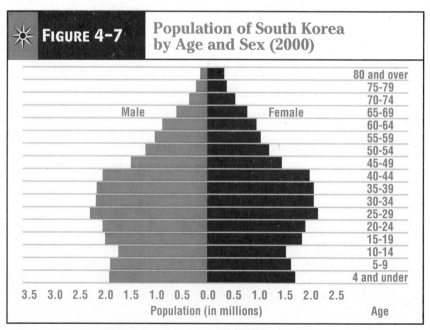

FIGURE 4-7 Population of South Korea by Age and Sex (2000)

Source: U.S. Census Bureau, International Data Base, 2000.

The vertical scale on the graph tells you what age group each bar represents. For example, the bottom bar on the graph stands for people between the ages of 0 and 4 years. The pyramid is made up of horizontal bars. Each bar is divided into two parts by a line down the center of the graph. The left side of the bar represents males in the population. The right side of the bar represents females.

At the bottom of the pyramid is a scale marked in percent (%). Notice that the scale begins in the middle of the graph at 0 percent. To read the percent of males, you must read from the center outward *to the left*. To read the percent of females, you must read from the center outward *to the right*. To find the total percent of the population in a particular age group, you must *add* the figures for males and females.

Reading Population Pyramids

Practice reading the population pyramid for South Korea. For what year are figures shown? In what age group are the largest number of males? Females? Add the figures for males and females in the 10 to 14 age group. What percent of the population is between the ages of 10 and 14 years? About what percent of the females in South Korea are between the ages of 40 and 44?

Look at the bars for people in South Korea between the ages of 25 to 29 and 30 to 34. These bars are longer than any of the others. This means that there are more people in South Korea between the ages of 25 and 34 than any other age group. Between 2000 and 2005, this age group will get five years older—they will be in the 30 to 39 age group. By 2010, these people will be in the 35 to 44 age group. Do you see what will happen to the shape of South Korea's population pyramid as these people grow older? The wide bars will move steadily toward the top of the pyramid.

Population pyramids change over time. The shape of a population pyramid is determined by a country's age structure and sex ratio. It may also be influenced by migration into and out of the country. The traditional pyramid shape is characteristic of a country with high birthrates and high death rates. Remember from Lesson 2 that countries with high birthrates and high death rates are in Stage 1 of the demographic transition. Some African countries have population pyramids with this shape. Another type of population pyramid has a narrow top, a wide base, and sides that curve inward. This shape represents a falling death rate and a high birthrate. Countries with these population characteristics are in Stage 2 of the demographic transition. A beehive shape characterizes a third type of population pyramid. Countries with low birthrates, low death rates, and a high average age have population pyramids with this shape. Some European countries such as England and Wales have population pyramids like this. These countries are in Stage 3 of the demographic transition. The fourth type of population pyramid has a tapered base that widens slightly as you move to the top. This shape represents a rapid decrease in birthrates.

Understanding Population Bulges

Large numbers of people in one or two age groups in the population are called a **population bulge.** The name comes from the long bars moving up the pyramid, as in the case of South Korea's 25 to 34 age group. The United States has such a population bulge. It was created by a high birthrate following World War II. This "baby boom" meant that a much higher number of babies than usual were born between 1946 and 1964. As these people become older, there will be a need for more doctors, hospitals, and services for the elderly.

It is possible to make some predictions about future population growth in a country based on population pyramids. For example, a country with a large population bulge at the bottom of its pyramid now will have a large number of people at the age to have children in a few years. That country may have faster population growth in the future. A country with very little bulge anywhere on its population pyramid may have slow population growth. A country with a bulge at the middle or top of its population pyramid may actually lose population in the future.

Using Your Skills

Ⓐ USING GRAPHICS

Use Figure 4-8 below to answer these questions.

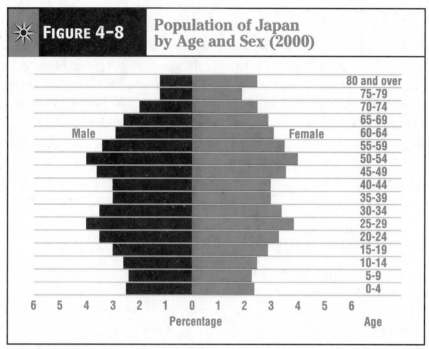

FIGURE 4-8 — Population of Japan by Age and Sex (2000)

Source: U.S. Census Bureau, International Data Base, 2000.

1. What age group in Japan has the largest number of people? _____

2. What age group in Japan has the second-largest number of people? _____

3. What age group in Japan has the smallest number of people? _____

4. The population pyramid of Japan shows two bulges. What age groups make up those bulges?

   _____

   _____

5. What is the total percentage of the population in the 80 and over age

   group? _____

6. Does the population pyramid show that men or women tend to live longer in Japan? How do you know?

   _____

   _____

B USING GRAPHICS

Use the population pyramids in Figure 4-9 to answer the questions.

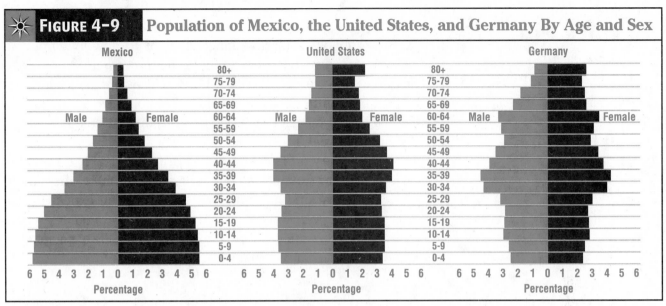

FIGURE 4-9   Population of Mexico, the United States, and Germany By Age and Sex

Source: U.S. Census Bureau, International Data Base, 2000.

1. Which country has the highest percentage of people between the ages
    of 0 and 9? _____

2. In what age groups does the United States have a large population
    bulge? _____

3. Which country has the smallest percentage of people between the ages
    of 0 and 9? _____

4. Which country has the greatest percentage of people at ages 40 and
    above? _____

5. What could happen in Mexico when the people now in the age groups
    of 0 to 4, 5 to 9, and 10 to 14 reach the age to start having children of
    their own? _____

    _____

6. Will the population of Germany most likely grow faster or slower when
    the people now in the age groups 0 to 4 and 5 to 9 reach the age to have
    children? Why? _____

    _____

7. Based on its population pyramid, do you think the population of the
    United States will grow quickly or slowly? Why? _____

    _____

Lesson ⑦ Interpreting a Life Expectancy Map

You probably don't give much thought to how long you can expect to live. Life expectancy is the term we use to describe how long the average person will live. For example, the average person born in the United States in 2001 could expect to live for 77 years. That means that a person born in 2001 could expect to live until the year 2078.

Where in the world you live can have a great deal to do with life expectancy. For example, a person born in a country where there is plenty to eat and good medical attention can expect to live longer than a person born in the same year in a country where food and doctors are in short supply. In general, life expectancy is higher in industrialized countries.

Life Expectancy Tables and Graphs

Information about life expectancy can be presented in several different forms. Look at Figure 4-10. It shows life expectancy in selected countries in Africa south of the Sahara. Notice that the highest average life expectancy is only 52 years. Compare this to the average life expectancy for the United States.

☀ **FIGURE 4-10**	**Average Life Expectancy in Africa**
Angola	47
Chad	48
Gabon	52
Gambia	45
Kenya	49
Namibia	46
Nigeria	52
Zimbabwe	40

Life expectancy information can also be shown on a bar graph. Figure 4-11 is a bar graph with the same information as the table above. Do you see how the graph makes it easier to find the country with the longest or shortest life expectancy?

Life Expectancy Maps

Information about the life expectancy of people in an entire region is shown easily on a **life expectancy map.** A life expectancy map uses shading, colors, or patterns to indicate life expectancy. A legend tells you what the different shades or patterns on the map represent.

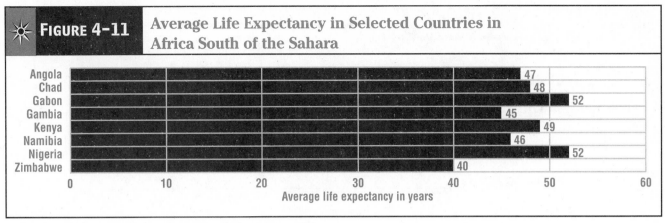

FIGURE 4-11 Average Life Expectancy in Selected Countries in Africa South of the Sahara

Source: U.S. Census Bureau, International Data Base, 2000.

A map cannot show life expectancy as exactly as a table or graph can. Instead, age groups are used. For example, one age group might include ages from 35 to 39, and so on.

You read a life expectancy map in exactly the same way you read any other map that uses shading or patterns. First, you read the title of the map to find out what area of the world is shown. Second, look at the legend to see what each shade or pattern used on the map represents. Then you read the information for particular countries and draw conclusions about life in each country.

Using Your Skills

Ⓐ USING GRAPHICS

Use Map 4-6: Life Expectancy in Africa South of the Sahara **on the next page to complete** Figure 4-12.

FIGURE 4-12 Life Expectancy Table

Country	Life Expectancy in Years
Burkina Faso	
Central African Republic	
Congo	
Ethiopia	
Ghana	
Côte d'Ivoire	
Madagascar	
Sudan	
Zambia	

❸ PRACTICING MAP SKILLS

Use Map 4-6: Life Expectancy in Africa South of the Sahara to answer the questions.

1. What is the title of this map? _____

2. Define life expectancy. _____

3. What does this shading ■ on the map mean?

   _____

4. How long can people in Mauritania expect to live? _____

5. How long can people in the Democratic Republic of the Congo expect to

   live? _____

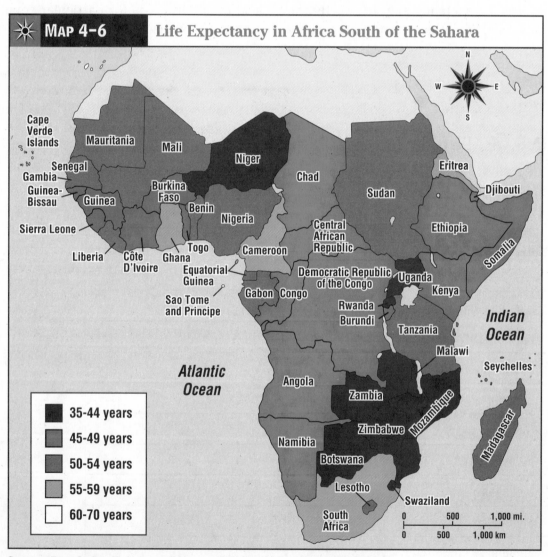

Source: Population Reference Bureau. 2000 World Population Data Sheet.

Lesson 8   Using Language Tables and Maps

WHAT YOU WILL LEARN

To gain and use information about world languages from tables and maps

READING STRATEGY

Create a diagram like the one below. Under each arrow list supporting facts for the main idea given.

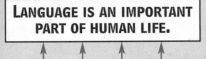

Would you like to take a trip around the world? Imagine flying your own plane as you land in Tanzania, Mexico, Hong Kong, or India. How will you talk to the people in the control towers? Will you need to brush up on your Swahili, Spanish, Chinese, or Hindi before your trip? You won't if you land at airports serving passenger airlines. All landing and takeoff instructions are given in one language around the world: English.

Language is a very important part of human life. We use language to talk with each other in our personal and professional lives. Language brings people together. People who speak the same language may share ideas as well as religious and political beliefs.

Language Tables

Language tables contain a variety of information on such things as where languages are spoken, the number of people worldwide who speak the language, the primary language of countries, and so on. Examine Figure 4-13. Notice that many countries are listed more than once. This indicates that more than one language is spoken in the country, or different regions of the country speak different languages.

Using the information in language tables, language maps can be created. These maps help geographers examine such topics as migration and the spread of languages.

The Spread of the English Language

A language map can lead us to ask some important questions about our world. For example, looking at a map that shows the places where English is the main language, one might ask, "Why is English the main language of Canada, the United States, the United Kingdom, Ireland, Australia, and New Zealand?" These countries were once ruled by what we now call the United Kingdom. Part of the United Kingdom is England, and this is where the English language originated. People from England spread the English language around the world through travel and conquest.

You might also ask why English is widely spoken in so many countries in Africa. The answer is the same: In most cases, those countries were once ruled by the United Kingdom. The rulers took their language with them.

Trade is another important factor in the spread of the English language. For many years the United States, Canada, and the United Kingdom have been among the richest, most powerful countries in the world. Many of the world's goods are made in these English-speaking countries. Many products from around the world are sold to these countries. English has become the language of trade. It is easier for people to buy and sell things when they can speak the same language.

Rank	Language	Countries in Which Language Is Widely Spoken	Number of People Worldwide (in millions)
1	Mandarin Chinese	Brunei, Cambodia, China, Indonesia, Malaysia, Mongolia, Philippines, Singapore, South Africa, Taiwan, Thailand	885.0
2	Spanish	Andorra, Argentina, Belize, Bolivia, Chile, Colombia, Costa Rica Cuba, Dominican Republic, Ecuador, El Salvador, Equatorial Guinea, Guatemala, Honduras, Mexico, Nicaragua, Panama, Paraguay, Peru, Spain, Uruguay, United States Venezuela	332.0
3	English	Australia, Botswana, Brunei, Cameroon, Canada, Eritrea, Ethiopia, Fiji, Gambia, Guyana, Ireland, Israel, Lesotho, Liberia, Malaysia, Micronesia, Namibia, Nauru, New Zealand, Palau, Papua New Guinea, Samoa, Seychelles, Sierra Leone, Singapore, Solomon Islands, Somalia, South Africa, Suriname, Swaziland, Tonga, United Kingdom, United States, Vanuatu, Zimbabwe, many Caribbean states	322.0
4	Bengali	Bangladesh, India, Singapore	189.0
5	Hindi	India, Nepal, Singapore, South Africa, Uganda	182.0
6	Portuguese	Brazil, Cape Verde, France, Guinea-Bissau, Portugal, Sao Tome and Principe	170.0
7	Russian	China, Israel, Mongolia, Russia, United States	170.0
8	Japanese	Japan, Singapore, Taiwan	125.0
9	German	Austria, Belgium, Bolivia, Czech Republic, Denmark, Germany, Hungary, Italy, Kazakhstan, Liechtenstein, Luxembourg, Paraguay, Poland, Romania, Slovenia, Switzerland	
10	Wu Chinese	China	77.2

☀ FIGURE 4-13 Most Widely Spoken Languages in the World

Source: *Time Almanac 2000.*

Using Your Skills

Ⓐ PRACTICING MAP SKILLS

Use an outline map of the world and the data from Figure 4-13 to create a language map. When a country is listed in more than one language row, use an Almanac or other reference source to determine the main language of the country. Be sure to include a map key.

Transportation in the United States

WHAT YOU WILL LEARN

To describe and discuss ways people move themselves and their products around the world

READING STRATEGY

Create a table like the one below. In the right column, write a result of the fact listed in the left column.

FACT	RESULT
The U.S. has one of the best transportation systems in the world.	
The U.S. depends on trade.	
The U.S. depends on other countries for the goods we need.	

TERMS TO KNOW

transportation, trade, interdependence

Do you know how much time you spend each day going from one place to another? If you were to keep track of this time each day of the week, the results might surprise you. Most of us spend many hours each week traveling. Moving people and goods from place to place is called **transportation.**

The United States has one of the best transportation systems in the world. We use roads, railroads, waterways, airways and pipelines to move ourselves and our products. The United States has about 5.3 million miles (about 8 million km) of roads, streets, and highways. It has more miles of railroads than any other country. Five of the 10 busiest airports in the world are in the United States. Trucks carry 39 percent of America's goods. About 13 percent of goods are transported by water. And about 6 percent of goods shipped in the United States travel by pipeline. Railroads carry about 42 percent of goods.

This story can be repeated endless times. Many of the products you use each day are made in some other part of the country. The raw materials that are used to make these products come from around the world. Transportation makes it possible to gather the raw materials and ship the finished goods to market. Transportation also makes it possible for workers to get to the factory to make the goods.

Transportation and Trade

Transportation is so important to the United States because our country depends on **trade.** Trade is the buying and selling of goods. No part of the United States has everything it needs.

A maze of highway overpasses in Dallas, Texas, illustrates the complex transportation systems in the United States.

People in different parts of the country trade with each other for the things they need. Cotton from Mississippi may be sold to a factory in New York. The money may be used to buy a car made in Detroit. A car bought in this way may then be used for a vacation trip to California. During the trip the car may use gasoline made from oil shipped by pipeline from Texas or by water from Louisiana.

Transportation and Interdependence

Different parts of the United States depend on each other for goods they do not produce themselves. The United States also depends on other countries for some things. In turn, other countries depend on the United States. Relying on each other is called **interdependence.** Put simply, it means that we need others, and they need us.

One reason we *can* depend on each other is because transportation makes it possible. Before good roads, railroads, and airplanes were developed, people had to depend more on themselves and others nearby. Goods could be shipped, but travel was slow and often expensive. People grew most of their own food and made most of their own clothing. Today shipping goods is fast and usually inexpensive. No matter where you live, your grocery store can offer you fruits from Texas, Florida, and California, meats from Iowa and Kansas, and fresh fish and seafood from the Atlantic and Pacific Oceans.

Using Your Skills

Ⓐ Reviewing Key Terms

Write the meaning of each word.

1. transportation _____

2. trade _____

3. interdependence _____

Ⓑ Recalling Facts

Answer these questions.

1. Why is transportation important to the United States?

   _____

2. What part does transportation play in trade?

   _____

3. How does transportation make interdependence possible?

   _____

4. Name a product that comes from another state or another country, such as a food, car, or appliance that you used today. Tell where it was originally grown or built, and tell how it was shipped to your city or town.

   _____

   _____

© PRACTICING MAP SKILLS

Use **Map 4-7: Transportation in the United States and Canada** below and
Map 4-8: Agriculture and Manufacturing in the United States and Canada
on page 146 to answer the questions.

1. What cities in the United States have both a major airport and a major
    seaport?

    _____

    _____

2. Compare the two maps. What connection can you see between the
    amount of agriculture and manufacturing and the number of highways
    and railroads? Why do you think this is so?

    _____

    _____

    _____

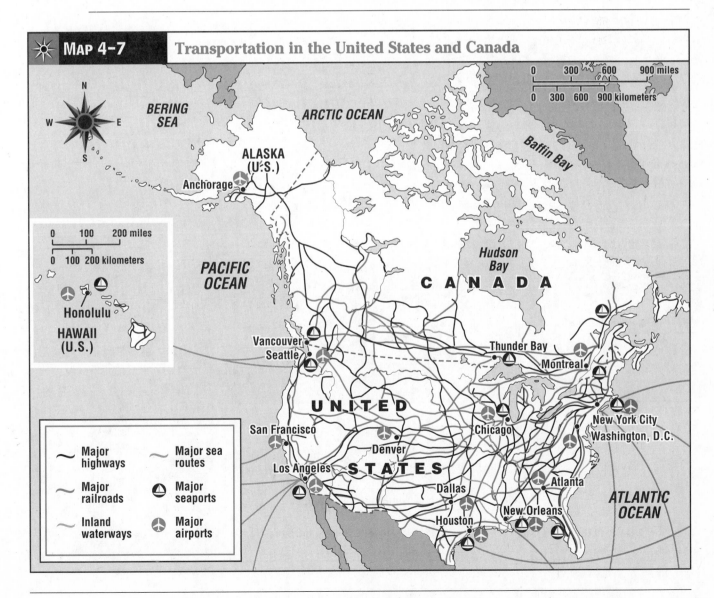

MAP 4-7   **Transportation in the United States and Canada**

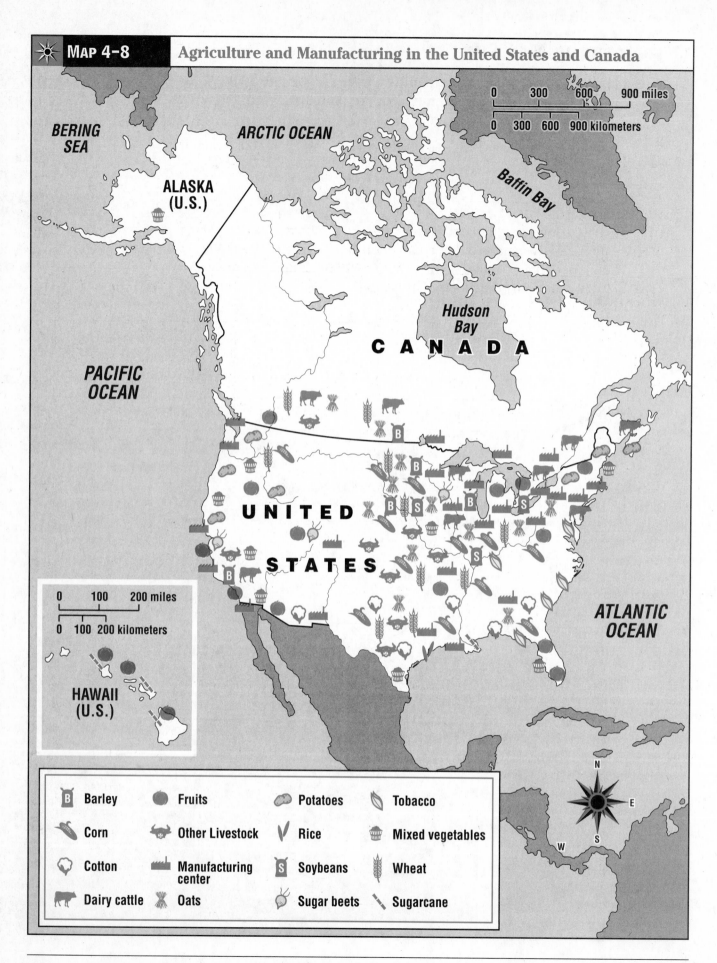

BERING
SEA

ARCTIC OCEAN

0   300   600   900 miles
0   300   600   900 kilometers

Baffin Bay

ALASKA
(U.S.)

PACIFIC
OCEAN

Hudson
Bay

C A N A D A

U N I T E D

S T A T E S

ATLANTIC
OCEAN

0   100   200 miles
0   100   200 kilometers

HAWAII
(U.S.)

N
W   E
S

Legend:

B   Barley
Corn
Cotton
Dairy cattle

Fruits
Other Livestock
Manufacturing center
Oats

Potatoes
Rice
S   Soybeans
Sugar beets

Tobacco
Mixed vegetables
Wheat
Sugarcane

United States's Trade With Other Countries

Look around you. Notice all the different things you see—walls, furniture, the clothing people are wearing. Outside are cars and trucks, and perhaps someone using a lawn mower. Have you ever wondered where all these things come from? Where was your desk made? And where did the raw materials to make the desk come from? Could you walk outside and find all the wood, metal, and plastic needed to make a desk? What about all the other things around you?

Almost anything that you buy will have a label or mark that tells where it was made. Your ballpoint pen may have been made in Japan, your shoes in Italy, your shirt in Taiwan, and your belt in Mexico. Some things, of course, will have been made in the United States. But chances are you can easily find things you own that were made in a dozen different countries.

Why the United States Trades With Other Countries

The United States is one of the richest countries on Earth. It has many natural resources. It has many factories that make huge amounts of goods. However, the United States is not **self-sufficient.** To be self-sufficient means to meet all of one's own needs. The United States cannot meet all of its own needs. For example, even though the United States produces a great deal of oil, it uses more that it can produce. The rest is bought from other countries. The

At this Singapore port, many items are imported from and exported to other countries.

United States must also buy goods it cannot produce. For example, the climate in the United States does not allow such things as coffee, tea, bananas, and rubber to be grown. These things must be bought from countries that can grow them.

The goods that a country buys are called **imports.** The goods that a country sells are called **exports.** No other country buys and sells more goods than the United States. The most important U.S. imports are oil, machinery, cars, metals, and foods that cannot be grown in the country. The most important exports are machinery such as computers, chemicals, metal goods, and farm products such as wheat.

The Balance of Trade

How do you suppose the United States pays for the goods it buys from other countries? If you said by using the money it gets from selling other goods, you are right. Suppose you are a wheat farmer in Kansas whose wheat is sold to Russia. You can take the money you got for the wheat and buy a new pickup truck that was made in Japan.

All of the money that a country makes from the sale of exports and the money spent on imports is added up each year. The difference is called the **balance of trade.** Some countries export more than they import. These countries are said to have a favorable balance of trade. In other words, a country with a favorable balance of trade sells enough to other countries to pay for all the goods it imports and have money left over.

Other countries buy more than they sell. These countries are said to have an unfavorable balance of trade. These countries do not sell enough to other countries to pay for all of the goods they import. A country that imports more than it exports has to borrow money to pay for the things it buys. Experts disagree about how much an unfavorable balance of trade harms a country.

The United States does not have a favorable balance of trade. Figure 4-14 shows the U.S. balance of trade for three recent years. A minus sign (–) before a number in the "Balance of Trade" column means that the United States bought more goods than it sold.

☼ FIGURE 4-14	United States Balance of Trade		
Year	**Value of Imports**	**Value of Exports**	**Balance of Trade**
1998	$ 912 billion	$682 billion	–$230 billion
1999	$1,025 billion	$696 billion	–$329 billion
2000	$1,216 billion	$782 billion	–$434 billion

Source: U.S. Census Bureau, Foreign Trade Division.

Using Your Skills

Ⓐ USING GRAPHICS

Use Figure 4-14 to answer these questions.

1. What was the value of imports the United States bought in 1998? _____

2. What was the value of exports the United States sold in 1998? _____

3. Was the United States balance of trade favorable or unfavorable in 1998? By how much? _____

4. How much more did the United States buy than it sold in 2000? _____

ⓑ USING GRAPHICS

Use Figures 4-15 and 4-16 to answer these questions.

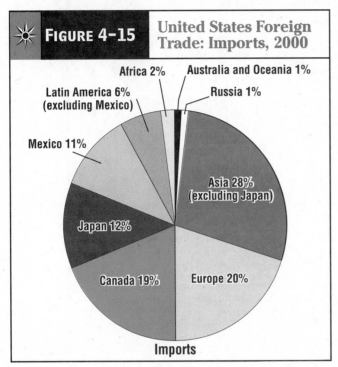

FIGURE 4-15 United States Foreign Trade: Imports, 2000

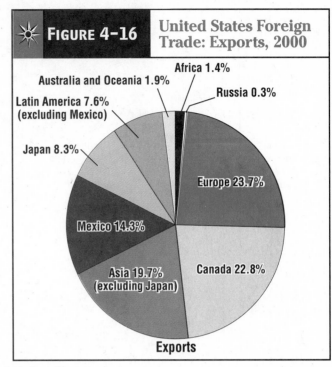

FIGURE 4-16 United States Foreign Trade: Exports, 2000

Source: U.S. Department of Commerce, International Trade Administration.

1. From which world region does the United States import the largest amount of goods? _____

2. Which two countries sell the most goods to the United States? _____

3. Which world region buys the most United States goods? _____

4. What percentage of U.S. exports does Japan receive? _____

5. What percentage of U.S. imports comes from Japan? _____

6. Which world region buys the smallest percentage of United States exports? _____

ⓒ PRACTICING MAP SKILLS

Use the information in the paragraph below to complete Map 4-9: United States Balance of Trade on page 150. Label each country named. Use shading to show whether the United States balance of trade was favorable or unfavorable. Make a legend to explain the shading.

The main countries with which the United States had a favorable balance of trade in 2000 were Argentina, Australia, Brazil, Egypt, and Panama. The United States had an unfavorable balance of trade with Bangladesh, Canada, China, Colombia, the European Union, India, Israel, Japan, South Korea, Malaysia, Mexico, OPEC countries, Russia, and Taiwan.

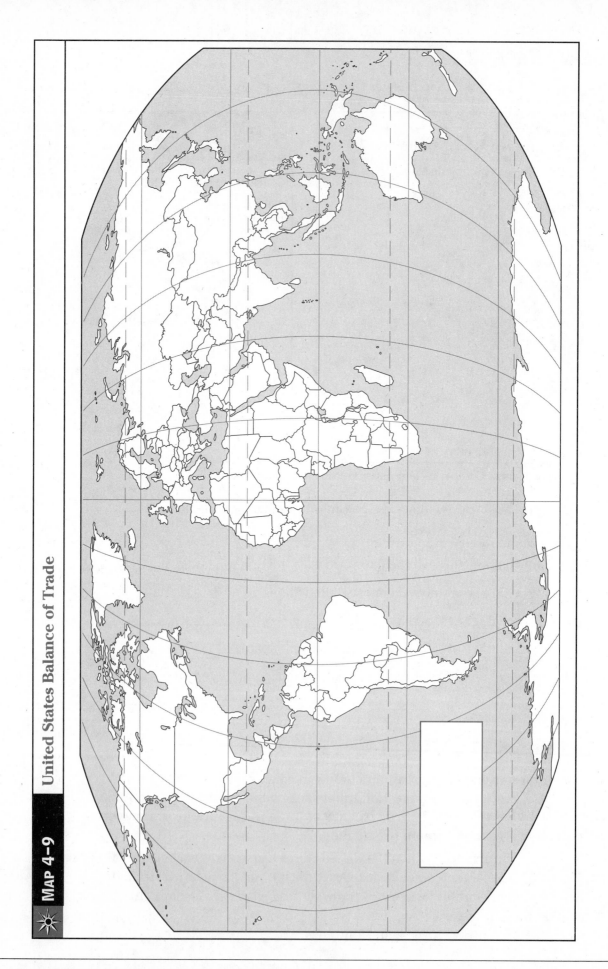

MAP 4-9

Global Interdependence

WHAT YOU WILL LEARN

To understand that all countries are interdependent

READING STRATEGY

Create a table like the one below. Fill in the raw materials from each region of the world used to make a pencil.

NORTH AMERICA	
SOUTH AMERICA	
EUROPE	
AFRICA	
ASIA	

How would you like to have thousands of people all over the world working for you? You do—right this minute. In fact, even while you sleep, people around the world are working in mines and factories and on farms to produce things you need. As you read this, ships and planes are crossing the oceans to bring these things to you.

You may be feeling rather special by now. But you needn't be. The fact is that all people, all over the world, work for each other. We all depend on others for things we cannot make for ourselves. We are all interdependent.

The Global Pencil

One example of how interdependent we all are may be in your hand right now. Or perhaps it is in your pocket, or your desk, or your notebook.

It takes the efforts of thousands of people from as many as 20 different countries and states to make one little pencil. You can imagine how many people it must take to make something like a car or a television set!

The roar of the chain stops as the <u>cedar tree</u> starts to fall. Much of the wood for pencils comes from trees in <u>Oregon</u>. The <u>chain saw</u> may have been made in <u>Japan</u>. The gasoline to run it started out as <u>crude oil</u>. Perhaps the oil came from <u>Texas</u>. But chances are good that the oil came from several places, such as <u>Mexico</u>, <u>Alaska</u>, <u>Saudi Arabia</u>, or the <u>North Sea</u>, located off the coast of the United Kingdom.

The logs are loaded onto a <u>truck</u>. The truck may have been made in <u>Michigan</u>. However, it could have been put together in a plant just across the border from the United States in <u>Canada</u>. And, of course, the trucks run on fuel made from crude oil.

The logs may be taken to a <u>sawmill</u> in <u>California</u>. The logs are sawed into small pieces before being sent to the <u>factory</u> in <u>Pennsylvania</u>. It is in Pennsylvania that the other parts that make up a pencil are added.

The "lead" in pencils is not really lead at all. Pencil lead is a mixture of several things. <u>Graphite</u> comes from mines in <u>Sri Lanka</u>. It takes the work of miners and dock workers in Sri Lanka to put the graphite on a <u>ship</u> built in <u>Japan</u>. The <u>ship owner</u> lives in <u>France</u>. The <u>ship company</u> that operates the ship does business from <u>Liberia</u>. The graphite is mixed with clay from <u>Mississippi</u> and <u>wax</u> from <u>Mexico</u>.

People and equipment are involved in shipping many items at a container port in Limassol, Cyprus.

For many people the most useful part of a pencil is the eraser. The <u>rubber</u> in the eraser likely came from <u>Malaysia</u>. The gritty stuff in the eraser that wears the pencil marks off the paper is <u>pumice</u>. Pumice comes from volcanoes in <u>Italy</u>. The piece of metal that holds the eraser in place is made of brass. Brass is made of zinc and copper. <u>Zinc</u> comes mainly from the <u>United States</u>, <u>Canada</u>, <u>Australia</u>, and <u>Ireland</u>. The <u>copper</u> may have come from <u>Bolivia</u>, <u>Chile</u>, or <u>Zambia</u>.

The pencil is almost finished. But first it must be painted. One of the main things that goes into the paint is <u>castor oil</u>. Farmers in <u>Africa</u> grow the castor bean plants from which the oil is made. After the pencil is painted, the name of the maker is stamped on it. The black paint used to stamp the name of the pencil maker has <u>carbon black</u> from the far north of Texas in it.

Now the pencil is finished, but it must still be sent to you. Hundreds of other people are involved in shipping and selling the pencil after it leaves the factory. People in any one of the 50 states could have played a part in bringing you the pencil you use every day.

Using Your Skills

Ⓐ PRACTICING MAP SKILLS

Read the description above of how a pencil is made. The underlined words tell you what goes into a pencil, or where work on pencils is done. Write each word in the correct location on Map 4-10: The Geography of a Pencil.

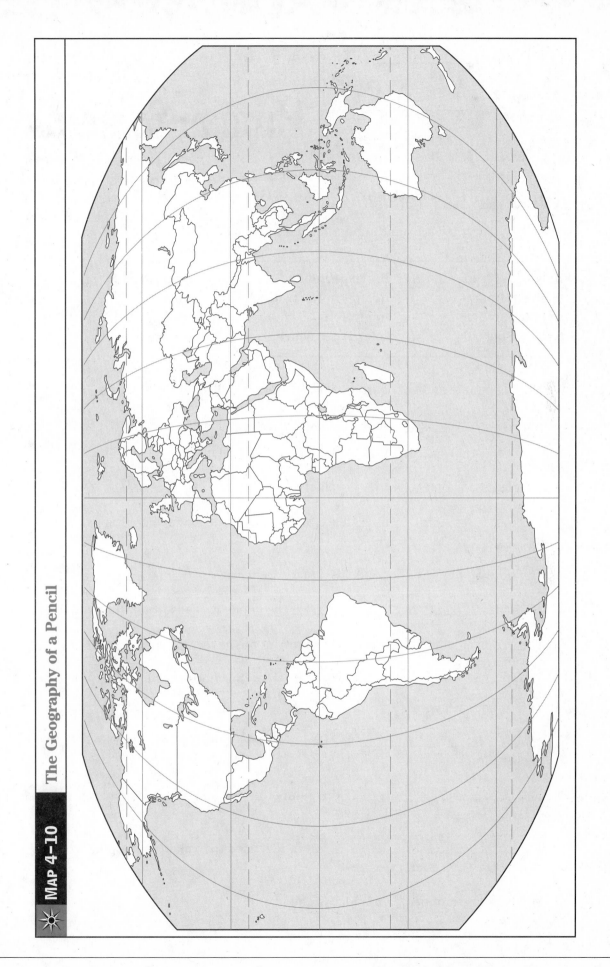

The Geography of a Pencil

MAP 4–10

Unit 4 Review

Human Systems

Ⓐ REVIEWING KEY TERMS

Write the correct term from the box in each sentence.

balance of trade	life expectancy	imports
urbanization	demographic transition	trade
population density	migration	refugees
transportation	interdependence	exports

1. Moving people and goods from place to place is called
   _____.

2. _____ is the buying and selling of goods.

3. People relying on each other is called _____.

4. _____ describes how long the average person will
   live.

5. The permanent flow of people from place to place is _____.

6. A country _____ the goods it needs from other countries.

7. The goods a country sells to other countries are called _____.

8. Countries that export goods worth more than the goods they import are
   said to have a favorable _____.

9. _____ flee their countries because of danger or
   persecution.

10. _____ is the number of people living in a unit area
    of land.

11. The _____ is a model used to explain the popula-
    tion history of a country.

12. The movement of people to cities is called _____.

UNIT 4 Review

❸ RECALLING FACTS

Write the letter of the word or words which will complete each statement correctly.

_____ 1. Which country has one of the best transportation systems in the world?

    a. Morocco   **b.** China   **c.** United States

_____ 2. Why is transportation so important to the United States?

    a. The United States has about 4 million miles of highways.   **b.** The United States depends on trade.   **c.** People like to travel to new places on vacation.

_____ 3. How many stages are in the demographic transition?

    a. four   **b.** three   **c.** two

_____ 4. Most industrialized countries have

    a. high birth and death rates.   **b.** high birthrates and low death rates.   **c.** declining birthrates and low death rates.

_____ 5. A line graph generally shows

    a. life expectancy.   **b.** kinds of resources.   **c.** changes over time.

_____ 6. The speed at which change is taking place is called

    a. life expectancy.   **b.** rate of change.   **c.** trend.

_____ 7. Refugees represent which type of migration?

    a. free   **b.** forced   **c.** reluctant

_____ 8. Which of the following continents has a population majority who are immigrants?

    a. Africa   **b.** North America   **c.** Europe

_____ 9. Urbanization that results from people looking for better job opportunities causes people to be

    a. pulled to urban areas.   **b.** pushed from rural areas.   **c.** migrant workers.

_____ 10. A special bar graph that shows population by age and sex ratio is a

    a. demographic transition pyramid.   **b.** life expectancy graph.   **c.** population pyramid.

_____ 11. People who make up a large group in the population are called a

a. population bulge.　　b. population density.　　c. demographic transition

_____ 12. Stage 1 of the demographic transition is characterized by

a. high birthrates and declining death rates.　　b. high birthrates and high death rates.　　c. declining birthrates and low death rates.

_____ 13. Which of the following factors was an important reason for the spread of the English language?

a. trade　　b. population density　　c. high life expectancy

_____ 14. A country pays for the goods it needs from other countries by

a. selling goods it has that other countries need.　　b. turning out more goods in its factories than its own people people need.　　c. saving its raw materials for its own use.

_____ 15. The making of a pencil is a good example of

a. self-sufficiency.　　b. interdependence.　　c. balance of trade.

_____ 16. A country that exports more than it imports

a. has an unfavorable balance of trade.　　b. is self-sufficient.　　c. has a favorable balance of trade.

❻ USING GRAPHICS

Use Figure 4-17 to answer these questions.

1. About how many people lived in India in 1985?

_____

2. About how many people lived in India in 2000?

_____

3. By how much did the population increase between 1985 and 2000?

_____

4. How would you describe the trend shown by this graph?

_____

5. About how many people are expected to be added to the population of

India between 2000 and 2025? _____

FIGURE 4-17 India's Population Growth

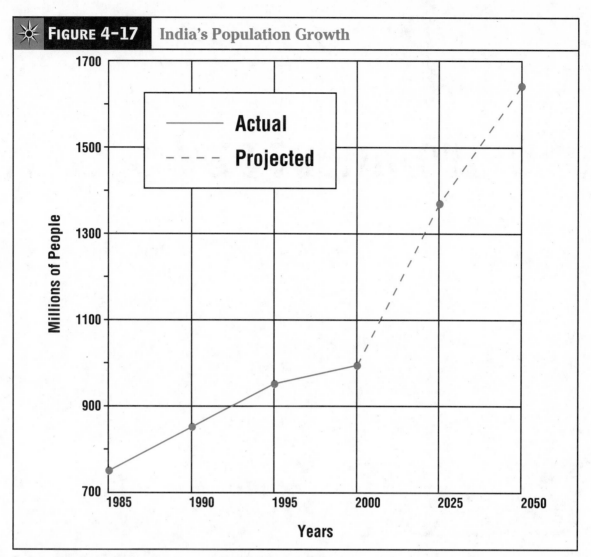

Source: Population Reference Bureau. 2000 World Population Data

Unit 5

Environment and Society

The steam coming from these cooling towers in England is evidence of the production of electricity.

Objectives

After completing this unit, you will be able to:

- identify ways in which human activity modifies the environment;
- understand how to deal with major environmental hazards;
- understand how people have adapted to difficult environments;
- understand the delicate balance between human activities and the physical environment;
- understand that the physical environment places some limits on human activities.

Humans have conflicting attitudes about our environment. We recognize the importance of our environment, but we also use it far beyond its capacity to clean itself. The result is what we call pollution. Pollution can affect the air we breathe, the water we drink, and the soil in which we grow our foods.

Not all dangers to the environment are caused by humans. Volcanoes spout dirt and ash into the air. Storms destroy homes and crops. Earthquakes rattle dishes and have caused entire buildings to collapse.

Environment and society is one of the six essential elements of geography. People may change their environment, or they may be changed by it. For example, hundreds of years ago, Native Americans built farming villages in the American Southwest. When the climate changed and became drier, Native Americans left their villages. Later, Hispanic and European settlers set up mines, farms, and ranches in the same area. These later settlers developed ways to bring water into the area for their needs. They dug wells and created irrigation systems. Rather than change their activities or their location, they adapted their environment to meet their needs.

A more recent example of how humans interact with their environment will be played out in the future. For the last 200 years, humans have been burning coal and oil at faster and faster rates. This burning has released a gas called carbon dioxide into the air. Carbon dioxide traps the heat of the sun close to the earth. As a result, the earth is slowly warming up. This warming could melt the ice at the North and South Poles and flood many cities and islands around the world.

The warming may also change the earth's weather, possibly causing crop failures in many areas. No one yet knows what changes will actually take place.

In this unit, you will study some causes and solutions to the problems of air and water pollution. However, you will learn that the relationship between humans and their environment is very complicated. We do not have nearly as many answers as we have questions.

Lesson 1 — Interpreting Resource Maps

WHAT YOU WILL LEARN
To gain and use information about places from resource maps

READING STRATEGY
Create a flowchart like the one below. Fill in each step involved in reading a resource map.

TERMS TO KNOW
resource, resource map, natural resource, manufacturing

We get information about places and regions in many different ways. One way to learn about a place is by a study of its **resources.** Resources are things people use—crops, minerals, animals, or plants. A **resource map** shows the things found or produced in an area. However, resource maps do not show exact locations, nor do they show every place where a resource is found. They show the general area, or sometimes the most important places where the resources are found.

Importance of Natural Resources

Natural resources are naturally occurring elements or substances that are found on Earth. The soil, water, plants, and animals are all natural resources. So are minerals such as gold, iron, and coal. People use natural resources in many ways. For example, farmers use soil, water, and animals to grow crops. Many natural resources are also used in **manufacturing,** the creation of products. Iron ore and coal are used to make steel, which is then used to make many other things, from cars to school desks.

The resources that are found in a particular place have a great deal to do with the way people in that place make a living. An area with much iron ore and coal may be a center of steelmaking. An area with rich soil and water may be a prosperous farming area.

Reading Resource Maps

You can compare the location of resources on a resource map with information on other types of maps, such as political, climate, or population density maps. This allows you to easily understand how the distribution of natural resources influences, or is influenced by other factors. You can also get an idea about a place's economic activities and the people's standard of living.

To read a resource map, you first need to identify the geographic area shown on the map. Some resource maps may include small areas such as a city or state. Others may include several countries or regions. Then look at the map legend to understand all colors, symbols, and patterns used on the map. Study the map to determine what resources are predominant in each area on the map. Are some resources concentrated in a particular place? Finally, compare the map to other maps showing physical features, climate, and natural vegetation of the area. Draw conclusions about the interaction of humans with the environment.

Ⓐ PRACTICING MAP SKILLS

Use **Map 5-1: Natural Resources of the United States and Canada** on page
162 to answer the questions.

1.   In which part of the United States is bauxite found?

_____

2.   What natural resource does Canada have that the United States does

not? _____

3.   What natural resource does the United States have that Canada does

not? _____

4.   Describe the relationship between mountainous areas and the location

of coal in the United States. _____

5.   What do Hawaii's resources tell you about the state's economic

activities? _____

Ⓑ PRACTICING MAP SKILLS

Use **Map 5-2: Agriculture and Manufacturing in Western Europe** on page
163 to answer the questions.

1.   What resources are found in Greece?

_____

2.   What resources are found in Finland?

_____

3.   In which countries are potatoes grown?

_____

4.   What do most of the manufacturing centers have in common?

_____

5.   In which countries are citrus fruits grown?

_____

6.   Think about the climate of countries along the Mediterranean Sea. How
     does this affect the types of food grown in this area?

_____

_____

MAP 5-1   Natural Resources of the United States and Canada

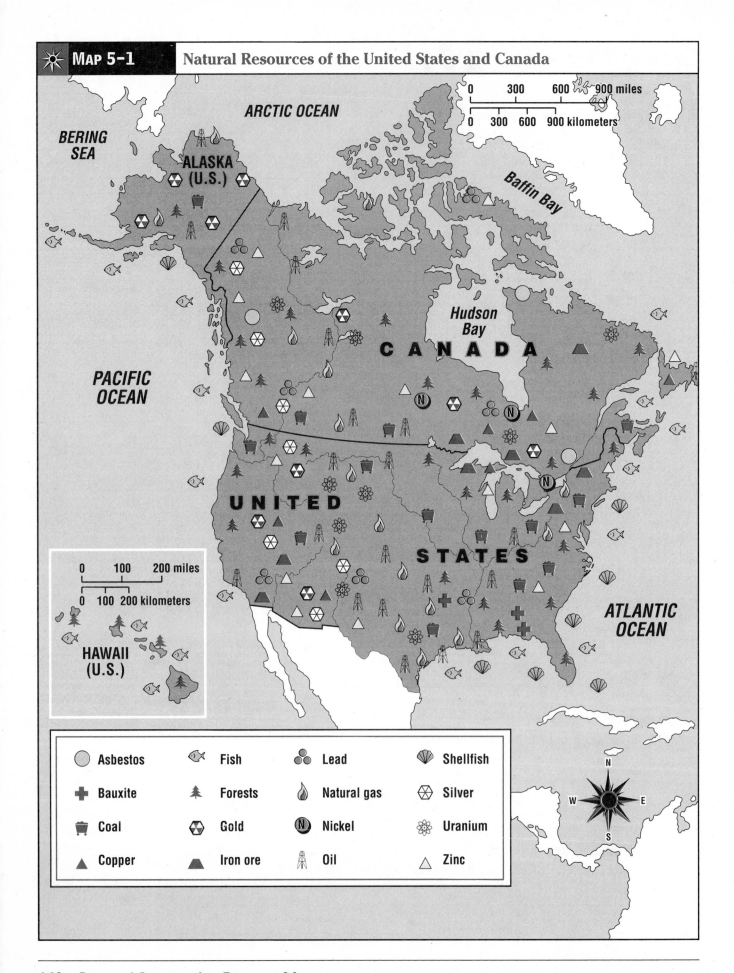

ARCTIC OCEAN

BERING SEA

ALASKA (U.S.)

Baffin Bay

0   300   600   900 miles
0   300   600   900 kilometers

PACIFIC OCEAN

Hudson Bay

C A N A D A

U N I T E D

S T A T E S

ATLANTIC OCEAN

0   100   200 miles
0   100   200 kilometers

HAWAII (U.S.)

Symbol	Resource	Symbol	Resource	Symbol	Resource	Symbol	Resource
⬤	Asbestos	🐟	Fish	⚬⚬	Lead	🐚	Shellfish
✚	Bauxite	🌲	Forests	💧	Natural gas	⬡	Silver
⬛	Coal	⬡	Gold	Ⓝ	Nickel	✳	Uranium
▲	Copper	▲	Iron ore	⚒	Oil	△	Zinc

N
W   E
S

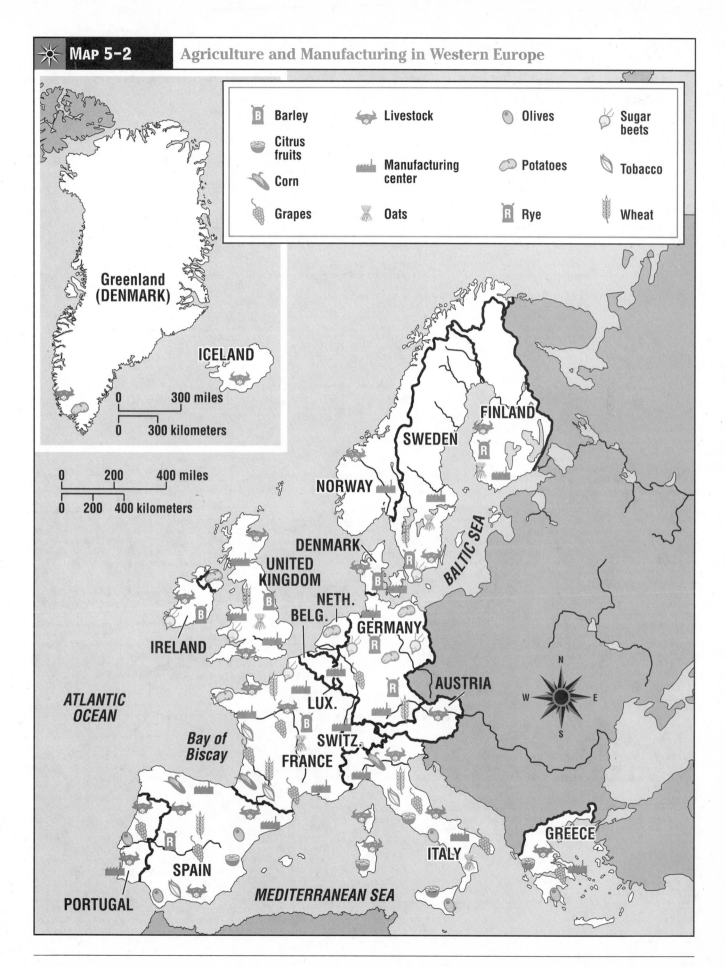

MAP 5-2 — Agriculture and Manufacturing in Western Europe

Legend:
- B — Barley
- Citrus fruits
- Corn
- Grapes
- Livestock
- Manufacturing center
- Oats
- Olives
- Potatoes
- R — Rye
- Sugar beets
- Tobacco
- Wheat

Greenland (DENMARK)

ICELAND

0 — 300 miles
0 — 300 kilometers

0 — 200 — 400 miles
0 — 200 — 400 kilometers

NORWAY

SWEDEN

FINLAND

BALTIC SEA

DENMARK

UNITED KINGDOM

IRELAND

NETH.

BELG.

GERMANY

LUX.

AUSTRIA

SWITZ.

FRANCE

ATLANTIC OCEAN

Bay of Biscay

SPAIN

PORTUGAL

MEDITERRANEAN SEA

ITALY

GREECE

N
W   E
S

C PRACTICING MAP SKILLS

Use Map 5-3: Natural Resources of North Africa and Southwest Asia below to answer the questions.

1. What natural resources are found in Saudi Arabia?

    _____

2. What natural resources are found in Iraq?

    _____

3. What natural resource seems to be the most widespread?

    _____

4. In which countries is zinc found?

    _____

5. In which countries is fish a resource?

    _____

    _____

    _____

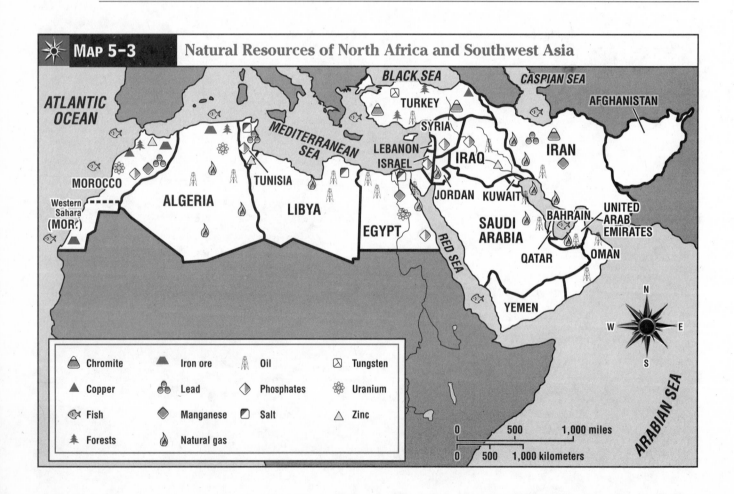

MAP 5-3   Natural Resources of North Africa and Southwest Asia

Legend:
- Chromite
- Copper
- Fish
- Forests
- Iron ore
- Lead
- Manganese
- Natural gas
- Oil
- Phosphates
- Salt
- Tungsten
- Uranium
- Zinc

Understanding Causes of Air Pollution

WHAT YOU WILL LEARN
To identify causes of air pollution

READING STRATEGY
Create a table like the one below. Fill in examples of indoor and outdoor air pollution.

INDOOR POLLUTION	OUTDOOR POLLUTION
1.	1.
2.	2.
3.	3.

TERMS TO KNOW
pollutant

A volcano erupts in Mexico, spewing smoke and ash thousands of feet into the air. A bus drops off a group of children at school. A carpenter builds shelves for a new kitchen. A power plant makes electricity for a city miles away.

What do all these events have in common? As unlikely as it may seem, they all play a part in air pollution.

Causes of Air Pollution

When a volcano erupts, it throws out huge clouds of smoke and ash, which can spread around the world. Volcanic smoke and ash can block some of the light of the sun and cause winters to be colder than normal for several years. When Mount Saint Helens erupted in the northwestern United States in 1980, the engines of many cars were damaged by dust they sucked in.

Air pollution can be caused by nature in other ways. Forest fires started by lightning can pollute the air with smoke and ash. Windstorms create dust clouds that can throw large amounts of dust into the air.

As powerful as nature is, however, human activities cause far more air pollution. This pollution is of two types: outdoor pollution and indoor pollution.

Outdoor air pollution comes from a variety of sources. Farmers create a great deal of air pollution. As they plow fields, dust is thrown into the air. Winds blowing across fields left bare after crops are harvested pick up still more dust. Another source of pollution on farms comes from the use of chemicals to kill weeds and insects. Many of these chemicals are sprayed by planes or tractors. The wind can carry tiny drops far from the fields.

Dangers of Air Pollution

Factories, power plants, cars, planes, ships, and even lawn mowers also cause air pollution. In fact, anything that burns a fossil fuel such as coal, oil, or natural gas adds to air pollution. Pollution from gasoline engines can reach such dangerous levels in large cities that children and people who have trouble breathing are asked to stay indoors. The gases from burning fuels can also cause eye and lung irritation. Some people can even die from the effects of air pollution.

Staying indoors may not keep a person away from all air pollution, however. Indoor air pollution is now known to be a serious health threat in the United States. In fact, the air in some buildings is worse than the air outdoors.

Indoor air pollution comes from many things. Figure 5-1 shows the most common indoor **pollutants.** Pollutants are harmful substances found in the environment.

Pollutants can build up to reach higher levels indoors than they do outside, where natural air currents carry them away. Indoor air levels of some pollutants may often be 2 to 5 times higher than outdoor levels. Indoor pollution is a greater problem now than it was a few years ago. One reason is that houses today are being built to be more airtight; windows and doors have better seals. As a result, pollutants such as cigarette smoke have a harder time getting out. Another reason indoor pollution is such a problem is that people spend up to 80 percent of their time indoors. As a result, even low levels of pollution add up to create health problems.

Air pollution from radon is largely a problem of air being trapped inside houses. Radon is a gas that you cannot see or smell. Radon comes from the natural breakdown of uranium, and is found in soil, rocks, and water. The gas can enter a house through the floor and walls. Radon from water wells comes into the house with water. If air can enter and leave the house easily, the radon escapes. However, a house with tight-fitting doors and windows may trap the radon. People who breathe high levels of radon over a number of years are more likely to get lung cancer. Map 5-4 shows areas in the United States that have a possible radon risk Notice that the potential for radon varies throughout the country. Many people may choose to have the house and the surrounding land tested for radon before they purchase a home.

Buildings not only trap indoor pollution, they also create it. Asbestos and formaldehyde are found in many building materials. When these substances get loose inside buildings, they can be dangerous. Asbestos is a substance formerly used to fireproof or insulate buildings. However, it is now known to cause certain types of cancer, and by law, may no longer be used in buildings in the United States. However, many older buildings have asbestos in them. Formaldehyde is a gas used as a disinfectant and preservative. It is often used in plywood and other building materials and can cause people to feel ill.

Two other common indoor pollutants are tobacco smoke and gases from burning fuels. Even people who do not smoke are affected by tobacco smoke. Secondhand smoke can intensify the symptoms of asthma, pneumonia, and bronchitis. The United States Environmental Protection Agency (EPA) estimates that smoke inhaled by nonsmokers causes 3,000 cancer deaths and about 40,000 deaths from heart disease each year. Children especially may be harmed by breathing air filled with tobacco smoke.

Gases from fireplaces, stoves, and heaters can also be harmful if they cannot escape from the house. In some cases, enough gases can collect to cause death.

☀ FIGURE 5-1	Indoor Pollutants	
Pollutant	**Source**	**Health Effects**
Radon gas	Rocks and soil	May cause lung cancer
Tobacco smoke	Cigarettes, pipes, cigars	Causes lung cancer and other diseases of the lungs
Asbestos	Pipe insulation; ceiling and floor tiles	Causes lung disease; cancer
Fungi, bacteria	Air conditioners	Cause allergies, asthma
Carbon monoxide	Stoves and heating systems	Causes headaches
Formaldehyde	Plywood, particle board, foam insulation	Causes eye, skin, and lung irritation; may cause cancer
Benzene	Certain types of cleaners	May cause leukemia
Styrene	Carpets, plastics	Causes liver and kidney damage

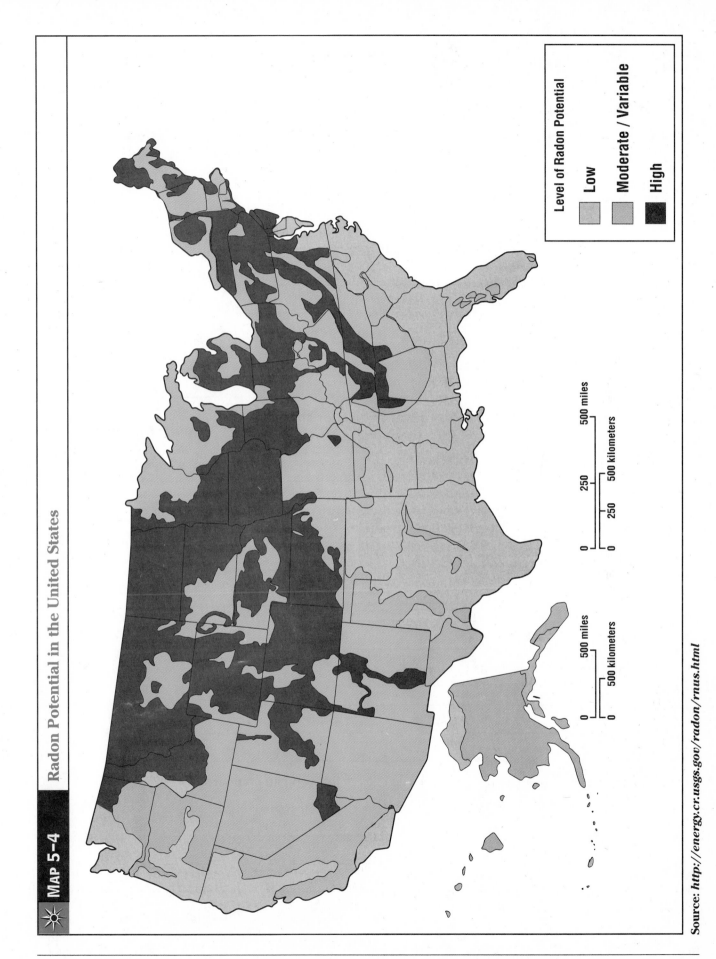

MAP 5-4   Radon Potential in the United States

Level of Radon Potential

Low

Moderate / Variable

High

Source: *http://energy.cr.usgs.gov/radon/rnus.html*

Ⓐ RECALLING FACTS

Answer these questions about air pollution.

1. Describe the two kinds of air pollution.

    _____

    _____

    _____

    _____

2. What are three things in nature that can cause air pollution?

    _____

    _____

3. Describe two ways in which people cause outdoor air pollution.

    _____

    _____

    _____

    _____

4. Why has indoor pollution become a problem?

    _____

    _____

    _____

5. Why is radon a dangerous indoor pollutant?

    _____

    _____

    _____

6. What kinds of health problems does Figure 5-1 tell you can come from indoor air pollution?

    _____

    _____

    _____

    _____

Do you know where the water you drink comes from? Of course, it probably comes out of a faucet, but where was that water before it became part of the water supply? Was it in a lake or river, or was it pumped from a well? If you live on a farm or ranch, chances are the water came from a well. If you live in a city, it's less likely that the water you drink comes from a well. Overall, about half of all Americans drink water from wells.

Danger in the Well

Some Americans have had the shock of learning that the water from their well is no longer safe to drink. In San Jose, California, for example, a chemical used in the manufacture of computer chips leaked from storage tanks into the groundwater. The chemical, TCA, may cause cancer. The drinking water for 20,000 people was contaminated. More than $40 million was spent to stop this waste from spreading.

The problem of **toxic wastes** has been growing for a number of years. Toxic wastes are solid, liquid, or gas wastes that are poisonous. They can cause death, illness, or injury to people and destruction to the natural environment.

Almost all toxic wastes begin with people. You and your family may be harming the environment with toxic wastes. Here is a list of some of the **hazardous,** or dangerous wastes that go into our trash every day. Remember that even if the product has been used, a small amount will remain in the container.

- HOUSEHOLD CLEANERS—drain openers, oven cleaners, wood and metal cleaners and polishes, toilet bowl cleaners

- HOME CARE PRODUCTS—paint thinners, strippers, and removers; glues, paints, stains, varnishes

- CAR CARE PRODUCTS—used motor oil, parts cleaners, antifreeze, waxes and cleaners, oil and fuel additives

- LAWN AND GARDEN PRODUCTS—herbicides, pesticides, wood preservatives

- OTHER—batteries, fingernail polish remover, pool chemicals

Some experts feel that our country's landfills are becoming more dangerous than the dumps made for hazardous wastes. Hazardous-waste dumps are required by law to be lined to keep wastes from leaking out. However, city landfills are not lined. Problems have arisen around many landfills as rainfall carries harmful wastes into underground water supplies. In a number of cities across the United States, everyone must drink bottled water because the city water supply has been spoiled by wastes.

Industry is one of the major producers of toxic wastes. In 1998 the United States produced about 7 billion pounds (about 3 billion kg) of toxic chemicals. This is about 26 pounds (about 12 kg) for every person in the country.

Industries use chemicals to make products that people want to buy. For example, automakers use paint on the new cars and trucks they manufacture. Papermills are left with contaminated water, a byproduct of producing paper. When an industry is finished with the chemicals, it must find a way to dispose of them. Many chemical wastes are pumped down deep wells. Sometimes the wells leak, and the chemicals seep into the groundwater. Other chemical wastes are stored in tanks. These tanks can corrode and leak, spilling toxic chemicals into the air and water.

The Superfund Law

Many years ago people did not give much thought to toxic wastes. Wastes were dumped on the ground, in rivers, or left out in the open. As a result, thousands of hazardous-waste sites were created. In 1980 Congress passed a law to help clean up these waste sites. This law was called the Superfund law because it set up a fund of $1.6 billion to clean up toxic-waste sites. At the time the law was passed, government officials said that the way Americans had been disposing of toxic wastes was "the most grievous error in judgment we as a nation have ever made." Toxic wastes were called "a ticking time bomb ready to go off."

Under the 1980 Superfund law, cleanup work was started at about 100 toxic-waste sites. Only 13 were completely cleaned up. It became clear that the problem was much bigger than had been thought. In 1986 a new Superfund law was passed. This new law set up a fund of $9 billion to clean up toxic-waste sites.

Map 5-5 shows how widespread the toxic-waste problem is in the United States. Find your state on the map. How many sites in your state are on the list of sites to be cleaned up under the Superfund law? Do you think the Superfund law will solve the toxic-waste problem in your state?

There are a number of problems that must be solved before toxic wastes can be cleaned up in the United States. The first problem is the cost. The cleanup will be very expensive—as much as $100 billion. Who should be responsible for the cost? Some people argue that federal, state, or local governments should pay for the cleanup. Others claim that private industries—those that created the wastes—should be responsible for the cost of cleanup.

Another problem is what to do with the wastes once they are cleaned up. Where will they be stored? No one wants to live next to a toxic-waste site. One idea is to haul liquid wastes out to sea in ships and burn them far out in the ocean. But what if the wastes are spilled while being loaded onto the ship? What if the ship sinks in a storm and the chemicals leak into the ocean? And if the chemicals are burned, the wind could carry dangerous smoke back to land.

Is Waste Reduction the Answer?

Many people believe that the final answer may lie in simply stopping the production of toxic wastes. This can be achieved through changes in the chemical processes involved in some manufacturing. Other changes in equipment, raw materials, and maintenance can also help reduce the amount of toxic wastes produced during manufacturing. Already some industries have found that by using these different methods, they can stop creating so many toxic wastes. This is called **waste reduction.**

Other industries have found that they can recycle wastes. For example, acids and solvents become contaminated during the manufacturing process. However, these acids and solvents can be processed to remove the pollutants, and then reused. Some experts feel that in the long run, waste reduction and recycling, along with cleanup efforts already under way, can solve the toxic-waste problem in the United States.

MAP 5-5   Superfund Sites on the National Priorities List

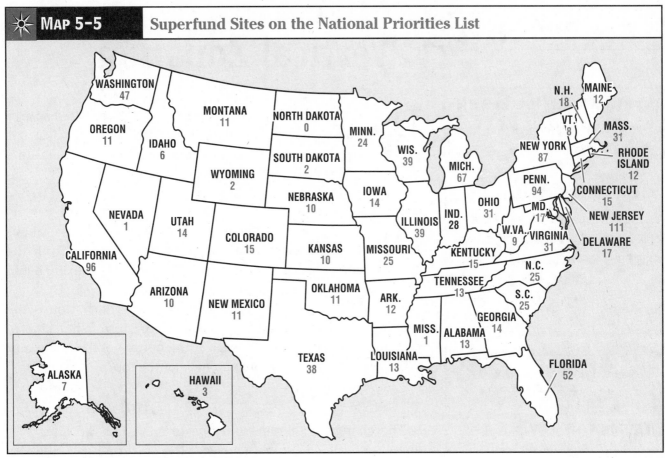

Source: *Environmental Protection Agency, 2000*

Using Your Skills

ⓐ RECALLING FACTS

Answer these questions.

1. What are toxic wastes? _____

2. How do you and your family add to the toxic-waste problem?

    _____

    _____

3. What makes up most toxic wastes? _____

4. What is the purpose of the Superfund law?

    _____

5. Use Map 5-5 to answer this question. How many toxic-waste sites in
    New York will be cleaned up under the Superfund law?

    _____

Lesson 4 Effects of Vertical Zonation

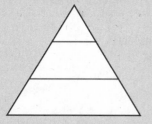
Do you live in the mountains? Perhaps you have visited an area with mountains. Many people like the mountains because it is cooler there in the summer. In fact, the higher you climb up a mountain, the cooler it will become. For every 1,000 feet (304.8 m) you climb, the air temperature will drop about 3.6°F (1.7°C). Visitors to Big Bend National Park in Texas can see this for themselves. The Chisos Mountains rise several thousand feet above the desert. Visitors may be sweating in 90°F (32.2°C) in the desert, but by driving just two miles (3.2 km), they can climb into the mountains and enjoy temperatures around 70°F (21°C).

Look at Figure 5-2. What is the temperature at the bottom of the mountain? What is the temperature at the top? What kind of clothing would you need to wear at the bottom of the mountain? What kind of clothing would you need at the top?

Effects of Elevation on Climate

The change in temperature due to elevation can affect the amount of rainfall an area receives. The cooler air gets, the less moisture it is able to hold. As warm moist air moves up a mountainside, it will be cooled. If the air cools enough, rain will fall.

India provides a good example of this process. During the summer, winds blow across the Bay of Bengal toward India, picking up moisture from the sea. As the winds climb higher and higher, more and more rain falls. Dhaka, India, in the lowlands near the sea, gets 49 inches (124.5 cm) of rain in four months. Only about 100 miles (161 km) away, the village of Cherrapunji receives an average of 328 inches (833.1 cm) in the same four months. What makes the difference? Cherrapunji is about 4,000 feet (1,219 m) higher than Dhaka. As the air rises and cools, it drops its moisture on Cherrapunji.

The change in climate due to elevation is called **vertical zonation.** Vertical zonation is especially important in countries near the Equator. People prefer to live where the temperature is not too hot nor too cold. Look at Map 5-6 of Mexico. As you would expect, the climate is very hot in the lowlands along the coast. What happens to elevation as you move away from the coast? Where would you expect most of the people of Mexico to live?

Mexico is divided into three zones based on elevation. The *tierra caliente,* or "hot land" lies at elevations between sea level and about 2,500 feet (760 m). The temperature in this zone may reach over 90°F (32.2°C) for most of the year. Freezing tempera-

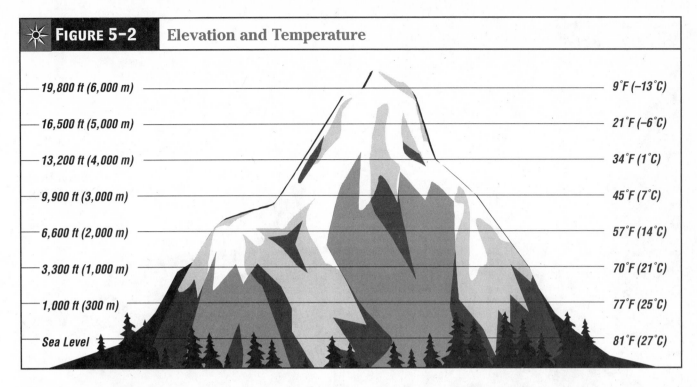

★ **FIGURE 5-2**   Elevation and Temperature

19,800 ft (6,000 m)	9°F (–13°C)
16,500 ft (5,000 m)	21°F (–6°C)
13,200 ft (4,000 m)	34°F (1°C)
9,900 ft (3,000 m)	45°F (7°C)
6,600 ft (2,000 m)	57°F (14°C)
3,300 ft (1,000 m)	70°F (21°C)
1,000 ft (300 m)	77°F (25°C)
Sea Level	81°F (27°C)

tures are almost unknown. The *tierra templada,* or "temperate land" lies between 2,500 feet and about 6,500 feet (2,000 m). Daytime temperatures in this zone range from 60°F to 72°F (16°C to 22°C). Most of the people of Mexico live in the *tierra templada.* Land at 6,500 to 10,000 feet (3,048 m) is known as the *tierra fria,* or "cold land." Here daytime temperatures average between 55°F and 65°F (13°C to 18°C). Freezing temperatures often occur at night during the winter months.

Vertical zonation can affect where people choose to live. It also affects the kinds of crops they can grow. Different crops need different amounts of rainfall and temperatures to grow well. Figure 5-3 shows some of the crops that can grow at different elevations.

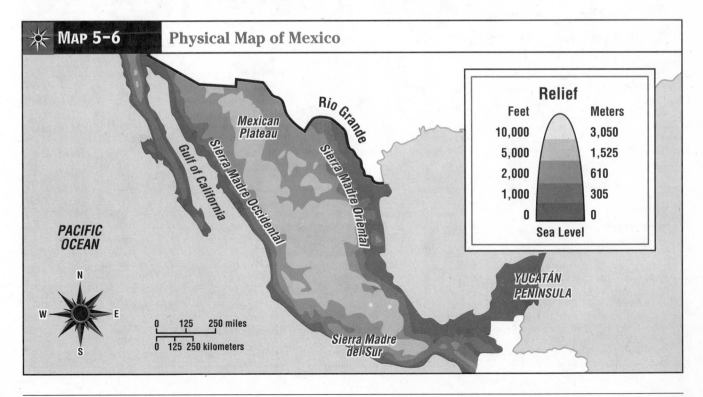

★ **MAP 5-6**   Physical Map of Mexico

Rio Grande

Mexican Plateau

Sierra Madre Occidental

Sierra Madre Oriental

Gulf of California

Relief

Feet	Meters
10,000	3,050
5,000	1,525
2,000	610
1,000	305
0	0
Sea Level	

PACIFIC OCEAN

YUCATÁN PENINSULA

N
W   E
S

0   125   250 miles
0   125   250 kilometers

Sierra Madre del Sur

FIGURE 5-3 Vertical Zonation and Agriculture

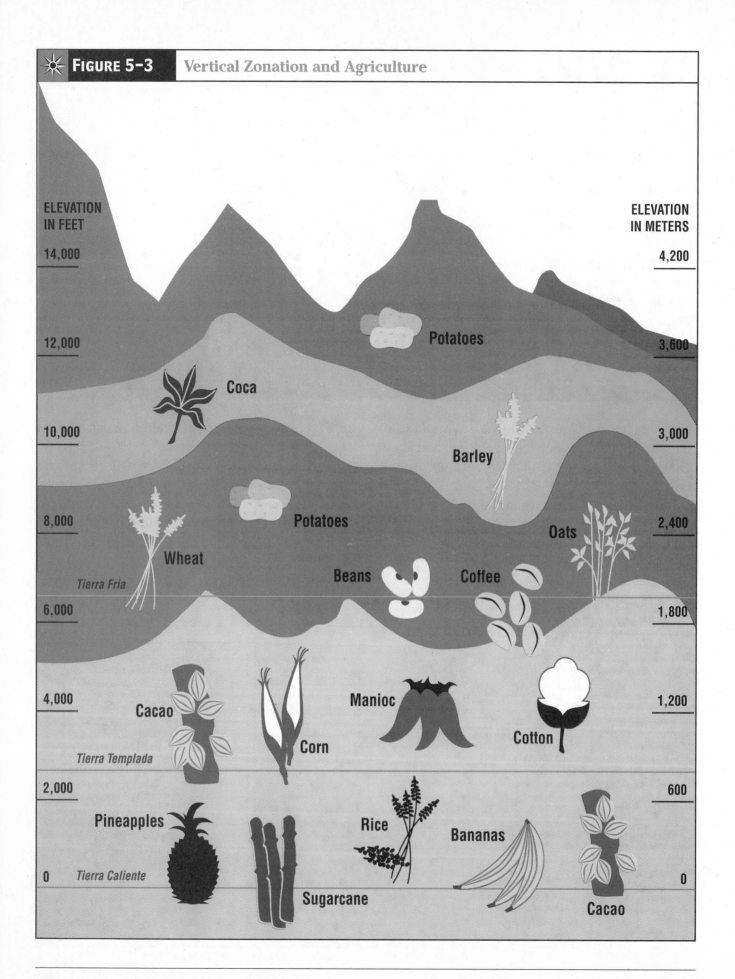

❹ RECALLING FACTS

Answer these questions.

1. What is vertical zonation? _____

2. What happens to temperature as elevation increases?

   _____

   _____

3. In addition to temperature, what other part of climate can be affected
   by elevation? _____

4. How does vertical zonation affect where people live?

   _____

   _____

5. How does vertical zonation affect agriculture?

   _____

6. Use Figure 5-3 to answer these questions.

   a. What crops can be grown at elevations between sea level and 2,500
      feet (760 m)? _____

   b. Which of these crops can also be grown between 2,500 and 6,500
      feet (760–2000 m)? _____

   c. At about what elevation can coffee be grown? _____

   d. What crop can be grown at the highest elevation? _____

   e. What crops could be grown in Mexico's *tierra templada*?

      _____

7. What is the elevation where you live? _____

8. How does elevation affect the climate where you live?

   _____

   _____

9. How does elevation affect agriculture where you live ?

   _____

   _____

   _____

WHAT YOU WILL LEARN

To be aware of danger to life and property from natural hazards such as hurricanes, tornadoes, and lightning

READING STRATEGY

Create a chart like the one below. Fill in the geographic area where each of the natural hazards occurs.

HAZARD	GEOGRAPHIC AREA

TERMS TO KNOW

tornado, lightning, hurricane, typhoon, windchill, earthquake, flood, flash flood, drought

The sound may be hard to hear at first over the pounding of hail on the roof, rain lashing at the windows, or thunder and lightning. People who have heard the sound say it is like the buzzing of 10 million bees. Others say it sounds like a train running through the living room. Once you have heard it, you will never forget it. It is the sound of a tornado about to strike.

Tornadoes

A **tornado** is nature's most violent storm. It is a violently rotating column of air from within a thundercloud. Tornadoes create winds that range from 75 mph to 300 mph (120 km/hr to 500 km/hr). Tornadoes can occur anywhere in the United States. However, they are most common in the United States over the Great Plains and Midwest (a region known as Tornado Alley) during the summer months. Map 5-7 shows the months of peak tornado activity.

The only safe place in a tornado is a strong underground shelter. Second best is the corner of a basement *toward the tornado*. Most injuries in tornadoes are from flying objects such as glass and lumber. If the building has no basement, go to a room, hallway, or closet *in the center of the house.* Get under a piece of furniture or pull a mattress over you.

People once thought that houses "exploded" in tornadoes. It was thought that opening windows would keep the air pressure equal inside and outside. *Opening windows is no longer recommended.* We now know that tornadoes simply blow houses down.

Thunderstorms

Thunderstorms can occur any place on Earth. And although tornadoes are usually born during strong thunderstorms, most thunderstorms do not make tornadoes. However, all thunderstorms create **lightning.** Lightning is the result of the buildup and discharge of electricity between the ground and a cloud. It is very dangerous. Lightning starts many forest fires each year.

The best protection against lightning is to stay indoors during thunderstorms. Stay away from open windows, metal water pipes, telephones, and any electrical appliances. If you are caught outdoors and cannot get to a building, the safest place is in a car with the windows rolled up. If you are on foot, stay away from high ground, wire fences, or trees that stand by themselves. Lightning often strikes the tallest object—which could be you standing at the top of a hill.

MAP 5-7   Continental U.S. Peak Tornado Activity

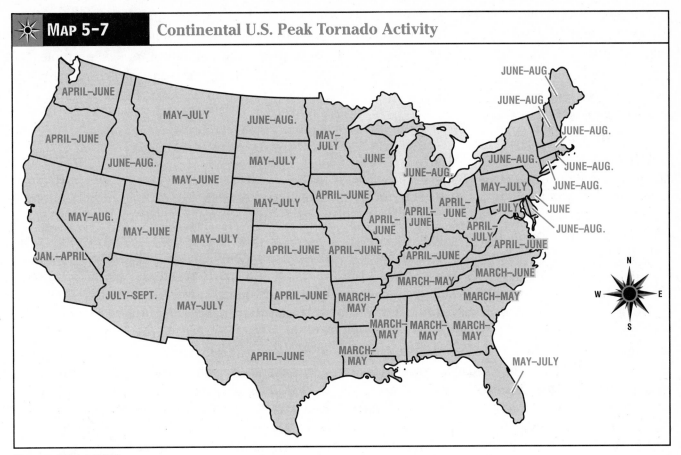

Source: *NOAA/NWS*

Hurricanes and Typhoons

Nature's largest storms are hurricanes and typhoons, types of tropical cyclones. **Hurricanes** originate over the Atlantic Ocean, while **typhoons** originate over the Pacific Ocean. These storms have winds that blow in a circular direction over an area of low air pressure. During a hurricane or typhoon, strong winds and rain move inland causing property damage and flooding. Tornadoes may also come with hurricanes and typhoons.

These storms are most dangerous to cities along the seacoast. Satellite data allow the movement of hurricanes and typhoons to be tracked. Early warning systems let people living in the path of the storm prepare for its arrival.

The safest place in a hurricane or typhoon is somewhere else. For example, when a hurricane warning is issued, drive as far as possible. Many people try to "ride out" the storm in order to protect their property. There is nothing anyone can do to protect property in a major storm.

Extreme Cold

Cold is another danger that takes many lives each year. However, it is not the cold itself that kills—it is the loss of body heat. A person caught outside in wet clothing and in high winds can freeze to death at a temperature of 50°F (10°C). **Windchill** is the rate of cooling as a result of wind or air movement. High windchill values can be dangerous even if the temperature is moderate. Windchill is what the temperature feels like when the wind is blowing.

Being prepared is the best safeguard against cold. If you will be outside in cold weather, dress warmly. Several layers of lighter clothing will keep you warmer than one or two very heavy layers.

Sometimes people are trapped in their cars by winter storms. If you must travel in snow or ice storms, carry food and extra clothing with you. Have blankets, sleeping bags, candles, matches, a shovel, and a tow rope with you. If you are trapped by snow, you can run the motor for a few minutes at a time to keep warm. However, you *must* keep snow shoveled away from the car. Otherwise the exhaust gases can enter the car and kill you.

Earthquakes

Earthquakes are a shaking and trembling of the earth. Earthquakes can occur any place on Earth, but there are some areas more likely to experience them than others. The area surrounding the Pacific Ocean is known as the Ring of Fire because of frequent earthquakes and volcanoes. This is an area of active tectonic movement. Remember from Unit 3, Lesson 1 that tectonic plates carry the earth's continents and oceans. Plates may collide into each other, creating earthquakes and volcanoes.

Most people are killed in earthquakes when buildings fall on them. If you are inside when an earthquake strikes, stand in a doorway. The strong doorway may protect you. You can also seek refuge under a desk or other sturdy piece of furniture. Do not run outside. Many people are injured or killed by falling debris such as trees or telephone poles while trying to run outside. If you are outside, go to an open area with no tall buildings nearby.

Floods

Floods occur when flowing bodies of water such as rivers, streams, and creeks overflow their banks, usually as the result of heavy rainfall. Flash floods pose the most immediate danger. **Flash floods** occur when small bodies of water rise quickly and swallow up the land around them. During heavy rainstorms, avoid low-lying areas. If you are in a vehicle that stalls in rising floodwaters, leave the car and move to higher ground.

Flash floods subside quickly and cause less damage than floods of larger bodies of water. Floodwaters rise on rivers over a period of days. The water rises because of heavy rainfall or from rapid snow melt. As the waters rise, the rivers overflow their banks and cover the land. Many areas of the world can experience flooding. In 1993 the Mississippi River flooded the midwestern United States. Other countries such as Italy, France, and Bangladesh experienced severe flooding in the 1990s.

Modern technology allows people to build dams to control flooding, and dikes and flood walls to keep out rising floodwaters. For example, the Nile River used to flood annually. Today, a series of dams keeps the Nile River within its banks.

Droughts

A natural disaster in which there is a long period of extreme dryness and water shortages is known as a **drought.** These natural disasters are more subtle than other hazards, but they can be just as destructive. During a drought, plants do not receive enough moisture to survive. As plants die, the animals that eat the plants lose their source of food. They also cannot find enough water as streams, lakes, and rivers dry up. During severe droughts, soil erosion occurs as winds blow away the exposed topsoil. Droughts can occur in many regions of the world. The Dust Bowl of the 1930s was one of North America's worst droughts. Since the late 1960s the Sahel region of Africa has experienced droughts. Even after rains come, the land may take years to recover.

Lightning lights up the sky in Seattle, Washington.

Using Your Skills

Ⓐ RECALLING FACTS

On a separate sheet of paper create a list of things you should do to protect yourself against tornadoes, hurricanes and typhoons, lightning, cold, and earthquakes. Discuss these things with your family. Make a family plan for what to do when bad weather threatens.

Ⓑ USING GRAPHICS

Use the table below to answer the questions.

☀	Windchill Table*								
	Wind Speed (miles per hour)								
Temperature (°F)	5	10	15	20	25	30	35	40	45
	Windchill (Equivalent Temperature)								
35°	33°	22°	16°	12°	8°	6°	4°	3°	2°
30°	27°	16°	9°	4°	1°	–2°	–4°	–5°	–6°
25°	21°	10°	2°	–3°	–7°	–10°	–12°	–13°	–14°
20°	16°	3°	–5°	–10°	–15°	–18°	–20°	–21°	–22°
15°	12°	–3°	–11°	–17°	–22°	–25°	–27°	–29°	–30°
10°	7°	–9°	–18°	–24°	–29°	–33°	–35°	–37°	–38°
5°	0°	–15°	–25°	–31°	–36°	–41°	–43°	–45°	–46°
0°	–5°	–22°	–31°	–39°	–44°	–49°	–52°	–53°	–54°

* Windchill temperatures shown in **dark type** indicate a danger of freezing exposed flesh.

1. If the temperature is 15°F and the wind is blowing at 20 miles per hour, what is the windchill? _____

2. If the temperature is 30°F and the wind is blowing at 30 miles per hour, what is the windchill? _____

3. You should be careful not to expose flesh at or below what windchill temperature? How can you tell?

    _____

    _____

Lesson 6 Human Adaptation to Difficult Environments

WHAT YOU WILL LEARN

To describe ways in which humans adapt to different physical environments

READING STRATEGY

Create a diagram like the one below. Fill in examples of human adaptation to the environment.

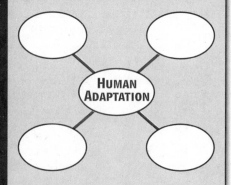

TERMS TO KNOW

technology, greenhouse effect

How would you like to live in a place where snow and ice cover the ground most of the year? Would you rather live in a place where rain almost never falls, and heat bakes the land year-round? Most of us would rather live someplace more pleasant. However, some people do live in places that are very dry, very hot, or very cold. How they live provides lessons for the rest of us.

Adapting to the Environment

The San of southwestern Africa live in one of the world's driest deserts. They were pushed onto this land many years ago by other people who moved onto the better land to the east. The San have a hard life. There is little food in the desert, and they often include bugs and frogs in their diet. They also dig what roots they can find from under the ground. However, they often go hungry. Because there is so little food, the population of the San grows slowly.

One of the few tools the San use is a pointed stick. They use the stick to dig up roots. Hunting is done with spears and bows and arrows. The San move about often, looking for new food supplies. Since they are always moving, they do not build permanent houses. A few sticks in the ground, bent over and covered with grass, make a home for the few days it is needed.

When the San move, they must carry everything with them. They have no animals to help them. The San do not weigh themselves down with many belongings. One thing they must carry is water. They gather ostrich-egg shells, which are very large, and fill them with water.

After the San have left an area, it would be very hard to tell that they had been there. The San have made little use of modern **technology.** Technology is the use of tools and skills to make life easier. Instead of using technology to change their world, the San have learned to live with their world as it is. They have adapted to their environment. Because they use few tools, they make few changes in their environment. Because they have no cars, they have no need for roads. They have very few belongings, so they have little to throw away. There are no San landfills. Because they have only simple tools and no permanent houses, they have no power plants to generate electricity. The San lead very hard lives, but they do not have major problems with air and water pollution. Nor do they create many such problems.

The Inuit are another example of a people who have learned to live in a difficult environment. They live in the far north of North

America and Asia. Snow and ice cover the land for most of the year.

For many years the Inuit used very little technology. For example, they made their houses of the one thing they have an abundance of—snow. These snow houses, or igloos, were heated by lamps which burn oil from animals such as seals. The Inuit wore fur clothing made from the skins of animals. They hunted with bows and arrows and spears. Most of their tools were made from animal bones or from pieces of wood they found washed up along the beach.

Inuit ways are changing. Some still follow the old ways, but the Inuit have been quick to adopt new technology. Bows and arrows have been replaced with guns. Skin boats and wooden paddles have given way to metal boats and gasoline motors. Sleds pulled by dogs are being replaced by snowmobiles. Home to an Inuit today is more likely to be a modern house than an igloo.

These changes have not come without problems. When the Inuit began to want guns and houses and snowmobiles, they had to have money to buy them. They made money by hunting and fishing. By using guns and modern boats, they were able to kill many more animals and catch more fish. Before long, there were not as many

An Inuit in Siberia, Russia, displays his modern transportation.

animals and fish. It became harder and harder to earn the money needed to pay for all the new things the Inuit wanted. Today, the number of animals the Inuit kill must be limited. Otherwise, all the animals might be killed off.

Using Technology to Change the Environment

Think about how other people in the world have dealt with the same kinds of problems that faced the Inuit and the San. Where it is too hot, people use air conditioning. Where it is too cold, people burn wood, gas, or oil or use electricity to heat their homes. If there is not enough food in an area to feed all the people who live there, food is imported. Factories produce goods to feed, clothe, and amuse us. All kinds of work have been made easier by the use of machines.

Few of us would want to live as the Inuit and the San live. However, the pleasant lives we lead do carry a price tag. We live in a world which makes great use of technology. Technology lets us feed, clothe, and house more people. It makes life more pleasant, but there is a catch. Technology solves many problems as it creates new ones. The pollution of our air, water, and land has been caused by our increasing use of technology.

One of the problems caused by the use of technology is called the **greenhouse effect.** The greenhouse effect is a slow warming of the earth caused by the burning of fossil fuels such as coal, oil, and gas. This warming started when people began burning very large amounts of these fuels in the 1800s. Burning these fuels creates a gas called carbon dioxide. Carbon dioxide traps heat from the sun. This makes the earth warm slowly over time. At the present rate of warming, the earth could be seven or eight degrees warmer in about 60 years. This does not sound like much, but it might be enough to cause changes in the earth's climate. Some scientists believe that the areas which now grow most of the world's food could become deserts. They claim that the ice covering the North and South Poles could melt. The melting ice could raise the oceans enough to flood many of the world's great cities.

Using Your Skills

Ⓐ RECALLING FACTS

Answer these questions.

1. What is technology? _____

2. How has the use of technology changed our world?

   _____

   _____

3. What is the greenhouse effect?

   _____

4. How may the greenhouse effect change our world?

   _____

   _____

   _____

Ⓑ RECALLING FACTS

Complete the chart below, showing how your life would be different without the use of technology. Remember: without technology you could use only tools powered by your own muscles. Use the headings shown below.

☀	Life Without Technology
With Technology	**Without Technology**
Food	
Clothing	
Shelter	
Transportation	

Lesson 7

Balancing Population and Resources

WHAT YOU WILL LEARN

To understand the problems associated with rapid population growth in developing countries

READING STRATEGY

Create a diagram like the one below and list three causes of world population growth.

```
CAUSES
1. ────▶ POPULATION
2.        GROWTH
3.
```

TERMS TO KNOW

developing country, birthrate, death rate

Have you ever gone to a store to buy something only to find that none was left? Perhaps you were told to come back the next day, or the next week. You may not have been pleased, but you probably did not suffer lasting harm. However, what if you had been shopping for food? What if all the food was gone?

More and more, food shortages are becoming a problem in **developing countries.** Developing countries are countries with a low standard of living and little industry. Although modern machinery has been recently introduced, many farmers still rely on traditional farming methods. The use of fertilizers and pesticides has increased over the last several years. But some developing countries still have trouble growing enough food to feed their growing populations.

Why World Population Is Increasing

Population growth is another issue for developing countries. People often tend to have large families. One reason is that parents depend on their children to take care of them in old age. A man and woman may also have many children to help work and support the family. Another reason for large families is the high infant mortality rate in some countries. Having many children makes it more likely that some will survive to adulthood.

However, population growth does not depend just on the **birthrate,** the number of births per 1,000 of a population each

In Rajasthan, India, some farmers still rely on traditional farming methods.

year. Population growth also depends on the **death rate,** the number of deaths per 1,000 of a population each year. In the last 40 years, the death rate in almost every country in the world has decreased. This has occurred mainly because of better medical care. People have also had access to more and better food.

Although the death rate has decreased in most developing countries, birthrates have continued to remain high in many of them. This has caused a huge increase in the world's population in just a few years. And as expected, most of this increase has been in the developing countries.

Look at Map 5-8. Each region of the world shown has two figures printed on it. The top figure shows the average number of children in each family in that region. The bottom figure shows the value of goods and services produced by each person in that region each year. The larger this figure is, the more money people in that country are likely to have to spend.

Rapid Population Growth

A large percentage of the population of developing countries is made up of children. Before better medical care, many children died at an early age. For example, in Africa in 1950, 182 children out of every 1,000 born died before reaching their first birthday. By 2000, only 79 out of 1,000 died. In South America the rate fell from 126 to 34. In Asia it dropped from 155 to 51. These figures are still far higher than in developed countries. In the United States, for example, only 7 of 1,000 children die before their first birthday.

The decreasing death rate in developing countries has caused the number of children to grow very quickly. Large numbers of children are a drain on a country's resources. Children need food, clothing, schools, doctors, and much more. Developing countries have to spend much of their money just feeding their people. Little money is left for better roads, schools, or factories to create more jobs.

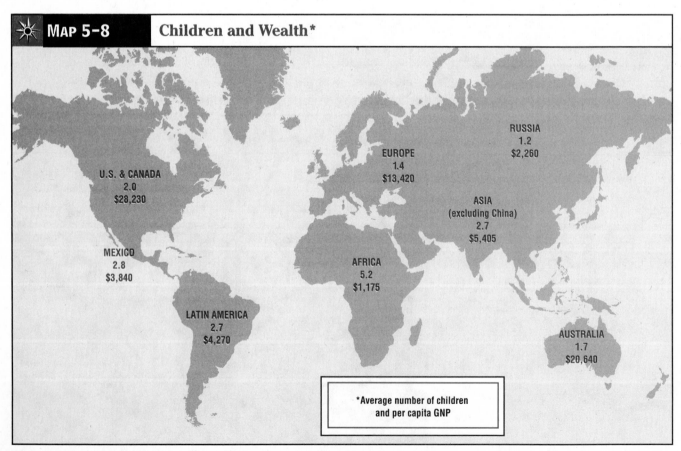

MAP 5-8 **Children and Wealth***

RUSSIA
1.2
$2,260

EUROPE
1.4
$13,420

U.S. & CANADA
2.0
$28,230

ASIA
(excluding China)
2.7
$5,405

MEXICO
2.8
$3,840

AFRICA
5.2
$1,175

LATIN AMERICA
2.7
$4,270

AUSTRALIA
1.7
$20,640

*Average number of children
and per capita GNP

Source: *World Population Data Sheet,* 2001

Using Your Skills

Ⓐ RECALLING FACTS

Answer these questions about Figure 5-4.

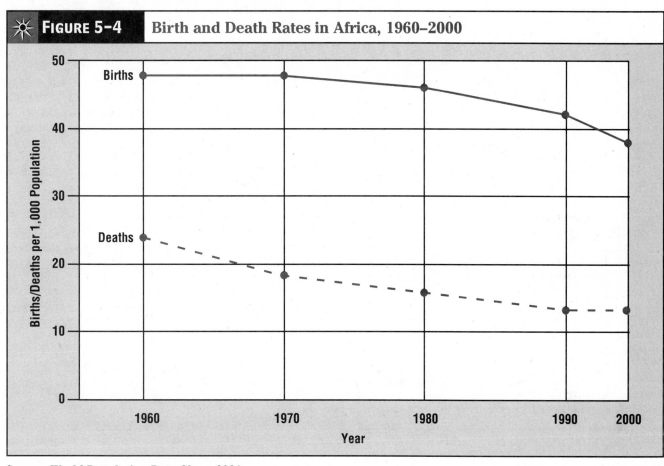

★ FIGURE 5-4 | **Birth and Death Rates in Africa, 1960–2000**

Source: *World Population Data Sheet*, 2001

1. What is the title of this graph? _____

2. What does the solid line on the graph stand for? _____

3. What does the broken line on the graph stand for? _____

4. What happened to the birthrate in Africa between 1960 and 2000?

   _____

5. What happened to the death rate in Africa between 1960 and 2000?

   _____

6. What will happen to the population of Africa if the birthrate remains
   high and the death rate continues to fall?

   _____

B RECALLING FACTS

Use Figure 5-5 to answer these questions.

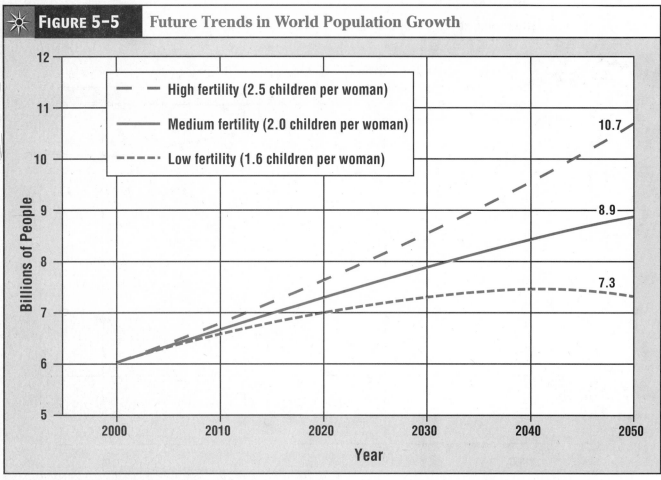

FIGURE 5-5 | Future Trends in World Population Growth

- — — High fertility (2.5 children per woman)
- —— Medium fertility (2.0 children per woman)
- - - - Low fertility (1.6 children per woman)

Y-axis: Billions of People

X-axis: Year

Source: *World Population Data Sheet,* 2001

1. What does this graph show?

_____

2. If the average world family today has 2.5 children, according to the graph, what will be the population of the world in the year 2050 if this continues?

_____

3. What would happen to world population if each family had only two children?

_____

_____

The Rain Forest—An Ecosystem In Trouble

Imagine that you are walking through a dense forest of huge trees. The forest is so dense that you need a flashlight to see where you are going. As you look up into the trees, you see different kinds of animals—animals you have never seen anywhere else. Most likely you are walking through one of the world's rain forests.

What's In a Rain Forest?

A rain forest is made up of tall trees that grow year-round in places that have a tropical climate. (You read about the world's climates in Unit 3, Lesson 3.)

Tropical rain forests make up only about 7 percent of the earth's surface. However, more than half of the earth's plant and animal species live there. There are more varieties of amphibians, birds, and insects in rain forests than anywhere else in the world.

A rain forest in Guatamala displays a typical abundance and density of vegetation.

Why Are Rain Forests Important?

Rain forests are home to millions of people. Many groups of people have lived in the world's rain forests for thousands of years. It is estimated that as many as 1,000 different cultures may be living in the world's rain forests. Groups such as the Yanomami in South America and the Mbuti of central Africa make a living in the rain forests by hunting, fishing, and gathering forest products.

Rain forests also provide many benefits to people living outside of the rain forests. Wood is one of the most important rain forest products. Teak, rosewood, and mahogany are used to make furniture around the world. Figure 5-6 shows some of the other products that are made from rain forest plants. Other important rain forest resources include petroleum and natural gas. Deposits in Southeast Asia, central Africa, and South America attract foreign businesses.

Rain forests provide scientific value. Scientists believe they have discovered only a small percentage of the plants that grow in the rain forests. Many of these plants have been used to make medicines. For example, specialized medicines used to treat a rare form of leukemia were created from plants in Madagascar's rain forest. Figure 5-6 shows some other medicines made from rain forest plants. Scientists believe that the drugs already in use are just a fraction of the potential medicines rain forests may hold.

Rain forests help to regulate and maintain the environment. They absorb a large amount of rain. Much of the rain evaporates from the leaves of the trees and goes back into the atmosphere as water vapor. Eventually the vapor condenses and comes back to the earth as rain. The thick vegetation of the rain forests helps prevent soil erosion. The plants also absorb carbon dioxide from the atmosphere and give off oxygen. In fact, tropical rain forests absorb more carbon dioxide than any other ecosystem on Earth. Scientists claim that this lessens the impact of global warming. Rain forests also help to control temperature by absorbing light and heat. By doing so, they help keep tropical climates from becoming too hot or too cool.

Rain forests also provide recreational value. They provide tourists with the opportunity to see beautiful vegetation and unique animals that cannot be found anyplace else on Earth.

Rain Forests In Trouble

Although the rain forests are home to unique cultures, plants, and animals, and provide many benefits, they are in danger. Thousands of square miles of rain forests are destroyed every year. This loss or destruction of trees is called **deforestation.** Experts believe that about 35 million acres (14 million hectares) of the world's tropical forests are lost every year.

There are several causes of deforestation. Some tropical forests have been cut down for the valuable timber or to clear land for farming. Some governments have ordered the clearing of rain forests to provide space for their country's growing population. Mining companies have cut down trees in search of petroleum or other minerals. Trees have

☀ FIGURE 5-6	Products from Rain Forests	
Ingredient	**Source**	**Product**
Rubber	Rubber tree	Tires, toys, and industrial raw materials
Rattan	Palm leaves	Wicker baskets, furniture
Cacao beans	South American tree	Chocolate, cocoa, cocoa butter
Kola nuts	Seed of a kola tree	Soft drinks
Palm oils	Palm hearts	Cooking oil
Sapayul oil	Sapote plant	Shampoo and conditioner
Chicle	Sapodilla tree	Base of chewing gum
Medicine	**Source**	**Treatment**
Cinchona	Cinchona tree	Reduces high fevers
Quinine	Bark of rubiaceae tree	Malaria
Rosy periwinkle	Tropical forest plant	Hodgkin's disease and other forms of cancer

also been cut down so that dams could be built to provide these areas with hydroelectric power.

Consequences of Deforestation

Deforestation has displaced many groups of people who live in the rain forests. It threatens to destroy many species of plants and animals. In addition, it can limit the many environmental benefits that rain forests provide. For example, destroying the rain forests contributes to an increase of carbon dioxide in the earth's atmosphere. Some scientists believe that the buildup of this gas can increase global temperatures. Known as **global warming,** this situation could lead to problems such as melting of the polar regions.

This, in turn, can lead to rising sea levels, and flooding of many of the world's coastal areas.

Saving the Rain Forests

In recent years, many conservation organizations throughout the world have been working with governments to save the rain forests. These organizations have made people aware of the importance of rain forests. They have set up protected areas, such as national parks, where rain forests are left undisturbed and intact. They have also worked with governments to set up ways of managing rain forests. By managing them properly, people can continue to benefit from what the rain forests have to offer while working to prevent their destruction.

Using Your Skills

Ⓐ RECALLING FACTS

Use the reading and Figure 5-6 to answer the questions.

1. Describe three reasons why rain forests are important.

    _____

    _____

    _____

2. Why are rain forests in danger?

    _____

3. Other than medicines, what kinds of products are made with ingredients from the rain forest?

    _____

    _____

4. Why are trees in the rain forest being cut down?

    _____

    _____

5. What are the consequences of cutting down the rain forest?

    _____

    _____

Environment and Society

Ⓐ RECALLING FACTS

Write *T* if the statement is true. Write *F* if the statement is false.

_____ 1. Nature's most violent storms are tornadoes.

_____ 2. Pollutants are harmful substances found in the environment.

_____ 3. Many dangerous wastes are pumped down wells.

_____ 4. Droughts occur suddenly and damage plants, animals, and humans.

_____ 5. Tropical rain forests cover half the earth's surface.

_____ 6. Most pollution is caused by human activities.

_____ 7. Anything that burns a fossil fuel such as coal, oil, or natural gas adds to air pollution.

_____ 8. Natural resources are naturally occuring things that are found on Earth.

_____ 9. The greenhouse effect is a slow warming of the earth caused by burning fossil fuels.

_____ 10. The change in climate due to time is called vertical zonation.

_____ 11. The safest place to be in a tornado is in an underground shelter.

_____ 12. People in developing countries tend to have small families.

_____ 13. Lightning often strikes the tallest object.

_____ 14. Hurricanes strike quickly and give people no time to get to a safer place.

_____ 15. The use of technology to make our lives easier has increased levels of pollution.

❸ RECALLING FACTS

Write the letter of the word or words which will complete each statement correctly.

_____ 1. A major threat to rain forests is (are)

      a. tornadoes.   b. deforestation.   c. pollution.

_____ 2. Which of the following groups lives in rain forests?

      a. Yanomami   b. Inuit   c. San

_____ 3. Indoor pollution is caused partly by

      a. too much air coming in.   b. too little air getting out.   c. smoke.

_____ 4. The Superfund law was created to help clean up

      a. toxic-waste sites.   b. tornado disasters.   c. flood damage.

_____ 5. Things that are found or produced in an area can be shown on a

      a. language map.   b. transportation map.   c. resource map.

_____ 6. What is the greatest danger to humans in an earthquake?

      a. lightning   b. windchills   c. falling buildings

_____ 7. Death rates in developing countries have decreased and birthrates have

      a. remained high.   b. also decreased.   c. decreased then increased.

_____ 8. For every 1,000 feet you climb up a mountain, the temperature will

      a. rise 3.6°F.   b. drop 10.6°F.   c. drop 3.6°F.

_____ 9. The peak months for tornadoes are the

      a. summer months.   b. fall months.   c. winter months.

_____ 10. Most of Mexico's population lives in the

      a. _tierra fria._   b. _tierra templada._   c. _tierra caliente._

C USING GRAPHICS

Use Map 5-9: Average Number of Tornadoes and Tornado Deaths by
State, 1950–1994 to complete the table and answer the questions.

☀	Average Number of Tornadoes and Tornado Deaths in Selected States, 1950–1994		
State	**No. of Tornadoes**		**No. of Deaths**
California			
Colorado			
Texas			
Illinois			
Tennessee			
Florida			

1. How many more tornadoes occurred in Texas than in California between 1950 and 1994?

   _____

2. How many more tornadoes occurred in Florida than in California between 1950 and 1994?

   _____

3. How does the number of tornado deaths in Texas compare to the number in Colorado between 1950 and 1994?

   _____

4. Which regions of the United States had the most tornadoes between 1950 and 1994?

   _____

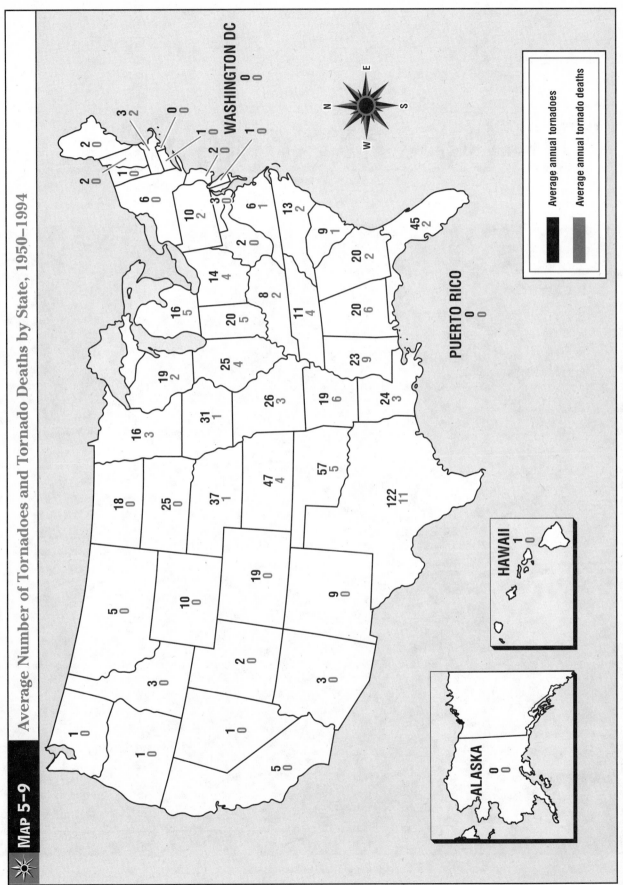

MAP 5-9 Average Number of Tornadoes and Tornado Deaths by State, 1950–1994

WASHINGTON DC
0
0

Average annual tornadoes

Average annual tornado deaths

PUERTO RICO
0
0

HAWAII
1
0

ALASKA
0
0

Data compiled from statistics found at: *http://www.spc.noaa.gov/archive/tornadoes/st-trank. html*

The Uses of Geography

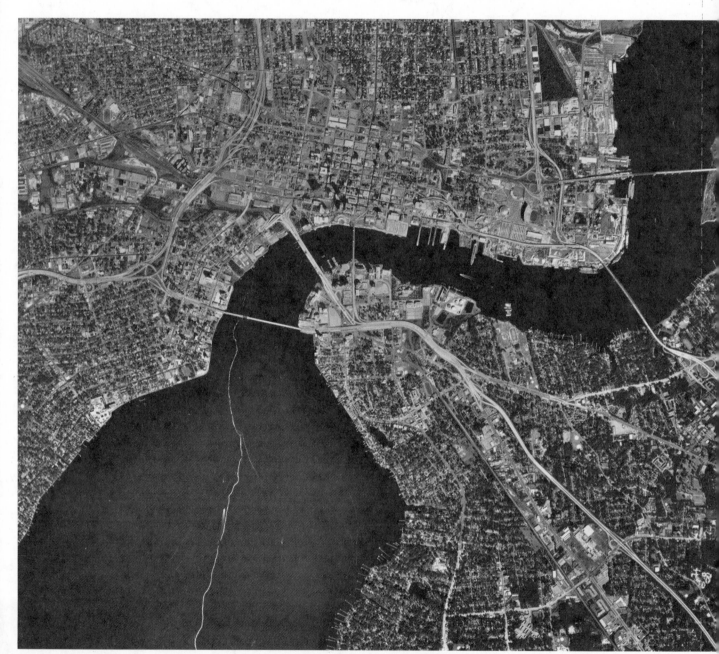

This satellite image shows St. John's River flowing through Jacksonville, Florida.

Objectives

After completing this unit, you will be able to:

- discuss how geography helps to interpret the past;
- understand how geography helps to explain the present;
- explain how geography can be used to plan for the future.

Amazing Statistics

- In this city, over 190 people pick up the telephone every second, on average.
- In this city, the people use 2,659,532 quarts of milk and an estimated 7,000,000 eggs a day.
- In this city, a baby is born every 4 minutes and 6 seconds.

These are some pretty amazing statistics. It is obvious from these numbers that the city described must be a huge metropolis. In fact it is; it's New York City. What is even more amazing is that these statistics applied to New York in 1929. Looking at how it was then, can you imagine what these figures would be like today?

What an Address

If you get tired of writing down your address, think about the people who live in Krungthep Mahanakhon (Bangkok), the capital of Thailand. The full name of their town is actually Krungthep Mahanakhon Bovorn Ratanakosin Mahintharayutthaya Mahadilok pop Noparatratchathani Burirom Udomratchanivetmahasathan Amornpiman Avatarnsathit Sakkathattiyavisnukarmprasit. With 167 letters, this name is enough to drive mapmakers and sign painters crazy.

Do you ever wonder why certain historical events happened the way they did? For example, why did Napoleon fail to successfully invade Russia? Why did industrialization in the United States begin in New England? Why are many cities located where they are?

Geography can explain many events and situations. Napoleon, who conquered many places, was unsuccessful because his troops had to face Russia's brutally harsh weather and had to travel large distances. Industrialization in the United States started in New England because that region had the natural resources and the sources of power that were necessary for industrialization to take place. Many cities throughout the world grew up near the coasts or on rivers, which provided water for farming and a means of transportation.

In addition to interpreting the past, geography can help us plan for the future. By understanding that some resources can be depleted, we can work to find ways to preserve them. Both governments and individuals can help by establishing recycling programs and by recycling paper, glass, and metal.

The uses of geography is one of the six essential elements of geography. Geography can help us understand the past. It can help explain how physical features developed in the past and why certain events happened the way they did. Geography can also help us explain the present so that we can plan for the future. For example, understanding population trends can help city planners decide whether to build highways or new schools. Knowing what resources are available in an area can help investors decide when and how to develop those resources.

Geography is more than just learning place names. It can help us understand the relationships among groups of people, as well as between people and their environment. This understanding can help people plan for a better future.

Lesson 1

Historical Change in Importance of Location

WHAT YOU WILL LEARN

To be aware that the significance and importance of locations change as cultures change their interactions with each other and with the physical environment

READING STRATEGY

Create a diagram like the one below. In each oval, fill in information about how the importance of Timbuktu's location changed over time.

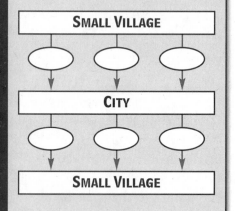

The soldiers creeping to the small Pennsylvania town on June 30, 1863, had no intention of making the town famous. All they wanted was to find shoes, for they had none. But five days later, the name *Gettysburg* had become one which would be written in history. One of the greatest battles of the American Civil War began there simply because soldiers of the two sides bumped into each other almost by accident. Today, Gettysburg is the site of a national military park that attracts thousands of visitors from around the world each year.

Why did the importance of Gettysburg's location change? The importance of Gettysburg's location changed because of events that took place there. The town is far more important today than it would be if the battle had been fought somewhere else.

Human interaction can change the importance of a location—it can become more or less important. The change can take place quickly, as in the case of Gettysburg, or slowly over hundreds of years, as in the case of Timbuktu.

The Story of Timbuktu

The African city of Timbuktu is a good example of a location whose importance changed slowly. At first a small village, Timbuktu grew into one of the most important cities of its time. Today, it is once again a village. What happened, and why, is one of the most interesting stories in geography.

Timbuktu is located in the western part of Africa, on a bend in the Niger River, at about latitude 17°N and longitude 3°W. Can you see anything about this location that would explain why Timbuktu became a great city? Other than its location on a river, there is very little in the physical environment of Timbuktu that would explain why it became a great city.

Trade's Impact on Timbuktu

Look at Map 6-1 showing trade routes in West Africa about the year A.D. 1000. Find the area marked Wangara. Gold was mined here. Now find the village of Taghaza. Salt was mined here. Find Timbuktu, which is between Wangara and Taghaza.

You can see that Timbuktu is located halfway between gold mines to the south and salt mines to the north. The people who had gold needed salt, and the people who had salt wanted gold.

By now you may suspect that trade, not just location, made Timbuktu a great city. However, it was Timbuktu's location that

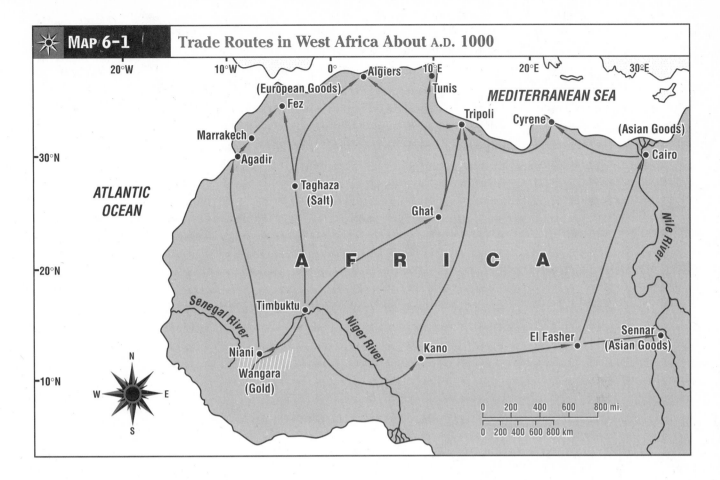

MAP 6-1 | Trade Routes in West Africa About A.D. 1000

20°W   10°W   0°   Algiers   10°E   20°E   30°E

(European Goods)   Tunis

Fez   **MEDITERRANEAN SEA**

Tripoli   Cyrene

Marrakech   (Asian Goods)

-30°N   Agadir   Cairo

ATLANTIC OCEAN

Taghaza (Salt)

Ghat

A F R I C A

-20°N

Senegal River   Timbuktu

Niger River

-10°N   Niani   Kano   El Fasher   Sennar (Asian Goods)

Wangara (Gold)

N W E S

Nile River

0   200   400   600   800 mi.

0   200   400   600   800 km

made it the ideal place for people to meet and exchange their goods.

The gold and salt mines in western Africa operated for hundreds of years. The gold was carried north to the Niger River. There traders from the south met traders from the north. The gold was traded for many kinds of goods from Europe—cloth, swords, beads, horses, and foods—but especially for salt. Salt was a necessary food. It was very important to these people who lived in a hot climate because they lost much salt through sweat each day.

The people of the area around Timbuktu needed salt so badly that sometimes they would trade a weight of gold for the same weight of salt. The salt that was so precious in Timbuktu was so common in Taghaza that houses were built of blocks of salt.

The king of the area around Timbuktu claimed much of the gold from Wangara for himself. He also taxed all the gold and salt that were brought in to be traded. As a result, the king and the traders became very rich.

A Center of Learning

Timbuktu became not only a center of trade, but also a center of learning. The rulers of Timbuktu became Muslims, followers of the religion of Islam. Muslims believe in education, because they believe that Muslims should be able to read the Quran, the book of Muslim teachings. Many Muslim traders came to live in Timbuktu. They brought their love of learning with them. The city became known for its teachers and libraries. One visitor wrote that "Here are a great store of doctors, judges, priests, and other learned men, that are bountifully maintained at the king's cost and charges. And hither are brought [many] manuscripts of written books . . . which are sold for more money than any other merchandise. . . ."

Timbuktu was a great city for hundreds of years. However, the riches of the area attracted many invaders. Shortly before the year 1600, an army from Morocco attacked. Over a period of many years, the area around Timbuktu was ruled by several different countries. Trade was broken up by wars, and the gold mines of Wangara ran out. Timbuktu once again became a poor village.

Timbuktu Today

Timbuktu is no longer a center of world trade and learning. It is still located at about latitude 17°N, longitude 3°W. Its location has not changed, but the *importance* of its location has changed.

The salt mines at Taghaza still produce salt for the people of West Africa. People come on camels and in jeeps to buy the salt, but the importance of the location of Taghaza has changed. No longer is it a stop on a trade route linking Europe with Timbuktu. No longer does gold from Timbuktu flow through Taghaza on its way to the coast to trade for goods from Europe.

Using Your Skills

Ⓐ RECALLING FACTS

Use the reading and Map 6-1 on page 197 to answer these questions.

1. What was important about Timbuktu's location?

   _____

   _____

2. How can people change the importance of a location? _____

3. How was the importance of Taghaza's location changed? How has it stayed the same?

   _____

   _____

4. How did trade change Timbuktu?

   _____

   _____

5. About how many miles did people travel from the north coast of Africa

   to trade European goods at Timbuktu? _____

6. About how many miles did traders from Asia travel across Africa to

   trade at Timbuktu? _____

7. For what is your town or city known? _____

   _____

8. What events or historic changes have affected the importance of your

   town or city? _____

   _____

Lesson ② Cultural Diffusion

WHAT YOU WILL LEARN

To describe ways in which people spread their ideas across the earth

READING STRATEGY

Create a flowchart like the one below. List in order the process by which Islamic culture spread around the world.

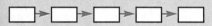

TERMS TO KNOW

cultural diffusion

Someone once said, "There is nothing so powerful as an idea whose time has come." The person meant that when people are ready to accept a new idea, great changes can take place.

The world in which we live has been greatly affected by the spread of ideas. With those ideas have come many other things: religions, foods, types of clothing, laws, and languages, to name a few. The greater part of the earth's surface has been affected by the spread of cultures, or **cultural diffusion.** When people move to a new area they take their culture, or way of life, with them. Two cultures largely shaped the world we live in today: the European culture and the Islamic culture.

The Islamic Culture

The Islamic culture began in Southwest Asia. It started with a religion, Islam, whose major prophet was an Arab trader named Muhammad. Muhammad died in A.D. 632. Then his followers, called Muslims, began to spread Islam to other lands. In little more than a hundred years Muslims ruled countries from Spain to India. Later Islam spread still farther, as you can see from Map 6-2.

Soldiers, scholars, and traders helped spread Islam to other parts of the world. And many people were willing to accept Islam. The religion stressed equality of all people, so any person could become a Muslim. Many people joined the new religion. They brought their own ideas and way of life with them. Muslims borrowed ideas from the many cultures of the lands they ruled. The Islamic culture became a mixture of the ideas from many different groups of people.

Location played an important part in the spread of Islam. Look at Map 6-2 which shows the spread of Islam. The first Islamic countries were between Europe, to the west, and India and China, to the east. At this time Europe was made up of many small lands ruled by kings. Most of the people were poor, and life was hard. At this same time, China was the center of a great culture which had books, fine silk, spices, gold, and many other riches.

A traveler from Europe named Marco Polo visited China from 1271 to 1295. After he returned to Europe, he wrote a book about his trip. As people read his book and became familiar with this new land, they wanted the riches of China. So trade began between Europe and China. As you can see from the map, this trade had to go through the hands of the Muslims. The Muslims became rich and very powerful from the profits they made from this trade. Such wealth and power allowed them to spread their culture.

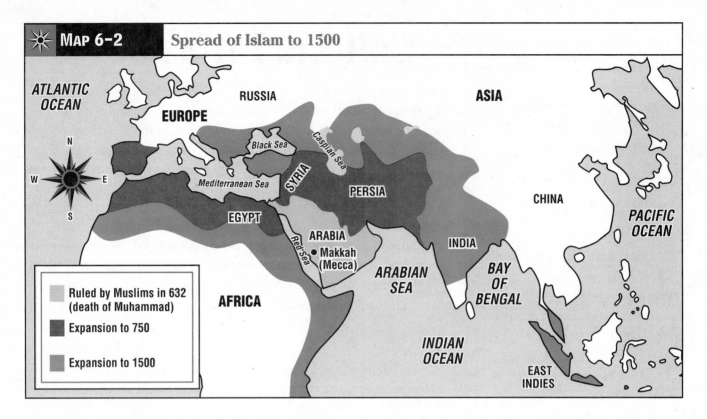

MAP 6-2 Spread of Islam to 1500

ATLANTIC OCEAN

EUROPE

RUSSIA

ASIA

Black Sea

Caspian Sea

Mediterranean Sea

SYRIA

PERSIA

CHINA

PACIFIC OCEAN

EGYPT

ARABIA
• Makkah (Mecca)

Red Sea

INDIA

ARABIAN SEA

BAY OF BENGAL

AFRICA

INDIAN OCEAN

EAST INDIES

Ruled by Muslims in 632 (death of Muhammad)

Expansion to 750

Expansion to 1500

Much of the world today is still influenced by Muslim people. North Africa, Southwest Asia, Central Asia, South Asia, and Southeast Asia are all areas where the Islamic culture is still strong.

The European Culture

The spread of European cultures came later than the spread of Islamic culture. In fact, the spread of European cultures owes much to the Muslims. It was through the Muslims that Europeans learned about Chinese inventions such as paper, printing, the compass, and gunpowder. These inventions helped Europeans grow more powerful and spread their cultures all over the world.

The compass, for example, helped European sailors find new trade routes to China. Once traders from Europe could sail directly to China from Europe, they no longer had to buy goods from the Muslims. All the profits went to Europeans. This helped European countries become stronger. Paper and printing meant that Europeans could write down their ideas and send them anywhere—in the form of books. And having many copies of books, printed on a printing press, instead of just a few copies written by hand, meant that ideas could spread much faster.

Gunpowder gave the Europeans a great advantage over people who were still using bows and arrows. With guns and cannons the Europeans were able to take control of more and more land.

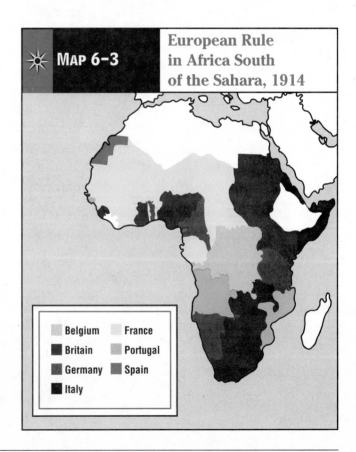

MAP 6-3 European Rule in Africa South of the Sahara, 1914

Belgium
Britain
Germany
Italy
France
Portugal
Spain

They eventually took control of whole continents: North America, South America, Africa, and Australia.

The most important way Europeans spread their cultures to new lands was by settling there themselves. After 1800, millions of Europeans moved to other lands. Between 1900 and 1914, almost a million people left Europe each year. This was the greatest movement of people in history.

With the Europeans came their languages, religions, and customs. The culture of the United States, for example, is largely influenced by British culture. In turn, the American culture is similar to the Australian, which also came from the British. The culture of much of Latin America comes from Spain and Portugal. As Map 6-3 shows, many African countries are influenced by the cultures of the European countries that once ruled them.

Using Your Skills

Ⓐ RECALLING FACTS

Use Map 6-2, Map 6-3, and the reading to answer these questions.

1. What is cultural diffusion?

    _____

2. Describe the areas covered by the Islamic culture by 1500.

    _____

    _____

3. What part did location play in the spread of the Islamic culture?

    _____

    _____

    _____

4. How did the spread of the Islamic culture help the spread of European

    cultures? _____

    _____

    _____

5. What was the most important way the Europeans spread their cultures?

    _____

6. What were the only two parts of Africa south of the Sahara *not* ruled by

    Europeans in 1914? _____

7. Which areas of Africa south of the Sahara were ruled by France? _____

    By Britain? _____

WHAT YOU WILL LEARN

That movements and human activities are concentrated in some areas and sparse in other areas, thereby creating patterns of centers, pathways, and hinterlands

READING STRATEGY

Create a table like the one below. Beside each place, or center of trade, list its importance in the process of triangular trade.

CENTER OF TRADE	IMPORTANCE
England	
New England	
West Indies	
Africa	

TERMS TO KNOW

raw material, manufactured good, profit, triangular trade, hinterland

Imagine you are flying high above the earth. As you look down, you see towns and cities scattered across the countryside. Each town or city has a downtown area with buildings close together. Around it are houses and other buildings that are farther apart. Outside the city, buildings get farther and farther apart. In some places it may be miles between buildings. Roads and railroads connect the towns with each other, and with the countryside. As you look down, you see bright, moving flashes of light. It is the sun reflecting off cars and trucks moving on the roads. Most of the cars and trucks are moving to and from the cities.

Centers and Pathways of Trade

What you see from high in the air is a model of how people trade with each other. The cities are centers of trade where goods are bought and sold. The areas surrounding the cities are where the goods are produced. The roads and railroads are the pathways over which the goods are carried to the cities.

If you could fly higher still, so that you could see a large part of the earth's surface at once, you would see much the same thing. It would be easy to pick out the countries where most trade was taking place. Many ships would be moving to and from some countries. Few ships would be moving to and from others.

There are two main elements of trade. The first element is **raw materials.** Raw materials are natural resources like oil, wood, coal, iron ore, and cotton. Useful things can be made from raw materials. For example, cotton can be made into thread and cloth. These can then be used to make clothing. Finished products from raw materials are called **manufactured goods.** Some examples of manufactured goods are cars, radios, and shoes.

Some countries produce mostly raw materials. Others produce mainly manufactured goods. As you might expect, there is a great deal of trade between such countries. The countries that have raw materials sell them to make money. They use this money to buy manufactured goods. The countries that make goods must buy raw materials to make those goods. Each time raw materials or manufactured goods are sold, the seller makes a **profit.** Profit is the money left over after all expenses are paid. Trade takes place because people can make a profit by buying and selling goods.

The Triangular Trade

The early history of the United States provides an example of how trade works. In the eighteenth century the land we know as the United States was ruled by England. The land was rich in raw materials such as fish, lumber, and cotton. England also ruled the islands in the West Indies, located southeast of the United States. Large plantations, or farms, on these islands grew sugarcane. Countries ruled by the English had to buy all their manufactured goods from England.

Trade between England and the lands it ruled worked in this way. Ships from New England, in the northeastern part of what is now the United States, carried fish from the region to the West Indies. There the fish was sold to feed the enslaved Africans who worked on the sugar plantations. Farmers paid for the fish with sugar from their crops. Ships then took the sugar to England where it was sold or traded for manufactured goods. The manufactured goods were then taken back to New England and sold. The money from the sale of manufactured goods was used to buy more fish.

This was called the **triangular trade** because the ships moved in a triangle from New England, to the West Indies, to England, and back to New England, where the process began again. The triangular trade worked in another way, too. It would begin in New England, whose fish was taken to the West Indies and traded for sugar. Then the sugar was taken back to New England where it was made into rum. The rum was taken to West Africa's Gold Coast. There it was traded for enslaved Africans. The enslaved Africans were then taken to the West Indies and sold to the sugar plantations.

The triangular trade had centers and pathways. The centers were the cities in New England, the West Indies, and England where goods were bought and sold. The pathways were the routes the ships followed across the ocean. The triangular trade also had **hinterlands,** or areas where raw materials were grown or gathered.

Using Your Skills

Ⓐ REVIEWING KEY TERMS

Match each term in Column A with its meaning in Column B.

Column A

_____ 1. raw materials

_____ 2. hinterlands

_____ 3. profit

_____ 4. manufactured goods

_____ 5. triangular trade

Column B

a.   the money left over after expenses are paid

b.   trade between New England, England or Africa, and the West Indies

c.   finished products made from raw materials

d.   areas where raw materials are produced

e.   natural resources

Ⓑ PRACTICING MAP SKILLS

Use information from the lesson to complete Map 6-4: Triangular Trade on page 204.

1.   Draw the pathways ships followed in the two different patterns of triangular trade.

2.   Label each pathway with the product ships carried between centers.

3.   Label the hinterlands with the product that came from each.

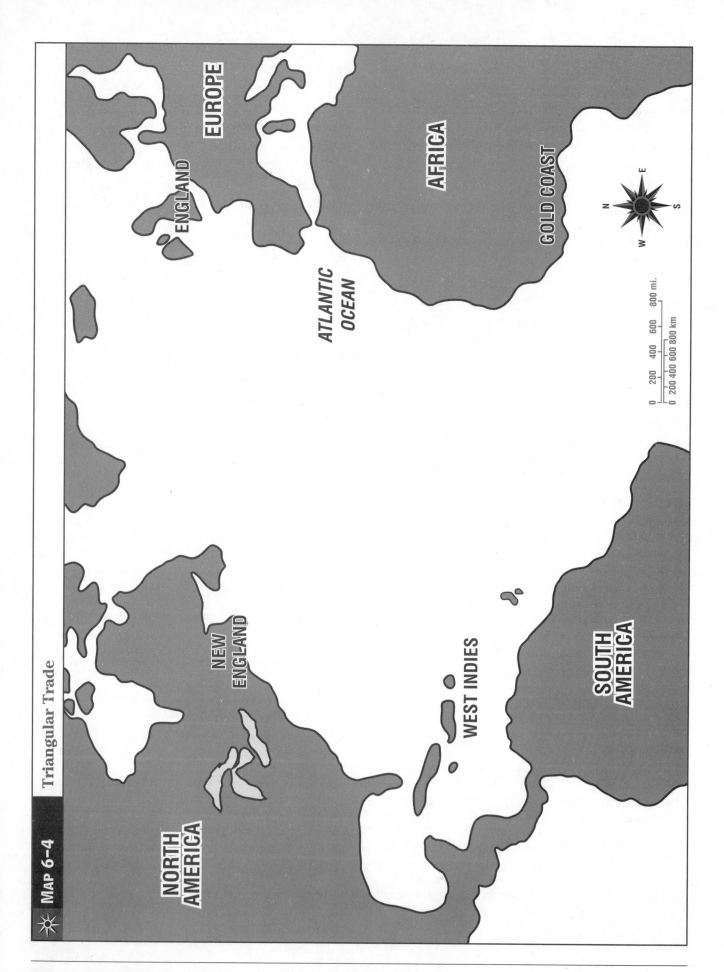

MAP 6–4 Triangular Trade

ENGLAND

EUROPE

AFRICA

GOLD COAST

ATLANTIC OCEAN

N
E
W
S

NORTH AMERICA

NEW ENGLAND

WEST INDIES

SOUTH AMERICA

0   200   400   600   800 mi.
0   200 400 600 800 km

The Industrial Revolution

WHAT YOU WILL LEARN

To explain how geographic factors contributed to the start of the Industrial Revolution

READING STRATEGY

Create a diagram like the one below. In the outer ovals, write the geographic factors that influenced the Industrial Revolution in the United States.

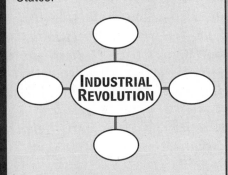

TERMS TO KNOW

Industrial Revolution, agricultural revolution, industrialization, capitalist, capital

How do you and your family get most of the things you need to live? Do you make any of these items yourself? If not, then where are most of the items made? Most likely they are manufactured in factories in the United States or in other parts of the world.

Goods we use for everyday living were not always manufactured in factories. Traditionally, most goods were made at home. However, by the late 1700s the way goods were made began to change. This change is known as the **Industrial Revolution.**

The Revolution Begins in England

Before the Industrial Revolution, goods were manufactured by hand or simple machines at home in rural areas. During the Industrial Revolution, however, more and more goods were made by power-driven machinery in factories. Factories became the best way of bringing together the machines and the workers necessary to produce goods. As a result, there was a huge increase in the number and variety of goods that were made.

The Industrial Revolution began in Great Britain, which includes England, Scotland, and Wales. There were several reasons why it started there, but many had to do with Britain's geography.

Britain had many natural resources. One resource was its fertile land, on which small farms prospered. However, in the 1700s wealthy landowners bought up much of the land, forcing the owners of small farms to move to cities to find work. The wealthy landowners introduced improved farming methods that resulted in greater crop yields. They also introduced improved methods of raising livestock. These changes in farming methods resulted in an **agricultural revolution.** The increase in farm products helped to feed the growing population in Britain's urban areas.

Britain had other natural resources that were necessary for **industrialization,** or the process of developing machines to produce goods. It had abundant supplies of coal, which were needed to fuel machines. A large supply of iron ore, which was used to make machines and tools, was also available. The region's fast-flowing rivers provided waterpower to factories. Navigable rivers were used to transport goods within the country, while many harbors allowed ships to transport goods overseas.

One of the first industries to develop in Britain was the textile, or cloth-making, industry. Inventors created machinery to do some of the work involved in making cloth, such as spinning. This machinery ran on waterpower. As a result, cloth makers built mills along rivers. Many small farmers who had lost their land came to the mills to find work.

As industries in Britain grew, private investors and banks were needed to provide money to build more factories and buy more machines. Soon, wealthy businesspeople called **capitalists** became as important as manufacturers in the growing process of industrialization.

The Revolution Spreads

By the early 1800s, the Industrial Revolution had spread to other parts of Europe and to North America. In the United States, the Industrial Revolution began on the northeast coast in New England. The soil in New England was poor, making farming difficult. As a result, people had to find other ways of making a living.

Like Britain, New England had many resources that made industrialization possible. Rapid-flowing rivers provided the waterpower necessary to run machines. Resources such as coal and iron were located nearby. Ports were used to ship goods from the factories to markets overseas.

New England also had many investors who could provide **capital,** or money needed for invest-

ment. As in Britain, the capital was needed to build more factories and machines.

Many workers in New England's factories were New Englanders. However, in the 1820s, many European immigrants arrived in the region looking for greater economic opportunities. Many immigrants took jobs in New England's growing industries.

Effects of the Revolution

For many centuries, most Europeans lived in rural areas. By the middle of the 1800s, however, more people lived in cities. The increasing number of factories brought people to cities to look for jobs. Look at Figure 6-1. What percent of the population in 1750 was urban? How did the population distribution change by 1850? How did the Industrial Revolution contribute to this change?

The Industrial Revolution was a turning point in history. It changed much of the Western world from a rural, agricultural society to an urban, industrial one. Industrialization provided people with a higher standard of living. However, it also created problems, such as pollution, that challenge the world today.

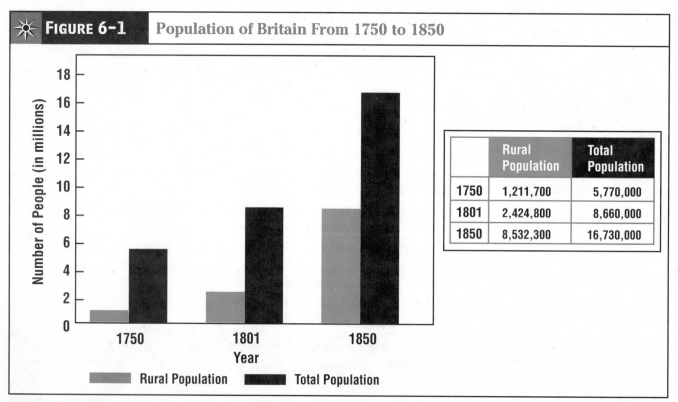

FIGURE 6-1 Population of Britain From 1750 to 1850

	Rural Population	Total Population
1750	1,211,700	5,770,000
1801	2,424,800	8,660,000
1850	8,532,300	16,730,000

Source: *Atlas of World History.* New York: Oxford University Press, Inc.

Using Your Skills

Ⓐ REVIEWING KEY TERMS

Write the meaning of each word.

1. agricultural revolution

   _____

   _____

2. Industrial Revolution

   _____

   _____

3. industrialization _____

4. capital _____

Ⓑ RECALLING FACTS

Use the reading and Figure 6-1 on page 206 to answer these questions.

1. How did the ways goods were made change as a result of the Industrial Revolution?

   _____

   _____

2. Why did the Industrial Revolution start in Great Britain?

   _____

   _____

   _____

3. In the United States, why did the Industrial Revolution start in New England?

   _____

   _____

4. How did the Industrial Revolution affect population distribution in Britain by the middle of the 1800s?

   _____

   _____

Lesson 5 The Expanding Desert

WHAT YOU WILL LEARN

To explain the causes of desertification and describe solutions to the problem

READING STRATEGY

Create a diagram like the one below. List the factors that have led to desertification, or loss of vegetation, in the Sahel.

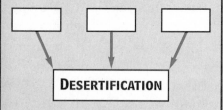

TERMS TO KNOW

Sahel, desertification, arable land, drought, cash crop, fallow, arid, famine

What do you think of when you hear the word *desert*? What images come to your mind? Where are some of the world's deserts located? Did you know that deserts can grow and shrink?

What Is Desertification?

The world's deserts were formed over a long period of time. Deserts are often separated from surrounding areas by landforms such as mountains. In some parts of the world, however, desert borders are not clear. Often, there is a transition zone, where a desert region blends into a more humid, or wet environment. The land that borders the desert generally includes vegetation such as sparse trees, shrubs, and grasses.

In western Africa, a region known as the **Sahel** is a transition zone between the Sahara to the north and the wetter areas to the south. The word *Sahel* comes from the Arabic word for "border." Vegetation such as grasses and shrubs grow in the Sahel. The region generally receives about 4 to 8 inches (10 to 20 cm) of rain, most of it between June and September. Many areas of the Sahel have been used for farming and for raising livestock.

Over the past 50 years, the Sahel has suffered from soil erosion and **desertification**—a process by which productive land turns into desert following the destruction of vegetation. When this happens, the soil cannot hold moisture and the desert encroaches upon it. As a result, the amount of **arable land,** or land suitable for growing crops, in the region has diminished.

This area of the Namib Desert in southern Africa includes a transition zone of sparse trees, shrubs, and grasses.

What Causes Desertification?

Desertification usually occurs in places that experience **drought,** or a long period of extreme dryness and water shortages. However, drought alone does not cause desertification. The major causes have more to do with the way people have used the land, such as in the Sahel.

The Sahel experienced a major drought that lasted from the late 1960s until the early 1980s. People there had traditionally made a living from farming and herding. Nomadic herders moved from place to place, finding food and water for their animals. Then they began using technology to drill deep wells, which provided a steady source of water. Many herders gave up a nomadic way of life and settled near the sources of water. They also raised more livestock. As a result, the land became overgrazed.

At the same time, the population of the Sahel was growing. More people turned to farming and the most fertile lands in the region were used to grow **cash crops,** such as cotton. Cash crops are grown to be sold or traded rather than used by the farmers themselves. To grow more crops, farmers in the Sahel began to change their farming practices. Instead of letting fields remain **fallow,** or idle, for 15 to 20 years to regain their fertility, the farmers began to rework the land within 1 to 5 years. Doing this did not give the land enough time to recover its nutrients. With the continuing drought, the land became **arid,** or dry, and the desert moved southward. Overgrazing, overfarming, and the continuous drought destroyed the Sahel's farmlands and grasslands.

What Problems Does Desertification Cause?

As the desert moved southward into the Sahel, people and their livestock moved to avoid it. As they moved southward, they continued to graze and farm the land, causing it to lose its richness and become arid. Droughts, which have always occurred in the semiarid Sahel, have recently become severe there and in other parts of Africa south of the Sahara. For example, in the early 1990s, drought in the Horn of Africa, which includes Eritrea, Somalia, Ethiopia, and Djibouti, caused widespread famine. **Famine** is an extreme lack of food. Since 1998 drought has killed crops and livestock across East Africa, threatening the lives of hundreds of thousands of people.

Desertification has caused other problems in the region. Unable to make a living by farming or herding, many people migrated to cities to work. This affected the region's economies. With fewer people farming, the countries in this region were not able to produce enough farm products to meet the needs of their people. Fewer farm products led to higher prices for these products.

The increased numbers of people migrating to cities also caused problems. Cities became overcrowded. They could not provide all the things that the increasing numbers of people needed to live.

Desertification is not just a problem for the Sahel. It is a worldwide problem. The United Nations estimates that desertification currently affects about 70 countries and will affect the lives of up to 900 million people.

What Can Be Done?

Satellites have been used in the last 25 years to keep track of the spread of desertification throughout the world. They take images of a particular area over a period of several years. In this way they can track changes in the land due to desertification. Monitoring the land can help countries become aware of the problem and do something about it.

People and governments are working to protect their lands. For example, farmers in Ethiopia have terraced more than 250,000 acres (about 101,172 ha) of land and planted 42 million young trees to hold soil in place. They also built earthen dams to store rainwater. Other countries are finding ways to better use their water resources, such as tapping groundwater to irrigate arid lands. Research is being done on crop rotation to keep the soil fertile. People are learning which plants can best adapt to an arid environment. They are also learning how grazing lands and water resources can be developed without being overused.

Using Your Skills

Ⓐ REVIEWING KEY TERMS

Match each term in Column A with its meaning in Column B.

Column A

_____ 1. arable land

_____ 2. desertification

_____ 3. drought

_____ 4. cash crops

_____ 5. famine

Column B

a. an extreme lack of food

b. crops that are grown to be sold or traded

c. the process in which land that once had vegetation has turned into desert

d. land suitable for growing crops

e. a period of extreme dryness

Ⓑ RECALLING FACTS

Use the reading to answer these questions.

1. Describe the general climate conditions of the Sahel.

   _____

   _____

2. What three factors contributed to desertification in the Sahel?

   _____

   _____

   _____

3. Describe the two problems caused by desertification in the Sahel.

   _____

   _____

   _____

   _____

4. What is being done to help prevent desertification?

   _____

   _____

   _____

   _____

   _____

⊖ PRACTICING MAP SKILLS

Use Map 6-5: World Desertification below to answer these questions.

1. What does the map show?

   _____

2. Which continents have areas that are at risk for desertification?

   _____

   _____

   _____

3. What part of the United States is at risk for desertification?

   _____

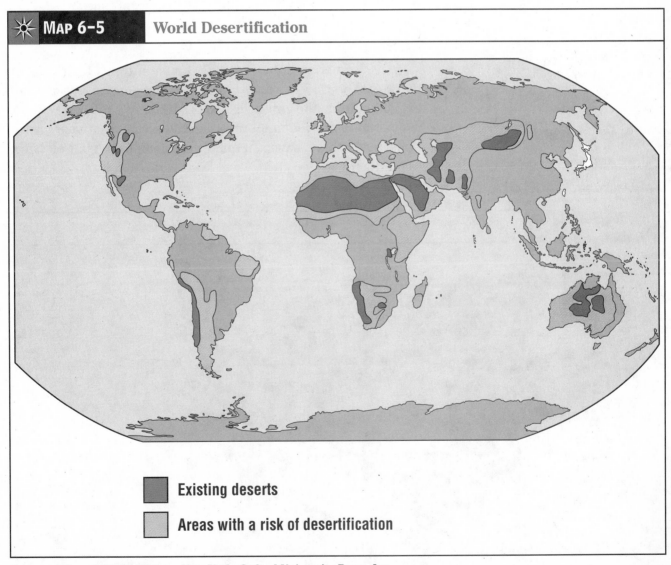

| ✳ MAP 6-5 | World Desertification |

Existing deserts

Areas with a risk of desertification

Source: *Atlas of World History.* New York: Oxford University Press, Inc.

Conserving Resources by Recycling

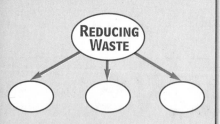
Do you like to pick up a hamburger, french fries, and a soft drink on your way to the park? When there is a good movie on TV, do you have a pizza delivered? Does your family ever eat frozen dinners? Do you ever wonder what happens to all the food and drink containers after you put them in the garbage?

Americans produce more garbage per person than any other people on Earth. Each American throws away about four pounds (2 kg) of waste each day—about 1,587 pounds (720 kg) in a year. All Americans together create more than one-third of the world's trash—200 million tons each year. That is enough to fill a line of garbage trucks that would circle the earth eight times!

Getting Rid of Garbage

In 1996 Americans generated 208 million tons of garbage. Of that total about 57 percent, or about 189 million tons, was buried in giant holes in the ground called **landfills.** As shown in Map 6-6, many states are running out of landfill space. By these projections, many states have run out, or are soon to run out of places to put their garbage.

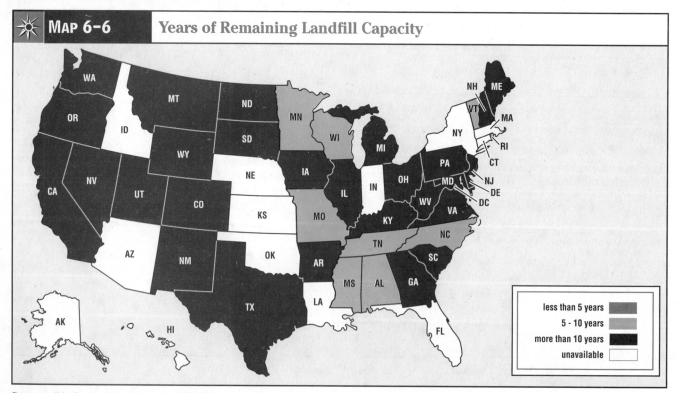

MAP 6-6   **Years of Remaining Landfill Capacity**

less than 5 years
5 - 10 years
more than 10 years
unavailable

Source: BioCycle Magazine, April 1999

Disposing of garbage is a problem, and no one expects the problem to go away. However, progress is being made in the battle to keep our planet from being buried under its own refuse. The growing mountains of garbage are being dealt with in two main ways: burning and recycling.

Burning Garbage

Garbage is being burned so that it will take up less room when buried. Over 100 plants in 32 states in the United States burn garbage in energy recovery plants. About 15 percent of the country's waste is burned at these plants. Some of these plants generate steam to power factories, or create electricity to run motors. The ash left after the garbage is burned must still be buried. However, this takes up only about half as much space as the unburned garbage would have. One problem with this way of getting rid of garbage is that the burning causes air pollution. For example, things made of plastic may give off dangerous gases when burned.

Recycling Garbage

Garbage is being saved and reused. There is an old saying: "One person's trash is another person's treasure." Many things that are thrown away can be saved and put to a new use. We call this **recycling.** Recycling saves money in several ways: (1) Less room is needed in landfills if things are reused instead of thrown away. (2) Valuable metals and other resources are saved when things are recycled. (3) Recycling often takes less energy than making new products.

Look at Figure 6-2. It shows what is in our garbage. Paper, glass, metals, and even some plastics can be saved and made into new things.

Recycling is growing in the United States. However, there is much room for improvement. Even the best recycling programs in the United States save only about 28 percent of the garbage. Some materials are recycled at much higher rates. For example, in 1999 42 percent of all paper, 40 percent of plastic soft drink bottles, and 55 percent of all aluminum beverage cans were recycled.

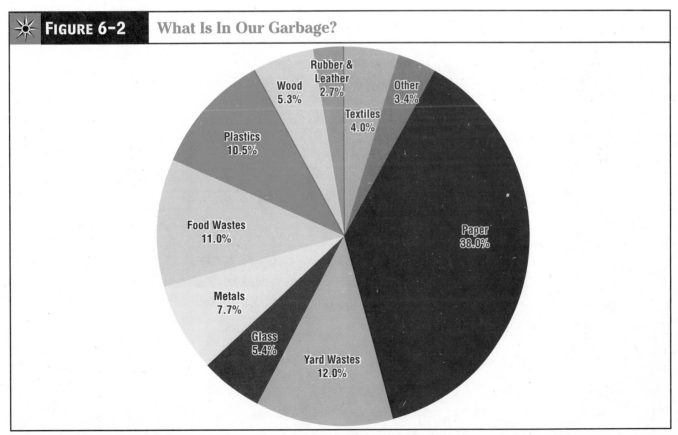

FIGURE 6-2 — What Is In Our Garbage?

Rubber & Leather 2.7%
Wood 5.3%
Other 3.4%
Textiles 4.0%
Plastics 10.5%
Food Wastes 11.0%
Metals 7.7%
Glass 5.4%
Yard Wastes 12.0%
Paper 38.0%

Source: Environmental Protection Agency. "Municipal Solid Waste in the United States: 1999 Facts and Figures."

In some recycling systems, all garbage is dumped into giant machines that separate the metal and glass from the other garbage. The metal and glass are sold to companies that use them to make new things.

The best recycling systems require people to separate their garbage themselves rather than dumping it all into one can or bag. Usually each color of glass must be kept separate. Tin cans must be separated from aluminum cans. Plastic bottles go into another pile. Separating the garbage at home keeps the costs of recycling down.

There are two reasons recycling is not used more widely. One reason is that many people do not want to go to the trouble to separate their garbage. Therefore, even the best programs get only about one-fourth of the people to take part. The second reason is that city and state governments have been slow to set up recycling programs. But as the garbage piles higher and the gates to more landfills are closed forever, more cities are starting to recycle. The states of New Jersey, Rhode Island, and Connecticut have passed laws that require people to recycle. Massachusetts and New Jersey have set up large plants to recycle garbage.

How You Can Help

Many experts feel that the only way to solve the garbage problem is to get each citizen involved. How can you help? Here are some ways that work.

1. **Don't buy things in containers that are made to be thrown away.** Buy products in glass bottles or metal cans. Avoid plastic and paper containers whenever possible. Reuse grocery bags whenever possible.

2. **Recycle paper, metal, glass, and even plastic.** School paper drives are one way to recycle. Some cities have recycling centers where you can take glass, metal, paper, used motor oil, etc.

3. **If there is no recycling program in your town, work to start one.** City leaders know it often costs more money to bury trash than it does to recycle. If enough people are interested in recycling, a program may be started.

As discussed in this lesson, there are many ways to deal with the garbage problem. But everyone agrees this problem won't go away. And the longer the garbage problem is with us, the more impact it will have on our daily lives.

Using Your Skills

Ⓐ RECALLING FACTS

Use the reading to answer these questions.

1. What problem are cities all over America having with their garbage?

_____

_____

_____

2. Describe the two ways in which people are working to solve the garbage problem.

_____

_____

_____

_____

3. How does recycling garbage help the garbage problem?

   _____

   _____

4. Why has recycling not been widely used in the United States?

   _____

   _____

5. How can you help solve the garbage problem?

   _____

   _____

❸ RECALLING FACTS

Use the table below to answer the questions.

World Garbage Output		
	Garbage Produced Yearly	
Country	Per Person (in pounds)	Total (in thousands of metric tons)
United States	1,587	202,321
Australia	1,521	13,097
Austria	1,124	4,124
Canada	1,080	14,989
Germany	1,014	37,697
Japan	882	50,698
Portugal	838	3,797

Source: *Statistical Abstracts of the United States*. "Organization for Economic Cooperation and Development," 1999.

1. Which of the countries listed in the table produces the most garbage per year? The most garbage per person?

   _____

2. Packaging for prepared foods is responsible for a large part of the garbage in the United States. In which two countries listed in the table would you expect to find few such foods? Why?

   _____

   _____

   _____

The Uses of Geography

Ⓐ REVIEWING KEY TERMS

Complete each sentence by using the correct term.

raw materials	cash crops	manufactured goods
cultural diffusion	arable land	

1. _____ is the spread of ideas and culture as people move to new areas.

2. _____ are natural resources such as oil, wood, and iron ore, from which useful things can be made.

3. Land that is suitable for growing crops is called _____.

4. Finished products made from raw materials are called _____.

5. _____ are crops grown to be sold or traded.

Ⓑ RECALLING FACTS

Write the letter of the word or words that will complete each statement correctly.

_____ 1. Two cultures that largely shaped the world we live in today are the
   a. European and South American cultures.
   b. Islamic and American cultures.
   c. European and Islamic cultures.

_____ 2. Recycling saves money by
   a. filling landfills with garbage.
   b. using more energy.
   c. reusing valuable metals.

_____ 3. One of the effects of the Industrial Revolution in Great Britain was a change in the population distribution from
   a. mostly urban to mostly rural.
   b. mostly rural to mostly urban.
   c. mostly male to mostly female.

_____ 4. Through the process of desertification, arable land becomes
   a. more fertile.
   b. a desert.
   c. a rain forest.

C PRACTICING MAP SKILLS

Use Map 6-7 below to answer the questions.

1. In 1750, where were most of Britain's coalfields located?

   _____

2. How was coal most likely transported to different parts of Britain?
   Why do you think this is so?

   _____

   _____

3. Where was the production of manufactured goods, such as linen and
   woolen cloth, concentrated? Explain.

   _____

   _____

4. Where were most of Britain's cities located? Why do you think this is so?

   _____

   _____

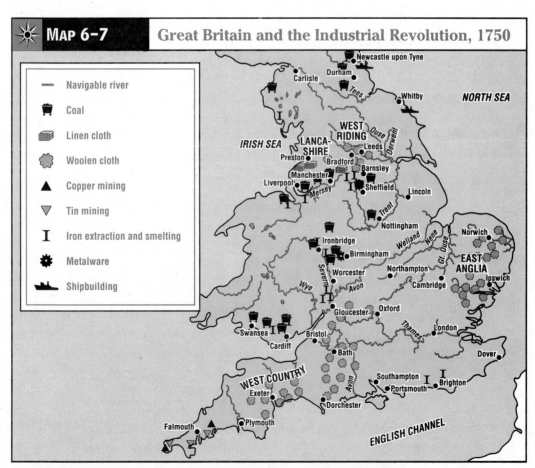

MAP 6-7   Great Britain and the Industrial Revolution, 1750

Legend:
- — Navigable river
- Coal
- Linen cloth
- Woolen cloth
- ▲ Copper mining
- ▽ Tin mining
- I Iron extraction and smelting
- ✦ Metalware
- ⚓ Shipbuilding

Map labels: Newcastle upon Tyne, Durham, Carlisle, Tees, Whitby, NORTH SEA, WEST RIDING, Ouse, Derwent, IRISH SEA, LANCASHIRE, Leeds, Preston, Bradford, Barnsley, Manchester, Liverpool, Mersey, Sheffield, Lincoln, Trent, Nottingham, Norwich, Welland, Nene, Gt. Ouse, EAST ANGLIA, Ironbridge, Birmingham, Ipswich, Severn, Worcester, Northampton, Cambridge, Wye, Avon, Gloucester, Oxford, Thames, London, Swansea, Bristol, Dover, Cardiff, Bath, WEST COUNTRY, Avon, Southampton, Brighton, Exeter, Portsmouth, Dorchester, Falmouth, Plymouth, ENGLISH CHANNEL

Source: *Atlas of World History.* New York: Oxford University Press, Inc.

Final Review

ⓐ PRACTICING MAP SKILLS

Use the political map Europe: Political on the next page to answer these questions.

1. Match each country with its capital city.

   _____ Sweden   a. Paris

   _____ Spain   b. Bern

   _____ France   c. Stockholm

   _____ Romania   d. Bucharest

   _____ Switzerland   e. Madrid

2. Match each city below with its absolute location.

   _____ Belgrade, Yugoslavia   a. 59°N, 11°E

   _____ Oslo, Norway   b. 64°N, 22°W

   _____ Prague, Czech Republic   c. 54°N, 27°E

   _____ Minsk, Belarus   d. 44°N, 21°E

   _____ Reykjavík, Iceland   e. 51°N, 13°E

3. About how far is it in miles between each pair of cities listed below?

   _____ Lisbon, Portugal, to Madrid, Spain
        a. 250 miles   b. 500 miles

   _____ Bern, Switzerland, to Belgrade, Yugoslavia
        a. 300 miles   b. 500 miles

   _____ Berlin, Germany, to Rome, Italy
        a. 600 miles   b. 1,000 miles

4. In what direction would you travel on each trip below?

   _____ from Sofia, Bulgaria, to Helsinki, Finland
        a. north   b. south   c. east   d. west

   _____ from Vienna, Austria, to Zagreb, Croatia
        a. north   b. south   c. east   d. west

   _____ from Oslo, Norway, to Warsaw, Poland
        a. northeast   b. southeast   c. southwest   d. northwest

Europe: Political

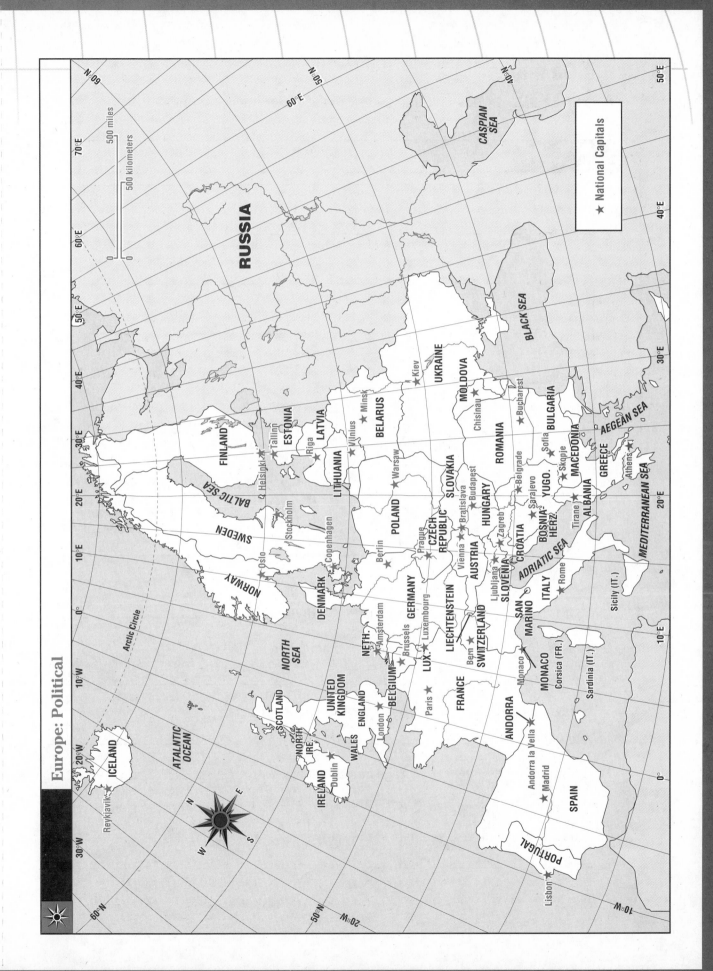

★ National Capitals

ATALNTIC OCEAN

ICELAND
Reykjavik

Arctic Circle

NORTH SEA

SCOTLAND
NORTH IRE.
IRELAND
Dublin
WALES
ENGLAND
London
UNITED KINGDOM

NORWAY
Oslo

SWEDEN
Stockholm

BALTIC SEA

FINLAND
Helsinki

ESTONIA
Tallinn
Riga
LATVIA

DENMARK
Copenhagen

Berlin
POLAND
Warsaw

LITHUANIA
Vilnius

BELARUS
Minsk

RUSSIA

Kiev
UKRAINE

MOLDOVA
Chisinau

BLACK SEA

CASPIAN SEA

NETH.
Amsterdam
Brussels
BELGIUM
LUX.
Luxembourg

GERMANY

Prague
CZECH REPUBLIC
Vienna
AUSTRIA
SLOVAKIA
Bratislava
Budapest
HUNGARY

ROMANIA
Bucharest

BULGARIA
Sofia

Paris
FRANCE

LIECHTENSTEIN
Bern
SWITZERLAND
Ljubljana
SLOVENIA
Zagreb
CROATIA
Sarajevo
BOSNIA HERZ.
Belgrade
YUGO.
Skopje
MACEDONIA
GREECE
Athens
AEGEAN SEA

MONACO
Monaco
SAN MARINO
ADRIATIC SEA
Rome
ITALY
Tirane
ALBANIA

ANDORRA
Andorra la Vella

Corsica (FR.)
Sardinia (IT.)

Sicily (IT.)

MEDITERRANEAN SEA

SPAIN
Madrid

PORTUGAL
Lisbon

500 miles
500 kilometers
0

N
W   E
S

Final Review   219

❸ USING GRAPHICS

Use the climograph of Valdivia, Chile, below to answer these questions.

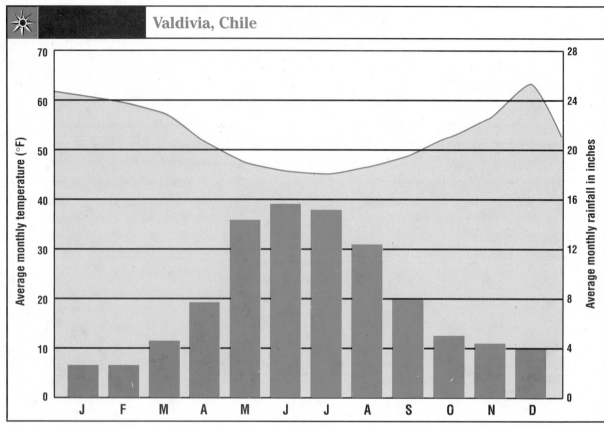

Valdivia, Chile

Source: www.worldclimate.com.

1. In what month(s) does the most rain fall in Valdivia? _____

2. In what month(s) does the least amount of rain fall in Valdivia?

    _____

3. What is the average monthly temperature for November

    in Valdiva? _____

4. What month has the highest average monthly temperature? _____

    the lowest average monthly temperature? _____

5. Which months of the year are part of the rainy season in Valdivia?

    _____

ⓒ PRACTICING MAP SKILLS

Use the elevation map Southwest Asia: Elevation below to answer these questions.

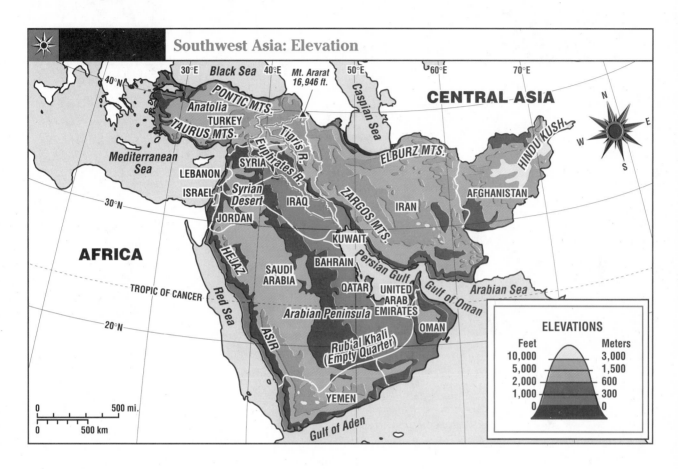

Southwest Asia: Elevation

1. Find Antolia on the map. What is its elevation?

   _____

2. Which area of the map has an elevation over 10,000 feet?

   _____

3. One area on the map has an elevation below sea level.

   Give the absolute location of that area. _____

4. What is the elevation of the Rub' al Khali?

   _____

5. At what elevation does most of the country of Iraq lie?

   _____

ⓓ Using Graphics

Use the population pyramid Population of Russia By Age and Sex,
2000 below to answer these questions.

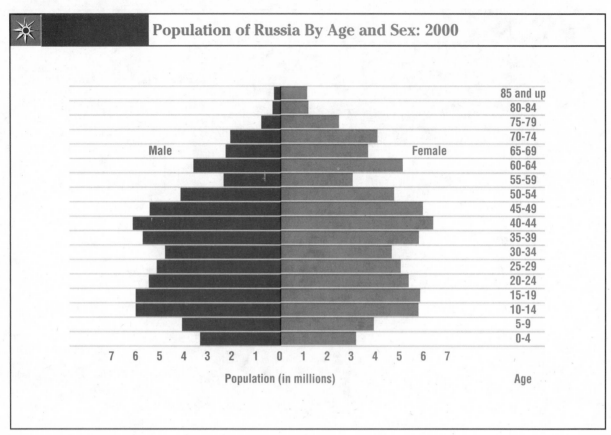

Source: U.S. Census Bureau, International Data Base, 2000.

1. What age group in Russia has the largest number of people?

    _____

2. What age group in Russia has the smallest number of people?

    _____

3. Will the population of Russia most likely grow faster or slower when the
    people now in the age groups 0 to 4 and 5 to 9 reach the age to have
    children? Why?

    _____

    _____

    _____

Ⓔ PRACTICING MAP SKILLS

Use the resource map Agriculture and Manufacturing in North Africa
and Southwest Asia below to answer these questions.

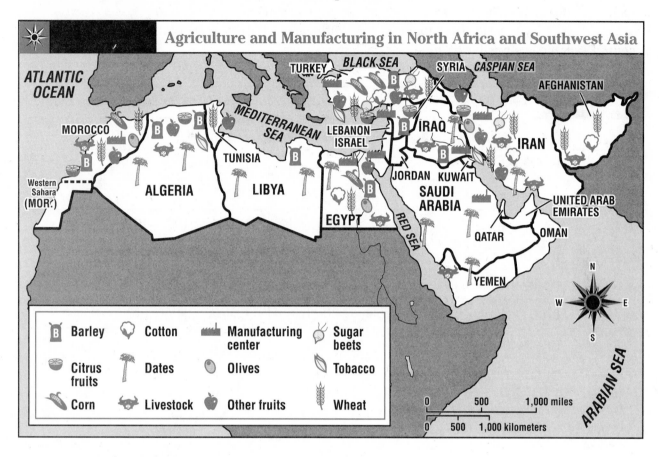

Agriculture and Manufacturing in North Africa and Southwest Asia

1. What crops are grown in Libya? In Egypt?

   _____

   _____

2. In which countries is raising livestock an agricultural activity?

   _____

3. Which countries have manufacturing centers located along the
   Mediterranean Sea?

   _____

4. Which countries have the most diverse agricultural activities?

   _____

5. Which countries have no major agricultural or manufacturing activities?

   _____

Glossary

This glossary contains all of the vocabulary words you have learned in the lessons of this book. The Pronunciation Key will show you the symbols used in the Glossary. A primary accented syllable is shown with capital letters. A secondary accented syllable is shown with small capital letters.

Pronunciation Key

Sound	As in	Symbol	Example
ă	hat, map	a	back (bak)
ā	age, face	ay	Asia (AY·zhuh)
ã	care, their	ehr	bareback (BEHR·bak)
ä, ŏ	father, hot	ah	rock (RAHK)
aù	house	ow	out (OWT)
ch	child, much	ch	China (CHY·nuh)
ĕ	let, best	eh	essay (EH·SAY)
ē	beat, see, city	ee	marine (muh·REEN)
hw	where	w	whale (WAYL)
ĭ	it, hymn	ih	system (SIHS·tuhm)
ī	ice, five	y	Ohio (oh·HY·oh)
		eye	iris (EYE·ruhs)
k	coat, look chorus	k	cat (KAT)
ō	open, coat, grow	oh	rainbow (RAYN·BOH)
ô, ȯ	order, all	aw	orchid (AWR·kuhd)
oi	voice	oy	coinage (KOY·nihj)
s	say, rice	s	spice (SPYS)
sh	she, attention	sh	motion (MOH·shuhn)
ù	put, wood, could	u	full (ful)
ü	rule, move, you	oo	super (SOO·puhr)
zh	pleasure	zh	Asia (AY·zhuh)
ə, ŭ	about, taken, term, stir, cup	uh	fiddle (FID·uhl), pearl (PUHRL)

A

absolute location (AB·suh·loot loh·KAY·shuhn)—exact location on the surface of the earth

acid (A·suhd) **rain**—rain or snow that carries pollution

agricultural revolution (A·grih·KUHL·chruhl REH·vuh·LOO·shuhn)—changes during the 1700s that resulted in better farming methods

air pressure (PRE·shuhr)—the measurement of the weight of air

altitude (AL·tuh·TOOD)—elevation

arable (AR·uh·buhl) **land**—land suitable for growing crops

arid (AR·uhd)—dry

axis (AK·suhs)—an imaginary line that runs from the North Pole to the South Pole through the center of the earth

B

balance (BA·luhns) **of trade**—the difference in value between a country's imports and exports

bar graph—graph that uses bars to show numbers

biome (BY·OHM)—a plant and animal community that covers a large geographical area

birthrate (BUHRTH·RAYT)—how many people are born each year per 1,000 population

C

capital (KA·puh·tuhl)—the money needed for investment

capitalist (KA·puh·tuhl·ihst)—wealthy business-person who provides money for investments

cardinal directions (KARD·nuhl duh·REK·shuhns)—the four primary directions of north, south, east, and west

cash crop—crop that is grown to be sold or traded rather than used by the farmers them-selves

cell—area on a map grid where a row and a column meet

circle graph—graph shaped like a circle

climate (KLY·muht)—the weather patterns in a place over a long period of time

climograph (KLY·muh·GRAF)—graph that shows both temperature and precipitation

compass rose (KUHM·puhs rohz)—symbol used on a map to show directions

condensation (KAHN·DEHN·SAY·shuhn)—process by which water vapor changes into liquid water

conic projection (KAH·nihk pruh·JEHK·shuhn)—map projection created by placing a cone over part of a globe

continent (KAHN·tuhn·uhnt)—one of the seven great divisions of land on the earth's surface

contour interval (KAHN·TUR IHN·tuhr·vuhl)—amount of elevation between contour lines

contour (KAHN·TUR) **line**—line on a map that connects points of equal elevation

contour (KAHN·TUR) **map**—map that uses con-tour lines to show elevation

convergent boundary (kuhn·VUHR·juhnt BOWN·duhree)—the place where tectonic plates move toward each other

core—the part of the earth located about 4,000 miles below the earth's surface

crust—the part of the earth located next to the mantle and about 3 to 30 miles below the earth's surface

cultural diffusion (KUHLCH·ruhl dih·FYOO·zhun)—the spread of a culture

culture region (KUHL·chuhr REE·juhn)—divi-sion of the earth based on a variety of factors, including government economic systems, social groups, language, and religion

D

death rate—how many people die each year per 1,000 population

deep-well injection (DEEP·wehl ihn·JEHK·shuhn)—the pumping of harmful wastes deep into the ground

deforestation (DEE·FAWR·uh·stay·shuhn)—the clearing away of trees

degree (dih·GREE)—unit of measurement of latitude and longitude

democracy (dih·MAH·kruh·see)—a government in which laws are made by leaders elected by the people

demographic transition (DEE·muh·GRA·fihk tran·SIH·shuhn)—a model used to explain the population history of a country or region

desertification (dih·ZUHR·tuh·fuh·KAY·shuhn)—the process in which land suitable for growing crops has been turned to desert

developed country (dih·VEH·luhpt KUHN·tree)—country with a relatively high standard of living and an economy based more on industry than agriculture

developing country (dih·VEH·luh·pihng KUHN·tree)—country with a low standard of living and little industrial development

divergent boundary (duh·VUHR·juhnt BOWN·duhree)—the place where tectonic plates move apart

doldrums (DOHL·druhmz)—calm area located between about 10°N and 10°S

drought (DROWT)—a period of dryness

E

earthquake (UHRTH·KWAYK)—strong shaking of the earth

economic system (EH·kuh·NAH·mihk SIHS·tuhm)—the way in which a country uses its resources to satisfy its people's needs and wants

ecosystem (EE·koh·SIHS·tuhm)—the relationship among all living and nonliving things that exist within a certain area

elevation (EH·luh·VAY·shuhn)—height above sea level

elevation (EH·luh·VAY·shuhn) **map**—map that shows elevation

energy (EH·nuhr·jee)—the power to do work

environment (ihn·VY·ruhn·muhnt)—one's surroundings

Equator (ih·KWAY·tuhr)—line of latitude that divides the Northern Hemisphere from the Southern Hemisphere

evaporation (ih·VA·puh·RAY·shuhn)—process by which water is changed into a gas

exponential growth (EHK·spuh·NEHN·chuhl grohth)—growth characterized by an extremely rapid increase

export (EHK·spohrt)—product sold to foreign countries

F

fallow (FA·loh)—idle

famine (FA·muhn)—an extreme lack of food

flash flood—flood that occurs when a small body of water rises quickly over nearby land

flood—the rising and overflowing of a body of water

food chain—the order in which living and nonliving parts of an ecosystem are interrelated

formal region (FAWR·muhl REE·juhn)—an area that has a common feature that sets it apart

free enterprise (EHN·tuhr·PRYZ)—an economic system in which people are free to decide what kind of work they will do, and to own businesses and keep the profits

Free World—region made up of countries with a democratic form of government

front—place where two types of air meet

functional region (FUHNK·shuhn·uhl REE·juhn)—a central area and the territory that surrounds it

G

geographic information system (JEE·uh·GRA·fihk IHN·fuhr·MAY·shuhn SIHS·tuhm)—software that analyzes information relating to geographic location

Global Positioning System (GLOH·buhl puh·ZIH·shuh·nihng SIHS·tuhm)—the satellites, receivers, and ground stations that allow the location of an exact position on Earth

global warming (GLOH·buhl WAWRM·ihng)—the increase in Earth's temperature caused by the buildup of carbon dioxide in the atmosphere

greenhouse effect (GREEN·HOWS ih·FEHKT)—a slow warming of the earth caused by heat being trapped by gases from burning fuels

grid—set of lines used to find locations on a map

groundwater (GROWND·WAW·tuhr)—water that sinks into the ground

H

hazardous (HA·zuhr·duhs)—dangerous

high latitudes (LAT·uh·toods)—lines of latitude from 60°N to the North Pole and 60°S to the South Pole

hinterland (HIHN·tuhr·LAND)—area where raw materials are grown or gathered

hurricane (HUHR·uh·KAYN)—large storm having high winds, heavy rains, and a storm surge

hurricane warning (HUHR·uh·KAYN WAWR·nihng)—notice that a hurricane is expected to strike a particular location within 24 hours

hurricane watch (HUHR·uh·KAYN WAHCH)—notice that a hurricane is within 24 hours of striking somewhere

I

import (IHM·POHRT)—product purchased from a foreign country

index (IHN·DEHKS)—alphabetical list of names

industrialization (ihn·DUHS·tree·uh·luh·ZAY·shuhn)—the process of developing machines to produce goods

Industrial Revolution (ihn·DUHS·tre·uhl REH·vuh·LOO·shuhn)—the changes that occurred in the 1700s in the way goods were made

interdependence (ihn·tuhr·duh·PEN·duhns)—reliance upon one another

intermediate direction (in·tehr·MEE·dee·uht duh·REK·shuhn)—the direction that falls between the four cardinal directions of north, south, east, and west

K

key—part of a map that tells the meaning of symbols

L

landfill (LAND·FIHL)—giant hole in the ground where trash is buried

landform (LAND·FAWRM)—feature of the earth's surface

latitude (LAT·uh·tood)—parallel lines on a map or globe running east and west; used to measure distance north or south of the Equator

legend (LEH·juhnd)—part of a map that tells the meaning of symbols

life expectancy (ihk·SPEK·tuhn·see)—how long the average person will live

life expectancy (ihk·SPEK·tuhn·see) **map**—map that shows the life expectancy of people in an entire region

lightning (LYT·nihng)—electricity passing between a cloud and the ground

line graph—graph that uses lines on a grid to show changes and trends

longitude (LAHN·juh·tood)—lines on a map or globe running north and south, used to measure distance east or west of the Prime Meridian

low latitudes (LAT·uh·toods)—lines of latitude between 0° and 30°N and 0° and 30°S

M

magma (MAG·muh)—liquefied rock

mantle (MAN·tuhl)—a layer of hot rock located next to the earth's core

manufactured (MAN·yuh·FAK·chuhrd) **good**—something made from raw materials

manufacturing (MAN·yuh·FAK·chuhr·ihng)—the making of products

map projection (pruh·JEK·shuhn)—a way of showing the earth on a piece of paper

mental (MEHN·tuhl) **map**—a person's internal image of a place

Mercator projection (muhr·KAY·tuhr pruh·JEK·shuhn)—map projection that shows true directions and land shapes but exaggerates sizes of landmasses

middle latitudes (MIH·duhl LAT·uh·toods)—lines of latitude between 30° and 60°N and 30° and 60°S

migration (MY·GRAY·shuhn)—the movement of people from one place to another

N

natural resource (NA·chuhr·uhl REE·SOHRS)—something that is found on or in Earth

north arrow (NAWRTH EHR·oh)—symbol used on a map to show directions

Northern Hemisphere (NAWR·thuhrn HEH·muh·SFIHR)—part of the earth north of the Equator

O

ocean currents (OH·shuhn KUHR·uhnts)—cold and warm rivers of seawater that flow on the surface of the oceans

P

perceptual region (PUHR·SEHP·chuh·wuhl REE·juhn)—region that reflects people's feelings and attitudes about an area

physical (FI·zi·kuhl) **map**—map that shows the earth's physical features

planar projection (PLAY·nahr pruh·JEK·shuhn)—map projection created by projecting the globe on a plane

plate tectonics (tehk·TAH·nihks)—theory that explains how the major features of the earth's surface were formed

polar easterlies (POH·luhr EE·stuhr·lees)—winds in the high latitudes

political boundary (puh·LI·tih·kuhl BOWN·duhree)—boundary around each political region

political (puh·LI·tih·kuhl) **map**—map that shows how humans have divided the earth

political region (puh·LI·tih·kuhl REE·juhn)—an area that has a particular kind of government

pollutant (puh·LOO·tuhnt)—harmful substance found in the environment

pollution (puh·LOO·shuhn)—something unclean in the environment

population bulge (PAHP·yuh·LAY·shuhn buhlj)—people who make up a large group in the total population

population density (PAHP·yuh·LAY·shuhn DEN·suh·tee) **map**—map that shows where on the earth's surface large numbers of people live

population pyramid (PAHP·yuh·LAY·shuhn PIHR·uh·MIHD)—graph that shows how the population is divided by gender and age

precipitation (prih·SI·puh·TAY·shuhn)—rainfall or other moisture

predator (PREH·duh·TAWR)—an animal that eats other animals

prevailing (prih·VAYL·ihng) **winds**—winds that blow in fairly constant patterns

Prime Meridian (prym muh·rih·DEE·uhn)—starting point for measuring longitude

profit (PRAH·fuht)—the money left over after all expenses are paid

R

rate of change—speed at which change takes place

raw material (muh·TIHR·ee·uhl)—material that can be made into other products

recycling (ree·SY·klihng)—reusing things instead of throwing them away

refugee (REH·fyu·JEE)—person who flees his or her country because of persecution or danger

region (REE·juhn)—a part of the world that is similar in some way

relative location (REH·luh·tihv loh·KAY·shuhn)—location in relation to the location of other places on Earth

relief (rih·LEEF)—difference in elevation between points on the earth

relief (rih·LEEF) **map**—map that shows the height of land above sea level

resource (REE·SOHRS)—something people use

resource (REE·SOHRS) **map**—map that shows the things found or produced in an area

rural (RUR·uhl) **area**—the countryside

S

Sahel (SA·hihl)—a transition zone in western Africa between the Sahara to the north and the wetter areas to the south

scale (skayl)—relationship between map distances and real distance on the earth

scale (skayl) **bar**—symbol used on a map to show distance

sea level (LEV·uhl)—average height of water in the world's oceans

self-sufficient (SELF-suh·FIH·shuhnt)—able to meet all of one's own needs

socialism (SOH·shuh·LIH·zuhm)—economic system in which the government owns most of the businesses and decides what kind of work people will do

Southern Hemisphere (SUH·thuhrn HEH·muh·SFIHR)—part of the earth south of the Equator

special-purpose (SPEH·shuhl PUHR·puhs) **map**—map that gives one particular kind of information

surface runoff (SUHR·fuhs RUHN·awf)—water that flows into rivers and oceans

symbol (SIHM·buhl)—drawing used on a map

T

table—information presented in list form

technology (tehk·NAH·luh·jee)—the use of tools and skills to make life easier

tectonic (tehk·TAH·nihk) **plate**—plate-like section of rock that is part of the earth's crust

temperature (TIM·puhr·CHOOR)—how warm or cool the weather is

time zone—division of the earth for the purpose of keeping time

tornado (tawr·NAY·doh)—the most violent storm in nature

toxic waste (TAHK·sihk WAYST)— harmful things people throw away

trade—the buying and selling of goods

trade winds—winds that bring cooler air toward the Equator

transform boundary (TRANS·FAWRM BOWN·duhree)—the place where tectonic plates slide past each other

transpiration (TRANS·puh·RAY·shuhn)—process by which plants put water vapor back into the air

transportation (TRANS·puhr·TAY·shuhn)—the moving of people and goods from place to place

trend—how an amount shown on a line graph changes over time

triangular (try·ANG·gyuh·luhr) **trade**—trade among New England, England, the West Indies, and Africa in the 1700s

typhoon (ty·FOON)—tropical cyclone that forms over the Atlantic Ocean

U

uniform region (YOO·nuh·form REE·juhn)—an area that has one feature that sets it apart

urban (UHR·buhn) **area**—a city or town

urbanization (UHR·buh·nuh·ZAY·shuhn)—movement of people to towns and cities

V

vertical zonation (VUHR·tih·kuhl zoh·NAY·shuhn)—change in climate due to altitude

W

waste reduction (WAYST rih·DUHK·shuhn)—decreasing the amount of waste produced

water cycle (SY·kuhl)—process by which the earth's water moves from the oceans to the air to the land and back to the oceans

water table—the boundary between groundwater zones

weather (WEH·thuhr)—the temperature and precipitation in a place on a particular day

westerlies (WEHS·tuhr·lees)—winds in the middle latitudes

wind—air that moves across the earth's surface

windchill (WIHND·CHIHL)—rate of cooling caused by wind or air movement

Winkel Tripel projection (WIN·kuhl TRI·puhl pruh·JEK·shuhn)—map projection that provides a balance between the size and shape of landmasses as they are shown on the map

Index

Maps